THERE IS A
BETTER WAY
TO MANAGE

THERE IS A BETTER WAY TO MANAGE

Hugh A. McLean

amacom

AMERICAN MANAGEMENT ASSOCIATIONS

Library of Congress Cataloging in Publication
Data

McLean, Hugh A.
  There is a better way to manage.

  Includes index.
  1. Management.   I. Title.
HD31.M385   1982   658   82-71315
ISBN 0-8144-5713-4   AACR2

© 1982 AMACOM Book Division
American Management Associations, New York.

First Printing.

To Martie

who has faith and impatience in proper balance

Preface

Years ago I began to notice that certain "traditional" practices in managing were not helpful in achieving important business results; in fact, they can wreck a business, as many organizations have found out the hard way. They force people to play games. Everyone loses. In addition, I began to see that traditional approaches to managing job responsibilities and handling progress reviews, performance appraisal, career development, compensation, and organizational improvement are incompatible with theory on the effective use of human resources. At some point I realized with embarrassment, if not horror, that I was using some of those approaches in my consulting assignments.

Certain that there had to be a better way of doing what managers do, I began experimenting with minor modifications that would "fix" things. I didn't have much success with window dressing. So I forced myself to brainstorm alternatives, to consider major changes in how things are handled. I had some success, but even major changes in some practices that were accepted well in the classroom didn't work out too well back on the job, and they soon disappeared. Finally I realized what it would take to achieve a better way of managing: Each practice would have to contribute to better management, and the practices would have to complement one another and work as a system. This book is my attempt to present such a system. No attempt is made to rehash all that has been written about management. Material was selected on the basis of what is most important to know and do in managing effectively. Much of it is intended for managing on a day-to-day basis, with the focus on accomplishing what's important.

New theory—the hierarchy of leader and follower behavior—sets the tone for the volume. This theory provides the framework for the practical "how to do it" material. Virtually every one of the how-to items in the book is unlike the traditional approach in some way. There is a fresh emphasis, a new slant, an advanced method, and a different and better way of managing connected with each practice that is part of the total management system presented here.

But that's not all. The system has built into it the processes that can lead to a still better way to manage, perpetuating the improvement cycle. A better way to manage is presented for use today, and the reader is encouraged to join the quest for a better way to manage tomorrow. The cases and examples come, without exception, from my personal experiences. I have made every attempt to conceal the identity of individuals and organizations and yet present the basic facts in each situation.

The material in the book is presented as the foundation for effective management practices, not as the answer to all management problems. Continuing management education and training are encouraged in order to build on the foundation. Although this book is not intended as a scholarly treatise, I believe the practices described in it will hold up well under scholarly scrutiny as being compatible with theory on the effective use of human resources. The book is not intended to impugn the work of any individual who has contributed to current management practice. It is presented simply as a better way of doing some of the basics.

Hugh A. McLean

Acknowledgments

To synthesize over 30 years' business experience is not an easy task. Writing it down has taken far more time than I anticipated. Gratefully, I acknowledge encouragement and help from many people who have profoundly touched my life in ways that are reflected in this book.

The book is, first, a reflection of my personal convictions about life and its purpose. There is abundant untapped potential in every person and every organization. Developing and using that potential are worthy endeavors. Realizing human potential, while achieving business results in honorable ventures, benefits the individual and society simultaneously. Everyone wins.

A second motivating force has been my wish to share my personal business experience and the insights I have gained from others who have shared their experiences with me. Out of these combined experiences, two types of bosses and their impact on my thinking must be acknowledged:

First, the type that I now see as a wretched model. Early in my career as a manager, I accepted out of sheer ignorance whatever bosses did as what bosses were supposed to do. Even then, I didn't like certain practices, and I tried to figure out the whys behind the behavior. As I gained more experience, I finally figured out that they simply didn't know any better; they were doing their best on the basis of what they knew.

The many examples of this model spurred me to face the fact that there ought to be better ways of managing jobs and people. To these unnamed people, I now acknowledge a peculiar debt: their example made me strive for practicality in the management system presented in this book.

It might seem strange to mention poor models in a statement of acknowledgments. Yet they have been important in my life, and I believe it's perfectly safe to mention them as a group, if not by name. I am confident that density of the perceptual screen through which they view the world would make it impossible for them to recognize themselves if they were to read the words herein. Hanlon's Razor explains my current tongue-in-cheek attitude toward this type: "Never attribute to malice what can be adequately explained by stupidity."

Second, the type that I now see as an excellent model. Early in my career as a manager, I noticed that people worked harder for some bosses, and they seemed to have more fun and get much more done. These bosses were so secure in their own abilities that they were willing to give their subordinates a crack at tough assignments, serve as their coach and counselor, and applaud their success. From these models, I learned that it was possible to be trusted, respected, and effective, all at the same time. These models would not choose to have their names listed here. They take delight in discussing the accomplishments of others. Their self-concept allows them to be boosters, concerned with helping others succeed.

I cannot avoid mentioning some names and omitting others. I hope those mentioned will understand why, and I sincerely trust those not mentioned by name will understand it in no way signifies less esteem for them as individuals or for their contributions to my work and my life.

Special appreciation is acknowledged to a few uncommon people who have made unique contributions to the contents of this book. Thomas B. Porter gave me encouragement and support as I entered a new field as an internal consultant with Standard Oil (Indiana) and began to explore the effective use of human resources. The example of Roy W. Walters, along with what I learned under his tutelage, gave me the courage to venture into external consulting. Walter R. Mahler provided me with the opportunity to broaden my business experience, confirm my career interests, and build my convictions about the need for a better way of managing what's important to a business. I am indebted to each of the writers mentioned in this book, because their research and experience have guided me in developing my own convictions.

My "firsts," after I ventured on my own as a consultant, will always be considered in a special category. The first to work with me on a full-scale test of the organizational improvement process was Robert N. Pratt, Senior Vice President, Kennecott Minerals Company, Kennecott Corporation. The first to use my help in setting up an objectives system at the corporate level as a model for the divisions was Martin Johnson, President, JSJ Corporation. The first to open the doors for me to have work projects in more than one division of a major organization at the same time was Jervis T. Cunningham, Manager, Personnel Administration and Development, Airco Incorporated. The first to plan with me the installation of a management system through a multiplant organization was John Johnstone, now President, Chemicals Group, Olin Corporation. The first editor to recognize the potential value of this book in management literature and to offer both encouragement and publishing expertise was Thomas Gannon, Acquisitions and Planning Editor, AMACOM Book Division, American Management Associations.

My gratitude is extended to many executives and managers who have joined me in the quest for a better way—by allowing me to work in their organizations, by their willingness to work with approaches new to them, by their candor in evaluating results. Only the problem of where to stop the list, and their right to privacy, keeps me from sharing their names as my valued friends and respected clients.

A Christmas gift from my family in 1975 heralded the formal beginning of what is now this published work. My son selected the gift—a handsomely bound book itself. Its title was *What I Know About Business;* its subtitle was *Authentically Described and Accurately Illustrated.* On the flyleaf, my son wrote, "It is high time you collect your thoughts on paper." The entire volume, apart from his inscription, was blank paper.

In a family council in 1979, the decision was made to make writing this book a high priority. It was time to do it, not just talk about doing it, my family told me. In addition to their moral support, each one of them contributed in a unique way to the book. The activities of my son, Michael, exemplify much of what I have come to believe about achievement motivation and human potential. His experience in the world of work corroborates my own; specifically, it has encouraged me to find a better way of handling performance appraisal, compensation, and managerial dialogues. The formal education of my daughter, Merrie, was put to the severe test in the critique of the initial drafts for clarity and consistency. Her keen insights into the concepts and approaches presented in the book, viewed from the context of her academic experiences in the fields of organizational behavior and communications, were enlightening and encouraging to me.

Many times over the years my wife, Martie, has said, "That ought to go in a book," as I related my experiences as a manager and later as a consultant. At the time she made those remarks, of course, she had no idea she would be so deeply involved in typing, critiquing, and retyping a manuscript based on those experiences. Her help in the formulation of the hierarchy of leader and follower behavior, and in the selection of terms to define each level, was a major contribution to this work.

My fond hope is that each individual who has made a contribution will recognize it in the pages that follow.

Contents

I

THE QUEST
FOR THE PERFECT
MANAGEMENT SYSTEM

Use the term *perfection* in connection with management systems and practices, and you'd better hurry up with the qualifying statements or be ready to be summarily thrown out by your audience. Here "the quest for" is intended to convey that while the perfect management system does not exist in this imperfect world of ours, it's worth searching for. In fact, that search is the driving force of this book. Ongoing efforts to reach the ideal system are paying off today, and building for tomorrow.

The ideal management system would work like a perfect machine: Each part would serve exactly according to the grand design, supplementing and complementing the other parts, all of them fitting together to make one functional unit suited to our particular needs. (It would include, of course, the mechanisms to accommodate changes in our needs.) The quest for a better way of managing a business and using human resources more effectively forces us to examine each part of our existing management system and the way the parts work together. The design of the perfect management system must be based on sound theory, with practical application to the day-to-day events of the business world. This is the topic of this first section. It should prepare us for examining the practical aspects of managing what's important to business success. As mentioned in the Preface, new theory—the hierarchy of leader and follower behavior—sets the tone for the practical models for managing that make up the bulk of the book.

In examining what we do in managing a business, we should consider these possibilities:

- What we do may be based on theory once considered advanced but now known to be unsound.
- What we do may be based on methods and practices once considered highly effective but now known to be unproductive and obsolete.
- What we do may be based on subsystems or parts that don't fit together and function as well as they would with certain improvements in design.

A look backward at the evolution in design of some existing management machinery, including some design disasters and mechanical failures, will give us perspective as we look ahead to the "coming generation" in design.

Read the book with the understanding that the best we have today may be made obsolete tomorrow by a still better way. But by using the system suggested on the following pages as a better way of managing, you may be the one to find it, moving us all ahead in the quest. In the words of English essayist William R. Inge, "There is no greater disloyalty to the great pioneers of human progress than to refuse to budge an inch from where they stood."

1

A Better Way

Bottom-line business results can elicit frightening extremes in management behavior—extremes that challenge our thinking about how an effective management system should work. For example, when things are going badly for a business—volumes lagging, profits dropping, forecasts gloomy—the clarion call goes out from the organization summit to turn the impending disaster around: Fix the problem! Find a better way and find it now! But when the business is doing well, there's no urgency to change anything. Rather, the subtle message is: Don't tinker! Leave well enough alone! Enjoy!

Immediately two questions come to mind. In the first case, does doing something different guarantee a turnaround of results? And in the second case, does continuing present practices guarantee continued success? The answer to both questions is, of course, no. Change alone doesn't guarantee improvement; it only guarantees that things will be different. And in a world of constant change, success today doesn't ensure success forever. We hope things will be better as a result of a deliberate change, but they may be worse. Most of us think of change as a means to achieve a better way of doing what needs to be done—or we wouldn't be making the change. So it's what we change to that counts. Is the change "another way" or is it "a better way"?

Fortunately, acceptance of change is part of our business heritage. Our economy encourages us to adopt changes that hold promise of improving our performance as individuals and organizations. A hallmark of successful companies is their ability to adapt to, if not create, continuing change in the marketplace.

In our quest for a better way of managing a business, we'll look first at why we might find a certain comfort in using traditional management practices. Then we'll consider the growing need for a better way of managing, the difference between a system that really works and a basket of miscellaneous parts, and the willingness to use a viable management system as the optimal way of realizing human potential and achieving business results.

The Comfort of Traditional Approaches to Managing

Traditional approaches to managing a business, the kind used by most managers in most organizations, are not inherently good or bad. We do what we do because it's the best we know, or because under the circumstances it makes sense to us. At times we rationalize what we do. Erich Fromm tells us that this is a common trait. He contends that however unreasonable an action may be, an individual has a driving urge to show somehow that the action is determined by reason, common sense, or at least morality. People often act irrationally, but they invariably try to give the appearance of reasonable motivation.

It's easy to rationalize the use of traditional approaches to managing. There's a certain comfort in carrying on the management practices of others around us, and in perpetuating the management systems in place. Three reasons for that comfort stand out. First, we cling to traditional methods out of habit—habit born of exposure and use. As newcomers to an organization, we are taught the accepted methods and procedures. We see what our bosses and peers do, and we quickly get in line. No matter how strange it might seem at first, over a period of time we become accustomed to doing things a certain way, and our habits become ingrained. The way we do it becomes *the* way. At the extreme, established practices are respected, even revered. Second, carrying on established practices requires minimal effort. There is no inertia to overcome, no selling of new ideas to those whose perceptual screens would block out the noonday sun. No burden of planning, controlling, and following up on changes. It's easy to do it the way we did it last year and the year before. The third reason has to do with our attitude toward risk. Have we "learned" that departure from traditional practice increases the possibility of criticism? Do we believe that staying with the traditional is always safe? Do we base our decisions on the wish to stay out of trouble?

As an example of traditional practices, think of how budgets are established and used. Too often, preparing the new budget is a matter of copying, with some revisions, last year's budget. Once approved, the budget becomes the master control, and it can influence business results in various ways. Depending on the traditions in the organization, an individual might believe that sticking rigidly to the budget is more important than the business objectives behind it. Or an individual might see the budget as a straitjacket restricting action on opportunities that may arise and discouraging innovations that require funding not provided for in the budget. Or tradition might allow an individual to ignore all but the overall budget figure and even encourage the juggling of funds.

Whatever the tradition in an organization, accepting the traditional way of preparing and using the budget satisfies all three of the comfort criteria. The problem, of course, is that this kind of comfort doesn't necessarily contribute to optimum business results.

The Need for a Better Way of Managing

The need for change, for improvement, for a better way of doing things is accepted in many aspects of life, and it should be accepted with equal or greater enthusiasm in managing a business. Change taking place at a dizzying rate throughout the world is bound to affect our business lives. Innovations and traditions each bring special problems and challenges to the workplace. And the emergence of new theory and additional research and experience add still another dimension to the challenge of managing effectively.

The British author H. G. Wells said: "Progress is always the result of the work of people who are dissatisfied with conditions as they exist." Charles F. Kettering of General Motors held that "the world hates change, yet it is the only thing that has brought progress." Whatever the motivation for progress, the drive to find and use a better way ultimately triumphs over the pain involved in coping with change. It's a matter of costs and benefits.

As an example, consider the technological development of today's computers. The earliest computers were welcomed because of what they could do for a business. Yet getting them manufactured, sold, and widely installed was no small task. Then came the training of people to operate them, and the task of programming the computers to meet specific needs of the organization. The inevitable then happened. Before the operators had learned how to use the equipment to the fullest extent of its capabilities, improvements were introduced. The size of the equipment was radically reduced, and the volume of data that could be processed in a given time was greatly increased. New capabilities were added. Again, management had to consider the cost-benefits trade-offs, and make a decision. Historically, opting for the better way has been a deliberate cost-benefits choice made at times to get ahead of competition, at other times simply for survival.

The changing world changes our business lives. The world is shrinking. We learn of events around the world as quickly as if they had happened next door. We can as easily be in touch with people thousands of miles away as with associates in the same office building. We know more quickly about competitive business moves and economic trends. All of these advances are wonderful for us, and equally so for our competitors. Modern communications add new time pressures to making decisions and taking actions.

Advances in automation require new approaches to managing. We smile when we read what the U.S. Commissioner of Patents H. L. Ellsworth said back in 1844 regarding inventions: "The advancement of the arts . . . from year to year . . . seems to presage the arrival of that period when further improvement must end." And in the late nineteenth century, the British Parliament was debating whether to close up the Royal Patent Office because all inventions of any significance had already been made. Are there those among us today who really believe no further improvement in the design and use of management machinery can be made?

Technology has changed not only our lives but the attitudes of workers as well. Those who lived through the depression of the 1930s look at work differently from those raised in the prosperous years following World War II. The expectations of workers have changed, and we must learn to deal with a variety of attitudes toward work.

Government regulation certainly adds to the complexity of

managing a business. Environmental protection and worker health and safety regulations take time and resources to manage. The paperwork involved in complying with the law is staggering. The actual tax burden in dollars may vary from year to year, but the burden of compliance with the accounting requirements is ever with us. In addition to our own federal, state, and local regulations, foreign governments can impose regulations that affect our personal and business lives. The classic example of this is the impact foreign oil has had and will have for many years on the world economy.

Whatever changes the future will bring in communications, automation, worker attitudes, and government regulations, we must be willing to adapt. We may need new management systems and skills in order to cope with the changes. At the least we are faced with the challenge of adapting existing systems and skills to the new situation.

Innovations and traditions. "Our reverence for the past must be continually qualified by our reverence for the future. The past constantly operates to enslave the present." These words from American newswriter Frank Crane challenge us to think about the possible benefits of innovation whenever we think about the known values of our cherished traditions. Crane also jars our thinking with these words: "Precedent is solidified experience. In the realm of ideas it is canned goods. It is very useful when fresh ideas are not to be had. The precedent is the haven of refuge for them that fear to decide."

Innovation involves risk. What are now cherished traditions were once experiments. Every current business practice had a beginning. A leader introduced a change to meet some perceived need, and the followers became part of the experiment with the new way. The mental struggle with the pros and cons is part of every decision to innovate. Once the decision is made, controls are installed to manage the risk: A change may be written into policy statements, described in procedure manuals, included in program plans, supported by new forms. Bulletins and formal statements may be issued by top management. In time the new practice is no longer looked upon as innovation. It becomes accepted and then established as a way of life. Thus the risky experiment becomes a cherished tradition.

Longstanding management practices may help or hinder an individual or an organization. Our attitude toward innovation and cherished traditions may be revealed by how we view these kinds of problem situations:

PROBLEM: *Recent innovations have proved unsatisfactory, yet further innovation is resisted.*

COMMENT: Could it be that to make further changes too soon would give the appearance of failure and cause someone to lose face?

PROBLEM: *Accomplishing a needed change is hampered by the mechanics of existing support systems.*

COMMENT: Ever hear of excuses such as: It's too late to do that because the computer system is already set up! It can't be changed now, the manual has just been printed! Impossible this year because there is no provision for that in the budget!

PROBLEM: *Practices needing to be changed are continued because the leader who introduced them is still in power.*

COMMENT: Why might we assume that a once innovative leader would now be against further innovation? Have past experiences caused us to lose faith in our ability to accomplish meaningful change?

PROBLEM: *A longstanding practice is continued unchanged in spite of today's changed circumstances.*

COMMENT: Could it be that we are too lazy to do the homework necessary to effect a change?

PROBLEM: *We are so busy doing our work that we don't have time to improve on the traditional methods of doing it.*

COMMENT: Is this simply a rationalization for avoiding our managerial responsibility for innovation?

Faulty assumptions about innovation and longstanding management practices can cause problems. Understanding the strength (if any) as well as the weakness (if any) of a management practice is an important step in making sure our assumptions are correct.

New Theory, Research, and Experience

Theory is essential to progress, but even the experts who conduct the research and develop theory are not infallible. Lord Kelvin, the eminent nineteenth-century physicist, believed X-rays would prove to be a hoax; he assumed radio had no future; he theorized that aircraft flight was impossible.

Here is a warning and a challenge to the reader who seeks a bet-

ter way: Not all beliefs, assumptions, and theories found in the literature on managing a business are sound. To paraphrase American author Lowell Fillmore: Remember that it is just as important to know
when to get rid of an old practice as it is to know when to get a new
one. Refusing to give up an unproductive or obsolete practice is a
common cause of personal and organizational failure. We certainly
can't afford to ignore the experts any more than we can afford to accept everything every expert believes. Looking at the total body of
management knowledge and experience as a benchmark for assessing
the unfamiliar is the safe way. Include this bit of theory about innovation: The best way hasn't been found yet.

New insights into managing people and organizations are continually coming to light. The research and experience of others becomes valuable to us, of course, only when we use it, adapted to our
particular situation. The critical test is application. Does it work?
Will it be used because it is so helpful that no external pressure is necessary to assure its continued use? Does it complement the overall
management system? Is it both a practical and a better way?

As an example of sound theory coupled with application problems, consider zero-base budgeting. The concept is that no expenditure is to be taken for granted year after year; each budget item must
be justified each year. It's a tool to review, analyze, and evaluate
budget requests. Who can argue against it as a management concept?
Yet the question remains, why isn't it immediately adopted and suc-
cessfully used by every organization with a budget? One answer is
that the current application of the theory is unwieldy. Most businesses would choke on the paperwork.

New insights gained from research and experience have to be
weighed against all that has thus far guided our thinking. Then
knowledge must be transformed into action. Wisdom is to know what
is worth knowing and to do what is worth doing. American philoso-
pher William Wetmore Story said, "Human wisdom is the aggregate
of all human experience constantly accumulating, selecting, and
reorganizing its own materials."

A System That Works Versus a Basket of Miscellaneous Parts

In searching for a better way of doing things, we usually have to
focus on one part of the whole. Then we have to make sure the
changes that improve the part contribute to the whole. Systems

thinking, well known in technology, is required. Reflect on the challenge of placing a man on the moon. Consider the number of subsystems required to make the mission possible. Imagine what would have happened if just one critical subsystem had failed to function properly. Examples of technical systems are everywhere around us: computers, telephones, automobiles. Each total system depends on the harmonious working of many subsystems.

Systems thinking is also essential in business. Each subsystem must function properly and in harmony with the overall system.

A discussion of a systems approach to business management would be incomplete without a few words on the temptation of smorgasbord design and on the test for balance. Smorgasbord design refers to putting together a management system based on a combination of items selected from the gamut of management practices without considering how each item fits with the others or whether together they form a cohesive overall management system.

Here are three suggestions if you insist on giving in to this temptation:

• Attach each currently popular practice to your system framework. Mention each practice, or ask others about each practice occasionally, so that whenever the subject comes up, others will know you're already using it and that you're somewhat of an expert on the subject. Staples for smorgasbord design include budgeting, time management, objectives, performance appraisal, compensation, forecasts, and strategic plans. Convince yourself this guarantees that you have the basics of sound management.

• Keep abreast of whatever is new and climb aboard the bandwagon. If it proves useful, proclaim you were among the first to use it. If it bombs, quickly declare you were among the first to find out it was no good. Typical in this category might be sensitivity training, transcendental meditation, outward-bound sessions, assertiveness training, transactional analysis, and various measures of leadership style. Convince yourself this protects your image as innovative, improvement-oriented.

• Drop whatever is not popular with your bosses. Do what they do. Listen and look for the signals indicating their attitude toward each practice. Convince yourself this gives evidence of your in-depth understanding of the real world of work and your loyalty to the organization.

Now consider those three suggestions from a different point of view:

• There is likely to be good reason for the popularity of a management subsystem. Try to understand how it works and the potential benefits of using it. Then look for possible side effects in connection with the total system. It's a better way if benefits outweigh costs and adverse side effects.

• It's a good idea to keep abreast of the times and know what's new or different. American author Napoleon Hill wrote: "One of the most valuable things any man can learn is the art of using the knowledge and experience of others." This includes knowing when and how to use a new way, and also when and why not to use it.

• Being aware of your boss's current thinking is a good idea—if it doesn't interfere with accomplishing what's important to the organization. After all, individuals are hired to contribute their energies and talents to the success of the business. Selling the boss on a better way of doing something should be accepted as making a contribution to the business.

Management system effectiveness depends on how the parts fit together, and whether the total cost-benefits ratio is so attractive that the system is used as designed.

Achieving balance among the parts. Making a cohesive management system out of management subsystems can be achieved through application of the following guidelines:

1. Understanding organizational objectives—the big picture—is essential to creating proper emphasis and harmony among the subsystems of management.

2. Understanding management theory and behavior theory is necessary in order to evaluate the parts and the whole of a management system. It's not enough to examine a system or subsystem against one theory or approach or research study. Every available comparison should be used.

3. Common sense is required in the design of each management subsystem. Ask these kinds of questions: Does it square with my own experience and harmonize with what I believe to be sound theory? Is it difficult to understand? Will users be willing to live with it day after day?

4. Trade-offs may be required to make a management system practical. Three questions must be asked repeatedly: What behavior

will this subsystem cause? What benefits will result for the business and the individuals involved? What side effects must be considered?

The subsystem is a better way if it increases individuals' ability and willingness to manage their entire job responsibilities and to find growth and fulfillment in accomplishing what's important to the success of the business.

The Willingness to Use a Viable Management System

No matter how good a management system or subsystem might be in theory, no benefits are derived until it is used. Moreover, the system must be used as designed to get the total potential benefits. Let's look briefly at four aspects of willingness to use a management system as designed: intellectual understanding; internalizing theory and practice; experimentation within the framework of the system; and staying on the cutting edge of innovation.

Intellectual understanding. The more we understand about how a management system works the better. If it makes sense to us, we're more likely to use it and use it well. But individuals can resist a system even when the benefits have been demonstrated. "Too busy" might be an excuse for not using a management tool that was designed to relieve "busyness" even when the purpose of the tool is understood. Excuses can be invented to rationalize intellectual understanding of a management system while refusing to use it.

Internalizing theory and practice. Theory and practice should go together. In order to understand why you do what you do, study the theory related to your behavior. Then observe the results of your behavior, striving to increase your understanding of the theory. For example, motivation theory suggests we feel successful and motivated to achieve further success when we receive reinforcement from someone we respect. This reinforcement may be for progress toward an objective or for the accomplishment of the desired end result. Examine your own experience as boss or subordinate, and see if the relationship of theory and practice holds up. As a boss, provide honest reinforcement and observe what happens. As a subordinate, observe your own feelings when you are on the receiving end of appropriate kudos from your boss.

Experimentation within the framework of the system. Theory for improvement and change should be built into the practices of a management system. A better way will encourage the quest for a still better way. The following steps encourage making full use of what you have as management tools and also encourage systematic experimentation.

STEP 1. Use the management system as it was designed to be used. Keep it as simple as possible, adding no unnecessary frills or complexities to adapt it to your particular situation.

STEP 2. When you get an idea for improving the system, test it against all the relevant theory. If the idea appears harmonious with much of the theory, continue the experimental cycle with increased confidence. If it goes against much of the theory, consider abandoning the idea or, at the least, proceed with extra caution.

STEP 3. Test the idea in relation to each of the other parts of the total management system. Try to determine how the idea will affect each of the other parts. Then examine the extent to which it will help or hinder the achievement of the organizational objectives. Summarize costs versus benefits and decide whether to continue the cycle.

STEP 4. Try out the idea if it still appears to have potential. Set up some kind of pilot test to learn more about how the promising idea works in practice. Be honest in evaluating the results of the pilot run. Go back and reevaluate your thinking in Steps 2 and 3. If it still looks like a better way, make it an official part of your management system and continue the experimental cycle at Step 1.

Staying on the cutting edge of innovation. "Man's mind stretched to a new idea never goes back to its original dimensions," said Oliver Wendell Holmes, Sr. Allowing the mind to explore and evaluate established and new concepts and practices is the first requirement for staying on the cutting edge of innovation. The second requirement is to take appropriate action. The following guidelines for thinking mind-stretching thoughts and then taking action have proved useful over the years. Making regular use of them led to the innovative approaches in the management system presented as a better way of accomplishing what's important to a business.

   1. Get reliable data. On a regular basis, get data on the impact of your management practices and on the conditions that exist in

your organization that affect business results and people. The organizational improvement process described in Chapter 19 provides reliable data of this kind from subordinates. In addition, use all other available sources for data—boss, peers, others with expertise or relevant experience.

2. Analyze and act on your own data. Examine what you do and why you do it that way. Use brainstorming techniques in your analysis and action planning, forcing yourself to think deeply and broadly. Invite your subordinates and boss to contribute their ideas. Analyze the results of your action plans, making improvement efforts an ongoing process in your business life.

3. Cling to an established practice if you can't improve it. Resist the temptation to change for the sake of change alone.

4. Be willing to make minor changes where they are all that's required to achieve the desired improvement.

5. Build on the ideas and experience of others. Innovation means introducing a better way, regardless of where the idea came from.

6. Be willing to look at a whole new approach to solving a problem or seizing an opportunity. Assess the ultimate value, not just the immediate effort required to accomplish the change.

7. Share your experiences with others. The sharing helps you to be honest with yourself in using the other guidelines and in recognizing your own psychological growth.

The Quest for a Better Way

All that has been written here applies to the remaining chapters. New approaches are blended with familiar fundamentals of management to form a better way of managing a business. And the mechanisms to guide and encourage further innovation are built into the system. There is an ever-growing need for a better way of managing. A systems approach is required, one built on sound theory and practical methods of implementing the theory.

You are invited to examine the parts and the total management system in the light of both theory and practical experience. And you are challenged to use the total system to find out its value in realizing human potential and achieving business results. The ongoing challenge is to learn to use the system so well that the built-in mechanisms to encourage innovation will result in a still better way.

2

Effective Use of
Human Resources

The system for managing and accomplishing what's important to a business is an outgrowth of many theories blended with much experience. In this chapter, a new way of thinking about leader behavior is presented as a way of achieving more effective use of human resources. The new system and new approaches build on well-known management fundamentals, and on the work of recognized researchers and writers. They debunk some traditions and ideas that have long needed to be labeled ineffective or destructive. The cry today is for gutsy, plain-spoken truths that leaders can easily understand and apply in day-to-day work situations.

The concept of leadership is intimately linked with the use of human resources in an organization. Let's define a *leader* as an individual who attempts to influence the thinking and thus the behavior of another individual or a group of individuals. By this definition, leadership can take place without regard to any organizational relationship. However, when a leader works with and through individuals and groups to achieve organizational objectives, we call it management. For our purposes, although leadership may be considered a broader concept than management, we shall use the term *leader* much as we use the terms manager, boss, superior, or executive. We'll use the term *follower* to refer to the role of subordinate in an organizational setting. Followers are the available human resources of the organization. Leaders (as bosses) attempt to influence the thinking and thus the behavior of followers (their subordinates) to achieve organizational objectives. How leaders think and behave affects how followers think and behave. How we behave as leaders in using our human resources is based on our assumptions and predictions. We believe that if we do *a, b* will follow, otherwise we don't do *a*.

Our beliefs, opinions, assumptions, convictions, hypotheses, generalizations, and predictions may lead to behavior that helps achieve our objectives as a leader and manager or to behavior that hinders the achievement of our objectives. Our assumptions may be unconscious, and they may be conflicting, but they do determine our predictions and thus our behavior. We cannot separate what we think from what we do.

The behavior of leaders and the effect on followers is summarized in the hierarchy shown in Table 1.

Level 1: The leader demands and the follower submits. At the lowest level of leader behavior, the leader demands, requires, and insists with authority that an order or assignment be carried out by the follower. There is no opportunity or provision for discussion or appeal. The demand carries with it the explicit penalty outcome for the follower if the assignment or directive is not carried out. The follower is virtually forced into submission through the leverage of the penalty. At the extreme, the subordinate in an industrial setting does what is demanded or leaves the organization.

Level 2: The leader pressures and the follower complies. The leader who pressures a subordinate into compliance with a directive or assignment is using fear and force, but not in the same way represented by Level 1. Pressure carries with it implied penalties for noncompliance. Because the leader or manager has such a wide range of penalties available, the threat becomes whatever the subordinate might as-

Table 1. Hierarchy of behavior.

Level	Leader Behavior	Follower Behavior
4	Encourages	Initiative
3	Requests	Cooperation
2	Pressures	Compliance
1	Demands	Submission

sume. Assumed penalties may be greater or lesser than what the leader intends the subordinate to understand. Pressure as used here involves more than persuasion. At one extreme, it means direct and blunt prodding, hounding, bearing down upon. In a discussion or other means of communication, the leader urges the subordinate repeatedly and insistently to comply. At the other extreme, pressure is applied to a subordinate a little more subtly, through hints, stories that obviously parallel a current situation, pointed joking, sarcasm, sugar-coated suggestions in the name of personal friendship and concern.

Level 3: The leader requests and the follower cooperates. The leader who asks for cooperation in following a directive or carrying out an assignment uses persuasion rather than threats or force. The persuasion is based on credible information and reasoning, and there is opportunity for discussion of the request. Cooperation from the subordinate is based on knowledge and understanding of the request, and how it is related to personal and organizational objectives. Discussion of the request adds to the ownership of the subordinate in the outcomes. Cooperation is given freely because the request is seen as an opportunity to make a meaningful contribution—no matter how small or large— to the organization.

Level 4: The leader encourages the follower to take the initiative. At the highest level of leader behavior, the leader has taught the subordinate to take the initiative in appropriate ways and continues to reinforce this behavior of the subordinate. Initiative is especially appropriate when it contributes to the achievement of organizational objectives. Initiative involves seeing what needs to be done and doing it without a specific request from the leader or other team members. It means leading the action, being enterprising, showing dynamism. It means taking the right risks. Encouraging initiative means to inspire, embolden, spur, reassure, give confidence to, hearten, cheer. Reinforcing initiative means to support, strengthen, and foster continued initiative. The leader or manager has a wide range of methods available for encouraging and reinforcing initiative. These include commendation for appropriate use of initiative given privately, publicly, and through the compensation system. Perhaps the most powerful reinforcement comes through adjustments in job content, that is, new assignments that provide further opportunities for growth and achievement.

Leader Behavior and the Power to Achieve Work Output

The concept of leadership involves the use of power. A leader tries to have an impact on an individual or a group for certain reasons. In a business organization, achieving work output is a recognized, legitimate reason for the leader to use power. When leader behavior is at Level 1 or Level 2, however, the basis for that power is dramatically different from the basis for it when leader behavior is at Level 3 or Level 4.

The basis for the power of the leader to achieve work output is expressed in relation to the hierarchy of leader and follower behavior, as shown in Table 2.

Achieving Work Output Through Levels 1 and 2 Leader Behavior

At Levels 1 and 2, the power of the leader to accomplish work through the efforts of others is based on the use of fear and force. Threats engender fear, which leads to compliance. Penalties provide the leverage to achieve submission to demands.

History offers many examples of work accomplished by followers who would acknowledge their efforts were heavily influenced by fear or outright force. As Erich Fromm explains in *The Sane Society*, "Despots and ruling cliques can succeed in dominating and exploiting their fellow man, but they cannot prevent *reactions* to this inhuman treatment." Fromm then comments on the reactions of those who are oppressed. One outcome may be apathy, deterioration of skills, and failure to perform as expected. Another may be hate that leads to the

Table 2. Leader behavior and work output.

Leader Behavior	Method of Achieving Work Output
Level 4 Encourages initiative Level 3 Requests cooperation	Cooperation and collaboration, fostered by a management system that meets both organizational and human needs
Level 2 Pressures compliance Level 1 Demands submission	Fear and force, fostered by the use of threats and penalties

destruction of the oppressive system. Yet another may be such a longing for freedom and independence that the seed of a better society is planted. Which reaction occurs depends on factors such as politics, the economy, and the existing spiritual climate. Fromm concludes his warning with these words, "But whatever the reactions are, the statement that man can live under almost any condition is only half true; it must be supplemented by the other statement, that if he lives under conditions which are contrary to his nature and to the basic requirements for human growth and sanity, he cannot help reacting; he must either deteriorate and perish, or bring about conditions which are more in accordance with his needs."*

The use of fear and force by a leader or manager in industry may in the short run produce certain desired results. But these negative approaches have rather severe limitations:

The outcomes of fear are unpredictable. The use of threats and penalties may produce results opposite to what is wanted. There is no way of knowing in advance to what extent initiative will be affected, what might occur as a result of letter-of-the-law compliance, how frequently the threats and penalties will have to be imposed in order to achieve the desired results, or what new behaviors will emerge. This is so because individuals are unique and will behave in ways that make sense to them as they see the situation and as they see themselves. The complexity of the forces behind behavior becomes apparent in considering some of the outcomes of fear in a business setting.

Fear may destroy initiative. Threats and potential penalties may make people decide to play it safe, to take fewer risks. This response may be manifested in the following ways: (1) Individuals may assume a low profile in group sessions, waiting to see the tide of opinion before committing themselves. (2) They may attempt to delegate up, that is, get their boss to provide the ideas and make the decisions they are responsible for. (3) They may avoid innovation in all its forms and devote their energy to justifying the status quo. (4) They may spend an excessive amount of time agonizing over objectives, alternative solutions, decisions, action steps.

Fear may encourage ridiculous compliance. Fear of the penalties for noncompliance may cause instructions to be followed exactly, even when the individual knows it's wrong to do this. For example, in a

* New York: Holt, Rinehart and Winston, 1955, pp. 18–19.

credit card operation, the backlog of unprocessed credit card applications had continued to grow in spite of all the manager's efforts until he issued an ultimatum: All work must be processed the day it is received, period! Failure to comply with the new rule meant dismissal. The effect was immediate. Desks were clean at quitting time. The turnaround was cause for much conversation at higher levels. Then after a few weeks, the trickle of inquiries about the status of applications turned into a flood of irate requests for action. An investigation showed what was happening. Applications that couldn't be processed properly before quitting time were being quietly "processed" into wastebaskets a safe distance from the worker's desk.

The use of fear is not self-sustaining. Threats have to be repeated; penalties have to be imposed again and again—much like using a pump that has to be primed each time water is needed or using a whip on a racehorse.

Fear may lead to costly new "games." Few managers, if any, would readily admit that they operate at Level 1 or Level 2. They rationalize their demands as necessary to get the job done in an emergency. They rationalize their pressure as the firm direction and follow-up required to get the subordinate to do the work.

The high cost of leader behavior at Levels 1 and 2 can be seen in the following: *The superior-subordinate working relationship is destroyed, leading to costs largely hidden from management control.* The subordinate may try to avoid the boss and thus avoid the unpleasantness of discussing the work and the penalties for failure. The subordinate may do only what is required, and the boss may see this as evidence that there is a need for more pressure or outright demands for improved performance. The subordinate may look for excuses to avoid assignments. This may mean feigning current work overload or pretending inability to do the work. The subordinate may look upon coaching by the boss as additional pressure, with implied penalties for failure to use the help.

There is no motivation to develop teamwork, adding to the hidden costs. Joining in team efforts under Levels 1 and 2 conditions means adding to the risk of penalties for failure. Alone, a subordinate at least has control over what he or she does in response to the superior. In a group, the failure of any individual to perform as required may lead to penalties for all group members.

The examples of the boss and/or of peers breed similar behavior in others, extending the costs. Subordinates may follow the example of their boss or peers, believing that the accepted way to get ahead in the organization is through demands, pressure, threats, and penalties. Limited exposure to better leadership models may lead subordinates to believe leader behavior at Levels 1 and 2 is necessary, normal, acceptable. To succeed, therefore, means they must follow the example, fit the mold.

The cost of avoidable turnover is a drain on the organization. When work satisfaction is low, subordinates look for opportunities to change their job situation. One way is to leave the organization, taking with them their talents and the knowledge and skills acquired on the job—and to a certain extent paid for by the company. Turnover of any kind costs money. Recruiting costs, training costs, and loss of productivity during the training period are involved.

The highest cost, and the one most likely ignored, is that of failure to develop and utilize the talents of the subordinate. Working under fear of penalties leads subordinates to play it safe, take fewer risks, refrain from innovation, suppress creativity, accept the status quo. Potential can never be developed to its fullest under such circumstances. Abilities are most likely to be developed and utilized under conditions that encourage appropriate risks, creativity, and innovation.

Achieving Work Output Through Levels 3 and 4 Leader Behavior

At Levels 3 and 4, the power of the leader to achieve work output is based on the voluntary cooperation and collaboration of followers. The leader takes steps to create the conditions whereby cooperation is freely given, and collaboration in achieving organizational objectives is standard behavior.

Cooperation and collaboration are fostered by a management system that meets both organizational and human needs. Organizational objectives need to be discussed openly so that followers know what the objectives are and understand what they mean in terms of commitment of time, effort, and resources of the organization. Followers need to see how their business objectives are established—that is, that their objectives support the achievement of higher-level objectives. And they need to see how accepting the responsibility offered them provides an opportunity to satisfy their personal needs or drives. There are four drives that are of special significance to management: competence, achievement, recognition, and realized potential.

Competence. The desire for competence is the desire to be able to do things, to make things happen, to control our environment. As adults in the world of work, the drive for competence is seen in our efforts to master our job and grow professionally. When we accept the challenge of important work assignments, and when we initiate action on important projects, we are responding to a very human desire for increased competence.

Past successes and failures influence what we are willing to attempt. Increased competence leads to increased competence. Therefore, the boss should provide work assignments appropriate for the subordinate's abilities and potential. Then, in the role of coach and booster, the boss should assist in making the assignment a successful experience, and provide reinforcement to the subordinate in every appropriate way. Building competence on the job requires an opportunity to learn and do, feedback on how things are going, help when it's needed, and appropriate reinforcement for the outcomes.

Achievement. Achievement-motivated people seek situations in which job objectives are difficult but attainable. They want the freedom *to do.* They want feedback on how they're doing. They think often about how to do their work and about what they might be able to accomplish. They make things happen. In so doing, their competence increases, which leads to achievement.

In the final analysis, all the activities and efforts of individuals don't mean much unless they produce results important to the success of the business. That's why achievement-motivated people, and management systems and leader behavior that reinforce achievement motivation, are important to business success.

Recognition by others. Recognition by others has to be earned—through demonstrated competence and achievement. Acknowledgment of competence and achievement is especially important when it comes from someone respected by the individual, such as the boss, higher levels of management, or experts in the field. Recognition by others differs from competence and achievement, although it is closely related. Competence is what we are actually capable of doing. How we see our own competence determines what we are willing to try. Achievement is its own reward for achievement-motivated individuals. Recognition by others permits us to compare our own competence and achievements with those of others.

Realized potential. Realizing one's potential is a lifelong quest rather than an actual occurrence. Who can say what limits there are to human potential? Yet this is a useful concept when we think in terms of self-fulfillment and continued self-development.

The basic ingredients of psychological growth and job satisfaction are responsibility, achievement, and recognition. They are closely related to realized potential. The opportunity for responsibility leads to the acceptance of responsibility. Working at the responsibility leads to increased competence and the achievement of outcomes related to the responsibility. The achievements are recognized by the individual, and recognition also comes from others. The success cycle leads to further and greater responsibilities. In each cycle, therefore, more of the potential of the individual is realized.

The steps to be taken by a leader to create conditions in which cooperation in achieving work output is freely given and collaboration in achieving organizational objectives is standard behavior are discussed in Sections II, III, and IV. Table 3 summarizes the effect of leader behavior and source of leader power on followers.

Leader Behavior and the Work Satisfaction of Followers

Work satisfaction of followers can be expressed along a continuum in relation to the hierarchy of leader and follower behavior, as shown in Table 4. Work satisfaction of followers is lowest at Level 1. Whether being forced to submit to the demands of the leader results in high or low work output, work satisfaction will be low.

At each higher level of leader behavior, there is increased work

Table 3. Effect of leader behavior and source of leader power on followers.

Leader Behavior	Source of Leader Power	Effect on Followers
Level 4 Encourages initiative Level 3 Requests cooperation	Cooperation and collaboration	Acceptance of responsibility, leading to competence, achievement, recognition by others, realized potential
Level 2 Pressures compliance Level 1 Demands submission	Fear and force	Unpredictable and costly reactions that may destroy initiative, may encourage ridiculous compliance, are not self-sustaining, have costs hidden from management control

Table 4. Leader behavior and work satisfaction.

Leader Behavior	Work Satisfaction of Followers
Level 4 Encourages initiative	Highest satisfaction
Level 3 Requests cooperation	
Level 2 Pressures compliance	
Level 1 Demands submission	Lowest satisfaction

satisfaction of followers. Examine your own experience. Think about how you felt when you were forced to perform as your boss demanded or face specific undesirable consequences. Then think of an occasion when you complied with your boss's wishes, under pressure, knowing there would be a penalty for noncompliance, but not being sure of exactly what it would be. How did you feel? Compare those feelings with an occasion when your boss talked with you about an assignment so you understood why it was considered necessary or important to the business, and then asked for your cooperation in handling it. Finally, think of how you have felt about doing work when you decided on your own what needed to be done to help the business succeed, so you took the initiative in doing it, and then received reinforcement from your boss for your initiative.

The work satisfaction continuum expresses the experience of followers at all organizational levels in all kinds of organizations. It should encourage leaders to examine their practices, and to learn to function as much as possible at Level 4 of the hierarchy of leader and follower behavior.

Leader Behavior and the Effective Use of Human Resources

What does understanding the hierarchy of leader and follower behavior contribute to effective use of human resources, and thus to better management of what's important in a business organization? Answers to the following questions may have formed in your mind already: Is there a "best" level for all circumstances? Is each level of the hierarchy appropriate under certain circumstances? What's involved in applying hierarchy theory in dealing with subordinates on the job? How does the theory of the hierarchy of leader and follower behavior hold up when compared to other, well-known approaches to the effective use of human resources? Let's discuss these issues to stimulate further thinking about the effective use of human resources.

The Use of Human Resources at Level 1

Level 1 represents the least desirable approach to effective use of human resources. Nothing good can be said about leader behavior that demands submission through the use of fear and force in a business situation. It's quite true that work output might be achieved under such conditions. But the costly effect on followers and on the success of the organization should strongly encourage every leader to avoid operating at this level.

Yet for some leaders and managers the use of fear and force at Level 1 is an accepted way of life. Their approach to leadership becomes more obvious when they sense any resistance to their ideas or plans. Subordinates may "hear" the bottom line of a demand from the boss to be similar to these examples:

"Just do it, Charlie. This is the way it's going to be, and if you want to work on my team, then get with the program."

"Now, look, Pat, this is the second time I've told you. There isn't going to be a third time, right? Not if you still want your job!"

Leaders and managers who behave at Level 1 are likely to do so for one or both of the following reasons: They are ignorant of the true cost of using fear and force to achieve work output. They lack the knowledge and experience that would show them there is a better way of getting the work done.

The Use of Human Resources at Level 2

Level 2 leader behavior, though not necessarily better than Level 1 in terms of effective use of human resources, is far more common. It's easier to imply penalties than to spell them out. And implied penalties, in the mind of the subordinate, can range from a slap on the wrist to outright dismissal. Frequency of Level 2 behavior doesn't make it right. Nothing good can be said about leader behavior that pressures compliance through the use of implied and assumed penalties for noncompliance.

Much work output is achieved under Level 2 conditions but, again, at a high cost to the organization. Many leaders and managers, in fact, are unaware of the extent to which they behave at this level. Subordinates may read between the lines of what is said, interpret the leader's body language, and have the following thoughts:

• Critical incident: "That's the only thing the boss will remember at salary review time if I don't do exactly what he says."

• Scapegoat position: "If everything isn't just about perfect, and top management isn't pleased with the reports, guess who takes the rap!"

• Career decision: "I really don't want this transfer. It's not what I'm good at. It's not what I want to do. The boss didn't come out and say so, but turn this down and my chances for moving up in the company are zero!"

Again, as at Level 1, ignorance of the true cost of using fear and force to achieve work output, and lack of the knowledge and experience of a better way of managing, are the principal reasons that leaders operate at Level 2.

The Use of Human Resources at Level 3

Level 3 leader behavior is appropriate whenever it's required. It's always appropriate for a manager to request cooperation from a subordinate when his or her services are needed to achieve a legitimate objective of the organization. Subordinates are not always able to see what needs to be done, what is a fair distribution of work, what talents are needed for a particular assignment, and what trade-offs have been agreed to at higher levels owing to current business priorities. Therefore, the leader has to supply the needed information and, in light of the situation, make assignments and ask for cooperative effort.

This same concept applies when more than one subordinate is asked to cooperate to achieve a result. One function of organizational structure is to coordinate the efforts of individuals and groups in order to accomplish tasks too great for individuals or subgroups to handle. Organizations survive and succeed through cooperative effort.

A request from a leader is more likely to be accepted and carried out voluntarily by a subordinate when there is adequate knowledge and understanding of the request. Cooperation is freely given when acceptance of the responsibility is perceived by the subordinate as a means of satisfying his or her motivational needs. Subordinates may form these kinds of thoughts from a request:

• Acceptance of "my turn": "The request makes sense from what I know. Someone has to do it. Everyone takes a turn at this kind of assignment, and this time it's my turn. OK."

• Confidence in my ability: "The boss trusts me, knows I can do it. Yes, I will do it."

• Opportunity for me: "I'm glad the boss asked me. This is the chance to show what I can do."

Leader power at Level 3 comes from a source quite opposite from that for Levels 1 and 2. Power, as a result of enlightened, freely given cooperative effort at Level 3, can be compared with power resulting from effort given begrudgingly out of fear at Levels 1 and 2. The high cost to the organization of achieving work output at Levels 1 and 2 discussed earlier can be compared to the abundant benefits to the organization when work output is achieved under conditions at Level 3.

The Use of Human Resources at Level 4

Leader behavior at Level 4 is the ideal. It encompasses all the benefits of behavior at Level 3 and more. Level 4 represents the ultimate acceptance of responsibility: voluntary collaboration in achieving the objectives of the organization, which includes providing the means of meeting the human needs of individual employees. Work satisfaction is greatest when an individual understands what needs to be done, takes the initiative in appropriate ways to achieve the desired results, and receives reinforcement for these efforts.

To achieve productive initiative requires a system of management controls that teach the doer how to determine what is and is not appropriate. The doer needs to have a working knowledge of what collaboration means in a given situation. To collaborate means to work jointly with others, work together, team up, join forces. This implies more than Level 3 cooperation in carrying out a superior's request. It builds on the concept that individuals are associates and teammates in a common endeavor, each with a distinct role to play. It reaffirms the need and value of organizational relationships, yet stresses that planners alone can't make the business succeed; doers must do what needs to be done. Collaboration is based on the recognition that contributing to the organization's success transcends one's location on the organization charts.

The Responsibility for Teaching Subordinates

The responsibility of the leader for teaching subordinates has been mentioned in connection with Levels 3 and 4 leader behavior. Voluntary cooperation and collaboration in achieving work output are more likely when subordinates understand:

- The major objectives of those at higher levels, and the major activities involved in achieving them.
- Their own responsibilities and objectives, the resources available to achieve them, and any restraints to be observed.
- How the continuing process of correlation works; that is, how objectives and action plans are dovetailed to assure teamwork.
- Why "no surprises for the boss" is an essential ground rule in the superior-subordinate relationship and for the success of the business.
- How "homework before help" benefits both superior and subordinate.
- How the reward system works, including how work assignments are made, how reviews of progress and accomplishments are handled, how compensation decisions are made, and what factors are involved in transfers and promotions.
- Why, and under what conditions, individuals have the responsibility to cooperate with others.
- Why, and under what conditions, individuals have the responsibility to take the initiative.
- How acceptance of responsibility in the organization and voluntary cooperation and collaboration can contribute to the satisfaction of many human needs, including those for personal competence, achievement, recognition from others, and realized potential.

Teaching subordinates to cooperate and take the initiative under the proper circumstances makes it unnecessary to resort to pressure and demands to achieve work output. The teaching process requires

effort, and it should be considered an appropriate business investment. Teaching and learning must be a joint venture. The value of
the three-step summary lies in its simplicity. It's easy to know where
you're at in applying the process. The three steps in the teaching
process are:

	Teacher	*Learner*
	Explains/Shows	Perceives
	Discusses	Thinks
	Applies	Tries

This process is suggested for teaching subordinates all aspects of
the system for managing what's important to the success of the business—that is, the system for realizing human potential and achieving
optimum business results.

Fundamentals of the Effective Use of Human Resources

The hierarchy of leader and follower behavior and related
issues—how the leader achieves work output, the effect on follower
behavior, and the work satisfaction of followers—reminds us of the
following fundamentals of the effective use of human resources:

1. A leader has to take risks in the delegation of responsibility in
order to develop the talents of subordinates.

2. A leader can't achieve the most effective use of human resources by using the least effective approaches.

3. A leader has to take action, put forth effort, in order to
achieve effective use of human resources, including: setting up job
content (responsibilities and objectives) of subordinates; teaching individual responsibility for contributing to the success of the business,
which includes the development and use of talent throughout the organization; coaching in ways that help and motivate subordinates;
and reinforcing systematic management practices, cooperation, teamwork, progress toward objectives, initiative, and important accomplishments.

In summary, leader behavior at Levels 1 and 2 is never appropriate. The outcomes of such behavior are unpredictable; the true cost of
its effect on followers is exorbitant. Leader behavior at Level 3 is appropriate whenever it's necessary to make assignments to get the work

done, and leader behavior at Level 4 is the ideal to strive for. The outcomes of behavior at Levels 3 and 4 lead to the development, utilization, motivation, and retention of talent in the organization, and to competence, achievement, recognition, and realized potential.

Comparisons with Other Theories

The reader is encouraged to compare and contrast the theory of the hierarchy of leader and follower behavior with other, well-known theories on the effective use of human resources. How we think and behave as leaders and managers is influenced by our assumptions about human nature and how to be most effective in our particular roles. Consider the impact of the following on your thinking, and thus your behavior:

- The strength of various human needs as explained by Abraham H. Maslow.
- The two sets of assumptions about human nature propounded by Douglas McGregor.
- How our value systems influence organizational behavior, according to Chris Argyris.
- The relationship of meaningful work and psychological growth, explained in the work of Frederick Herzberg.
- How concern for people and concern for production should be linked together, as explained by Robert R. Blake and Jane S. Mouton.
- The continuum of management styles described by Rensis Likert.
- The relationship of freedom and responsive behavior, explained by Erich Fromm.
- The meeting of basic human needs by coping with reality and showing responsible behavior, as suggested by William Glasser.
- The concept of developmental supervision, defined by M. Scott Myers.
- The movement toward a flexible and adaptive management structure, as outlined by Warren G. Bennis.

In the work of each of these well-known authors, it's possible to differentiate the least effective from the most effective use of human resources. Whose responsibility is it to implement the theory? And is there a management system that has the theory built in?

Implementing Theory—Whose Responsibility?

The quest for effective use of human resources is not merely a game for the social scientist or the subject of a speech by an altruistic executive. It's the responsibility of every individual in a business organization. Every manager should be personally involved in the quest. Keeping up with pertinent research, learning from personal experimentation and the experience of others, sharing experiences with others—these are activities worthy of managers at every level in the organization. Every subordinate should be an active participant in the quest also. As human resources, all individuals should be involved in the development and use of their talents for the benefit of themselves and of every other person connected with the organization.

More than theory is involved in the quest for the effective use of human resources. Theory has to be coupled with practical application. The foregoing well-known theories served as background against which the practices of the system for managing what's important to a business were tested and developed. The hierarchy of leader behavior and its effect on follower behavior and organizational performance were developed from firsthand experience attempting to make effective use of these well-known theories about people and organizational systems.

The hierarchy of leader and follower behavior summarizes, in terms readily understood by leaders and followers, much of what has been said before about effective use of human resources, and adds some new insights. It provides a single, fresh, theoretical base for the practices that make up a better way of managing and accomplishing what's important to business success. Use the system as designed, follow the practices suggested, and you will be implementing theory that will lead to the most effective use of human resources in your organization.

3

The Evolution in Design

A management system designed to achieve business results and realize human potential has to be built around the job content of individual positions—responsibilities to be managed and objectives to be achieved in fulfilling those responsibilities. Let's look at the evolution in design, beginning with the first appearance of an important management concept in the literature. The concept deals with job content and using job content in managing. Perhaps no other idea has had such an impact on so many individuals in business organizations. The concept has been used and abused. It has received much credit for phenomenal business successes, and it has been held in contempt as the cause of dismal business failures. It is so important as a management tool that no discussion of a management system can ignore it. We must, therefore, examine the evolution in using job content in managing. We'll start with the coining of the well-known phrase "managing by objectives."

Peter Drucker said it first: "To manage a business means . . . to manage by objectives." That was back in 1954, when his book *The Practice of Management,** now hailed as a classic in management literature, was first published. The evolution that has taken place in using responsibilities and objectives in managing since Drucker coined the

* New York: Harper & Row, 1954, p. 12.

phrase is fascinating. Managing by objectives, or simply MBO, continues year after year as a popular topic in management circles. There is widespread agreement that MBO is no fad. Fads usually bloom and fade in much less than 25 years. Why the sustained interest? Managers have recognized that what Drucker said in 1954 was right. And they are still struggling to find the best way to do it—to actually manage their businesses on the basis of the responsibilities and objectives they have established.

Looking back at the evolution in design of a management system using responsibilities and objectives is a way of gaining perspective on where we are today, which can help us to master our circumstances and to change the way things are to the way we wish them to be by our deliberate action. To the extent that we take deliberate action to create the future, to make the desired results come to pass, we are managing the business by objectives.

Before we trace the evolution in using objectives, let's acknowledge two obvious facts. First, objectives existed before Drucker. He did not invent them. Call them by any name you will, objectives have been around since time began. Second, responsibilities and objectives have been used in managing as long as business has existed. To paraphrase Drucker, how else can you manage a business?

So what did Drucker do? He forcefully called to our attention the importance of using responsibilities and objectives in managing a business. Others have followed, adding their contributions. From Drucker's pronouncement to today, an evolution has taken place in the design of this critical part of a viable management system. Let's consider some of the aspects of this evolution. It started with the early struggles, grew into full-scale experimentation, settled into a traditional stage, and is now emerging into a developmental era with a search for a better way.

Stage I: The Early Struggles

The earliest attempts at the systematic use of responsibilities and objectives in managing in the mid-1950s quite naturally followed the suggestions made by Drucker. Drucker identified eight areas in which objectives should be set: market standing, innovation, productivity, physical and financial resources, profitability, manager performance and development, worker performance and attitude, and public responsibility. He knew the first five areas would have general acceptance but that some would protest the inclusion of the last three areas—the "intangibles." He argued that their neglect would result in the loss of performance in other areas and ultimately in the loss of business life.

Influenced by Drucker's thinking, many companies attempted to use the eight areas of responsibility as he outlined them. They ran into difficulties. At the very top levels of larger organizations, some of the areas seemed to fit very well, but other areas seemed less relevant to the real world. Many executives had never given much thought to certain areas of responsibility suggested by Drucker. So, those executives interested in using his ideas accepted the challenge to broaden their thinking and increase their contribution to their company, stockholders, and society by attempting to use each of the eight areas for setting objectives. This was a major step forward in managing an entire job by objectives.

However, in a way this added to the difficulties. The executives still faced the problem of setting objectives under each area of responsibility, including the intangible areas that Drucker insisted were central to the management of an enterprise. It was difficult enough to set objectives in areas that were familiar. When it came to the unfamiliar areas, the whole exercise seemed impractical. Another difficulty was that as the objectives system was expanded to lower levels, many managers tried to use the same eight areas of responsibility, and found them to be inappropriate. Trying to "force fit" the eight responsibility areas to most jobs was a frustrating exercise.

The companies trying to follow Drucker's suggestions found he was right—it is, indeed, tough to decide what should be measured, and how to measure it for each area of responsibility. With no models to follow, and no experience with the process, it was truly a struggle to get started.

The focus of the first stage, then, was the struggle to define areas of responsibility that fit the particular job, and to decide what to measure and how to measure it. And it was becoming clear that writing objectives documents was only the beginning of the process of using objectives to manage job responsibilities. There was, indeed, a need for experimentation, building on the foundation laid by Drucker.

Stage II: The Experimentation Period

The experimentation stage took place in the late 1950s and the 1960s. The period was marked by both successful and unsuccessful attempts to install management systems built around responsibilities and objectives. The definitions of success and failure varied widely. Standards of what constituted an effective system were slowly developing as experience accumulated and was shared.

The experimentation stage brought us closer to where we are today in the evolution of a practical management system. Each of the following items had real impact during the period. Some are still recognizable today. To dramatize the experimentation stage, the extremes experienced by many organizations are indicated. It's likely that every organization involved in MBO programs during the period would identify with one or more of the following items.

The bandwagon. Having an in-company management by objectives "program" became the thing to do. It was popular. Executives had something new to talk about inside and outside the company. The burst of enthusiasm at the top had its effect throughout the organization. Buzz words abounded. The flurry of activity involved in talking about objectives and writing objectives gave managers the feeling that they were now managing by objectives.

The bandwagon was more form than substance. Pronouncements from top management, meetings and booklets to explain the program, training in writing objectives, revised performance appraisal forms, and talk, talk, talk made the new program obvious. However, substance was lacking. Managers were groping for ways to make the program work. A year or two after the initial burst of enthusiasm, it was common to find little evidence that the program had made a positive impact on management practices or business results. More often the result was a negative impact on morale and the creation of a variety of ingenious ways to "beat the system."

The literature explosion. As interest in managing by objectives grew, writers responded with their interpretation of Drucker's thinking, and added their own. External consultants wrote books and articles and collaborated with internal personnel in case histories of the experience of their organization. Within an organization, instructions, theory, and encouragement from top management were often combined in memorandums and booklets. A variety of names and phrases related to MBO were introduced. Some phrases were picked to avoid the use of the word *objectives*. This usually occurred when an earlier attempt at managing by objectives had had disastrous results and there was a desire to start fresh under banners such as Goals, Targets, Commitments, Results.

The literature, considered as a whole, added a great deal to management thought. Unfortunately, mixed in with the sound fundamentals were untested theories and approaches. Many of the approaches tried were based on the latest research findings and experience available at the time. But by today's standards, some were not sound. Some of the literature was created to sell a particular viewpoint for the benefit of the author, who might have been a personnel specialist, consultant, or trainer. Some of the theories and approaches were simply shallow thinking, probably owing to lack of experience in managing in the real world.

Public courses. Conferences, seminars, and workshops on MBO were numerous during this period. The philosophy behind MBO was usually reviewed in depth, and much time was spent on writing objectives. Participant ratings of a course were critical to its future, so leader behavior and course design made sure the participants completed the course evaluation worksheets while in a state of euphoria about managing by objectives. A "good" or a "great" course meant the course leader was stimulating, entertaining, had lively comebacks to questions, told new jokes or told old jokes in new ways, spoke with professional authority, drew diagrams and graphs and offered other colorful visual presentations, and what have you.

But who could judge course content? Who could question the validity of the suggested models, forms, and procedures, based on the new MBO concepts? So, the stage presence of the course leader determined what was accepted by the participants.

Two outcomes of public courses were common. First, participants became very enthusiastic about the concepts and potential benefits of MBO. They hoped to install an MBO program in their own organization after attending the course. Second, they were unable to accomplish the installation of the program back on the job because they didn't have a practical, sound system to work with. In most cases, a year later, there was little or no evidence that the public course had led to systematic use of objectives in managing the business.

Job descriptions and MBO. Existing job descriptions had a great impact on the definition of areas of responsibility and objectives. Job descriptions were usually written in terms of activities rather than end results. The carryover of lists of activities from the job descriptions to the objectives documents was a natural one. As Drucker noted, it's tough to determine what to measure and how to measure it. Copying activities from the job description was easier.

Number of objectives. Long lists of objectives growing out of job descriptions posed two problems. One was the difficulty of managing a large number of objectives, of physically keeping track of progress. The other was dealing with the priorities involved in trying to manage the entire job by objectives. Some writers of the day argued that too many objectives tended to take the drive out of an objectives program. Minor objectives, they said, received attention to the detriment of major objectives. The selection of a small number of objectives covering major areas of responsibility seemed to be a practical solution to the problems of managing long lists of objectives and deciding priorities among them. As a working rule, two to five objectives came to be considered an appropriate number for any position. But selecting a small number of major objectives meant that only a part of the job was to be managed by objectives. In cases where a number of minor duties were combined, objectives tended to be broad and general rather than specific. In either event, this experimentation led further away from the concepts outlined by Drucker.

Improvement objectives. One approach that resulted in reducing the total number of objectives to be managed was to select areas of the job where improvement was needed and write one or more objectives for each of these areas. Although this approach didn't attempt to manage the entire job by objectives, it did encourage individuals to think through possible improvements under the following headings: (1) correcting problems, (2) handling routine operations, (3) introducing new and better ways of doing the work, and (4) individual development. Ease of measurement was a big factor in setting objectives for improvement, and it became convenient to blame the MBO system for any failure to achieve significant business results.

Assigning weights. In the attempt to reach agreement on the importance of specific objectives, the practice of assigning weights or percentage values was introduced. The idea was to encourage a more balanced effort from the subordinate by identifying, for example, objective A as 40 percent, objective B as 40 percent, and objective C as 20 percent of the job. Unfortunately, the weights, and the objectives themselves, were allowed to become fixed and to stay fixed in spite of changing circumstances. This rigidity created a host of problems that did not contribute to effective management, and no practical method of maintaining flexibility with regard to objectives or weights was developed.

Subjective judgments were required both in setting up the weights and in evaluating the extent to which each objective had been achieved. These subjective judgments affected business plans, budgets, performance appraisals, and compensation and promotion decisions. Abuses were blamed on the MBO program, not on the individual responsible for the judgments.

The purpose of experimenting with assigning weights to objectives was to simplify and improve the system. The outcomes were largely counterproductive.

Action plans. The introduction of a system for managing by objectives called for a heavy emphasis on setting, writing, and reaching agreement on objectives. Some managers new to the MBO approach naively assumed that once objectives were agreed upon with their subordinates, achievement of the results would naturally follow by allowing the subordinates full freedom in working toward their objectives. It didn't take long for this hands-off attitude to change. Superiors were uncomfortable having objectives alone as a means of following up on their subordinates' progress and performance. Managers not used to real delegation, and not knowing how to live with the risks involved, wanted more assurance that their subordinates' objectives would be reached. Knowledge of the activities being carried out to achieve objectives filled this need. So, there was a requirement for action plans to be developed and added to the objectives document.

Several problems were compounded by this experimentation. First, the paperwork grew from a few precise statements of end results to pages of detailed activities. The amount of detail depended on the demands of the superior. Second, the activities dominated the objectives document by sheer numbers of words, and came to dominate the objectives program. Objectives were the future. Action steps were now, observable, inviting attention. Follow-up focused more on activities than on end results. Third, the need to have action plans to achieve each objective led to increased caution in setting objectives and to more pressure to achieve objectives. Fourth, putting action steps on the same piece of paper as objectives had the effect of "locking them in." Carrying out the stated action steps became as important as achieving the objectives. Rigidity in the system increased. Fifth, time and effort were required to prepare action plans to fill the available space on the objectives document. In some cases, the action plans were meaningless duplicates or digests of plans already prepared. In other cases, the plans were far too sketchy in relation to the importance of the objective and the difficulties and complexities involved in accomplishing it. So much planning was required that some managers complained there was no time to do the work. Or by the time the detailed planning was completed, the situation had changed and the planning had to be redone.

Reviews of progress and accomplishments. Naturally, some kind of review process was needed to follow progress toward objectives and/or accomplishment of objectives. There was also a natural apprehension about how the objectives would be used—to reward? to punish? Meeting objectives became all important. Failure to meet objectives was a no-no punished in a variety of ways, including negative ratings, which in turn were tied to compensation and promotion decisions. There was little stress on analyzing results as a learning process or on evaluating results in terms of their importance to the success of the business.

Formal reviews were usually done annually. Written reports were often required of subordinates. The requirement to account for results versus each objective encouraged setting a small number of readily measurable objectives and making easily attainable objectives appear difficult. In addition to results data, the reports of activities carried out to achieve the results were used to fill the space on the report forms, especially when results did not meet or exceed the objectives. Rewriting the reports until the boss was satisfied became an accepted practice.

Rather than have the subordinate prepare a written report, some companies required the boss to prepare the report and discuss it with the subordinate. The discussion part was frequently omitted, with the excuse that there was no time "due to the press of business." Actually, bosses were under great pressure to think of something to say that would be acceptable to the subordinate and to higher levels of management, and that would at the same time represent them well as the immediate superiors. The safe way was for bosses to make reports with an eye to their own future, and not bother the subordinate with details that would require lengthy explanations or delicate confrontation.

Verbal reviews of progress were sometimes held semiannually, sometimes quarterly. After looking at the data, the boss usually evaluated the situations and then launched into what the subordinate should have done and what should now be done. The boss selected the areas most obviously in need of improvement, namely, objectives not reached. The process was seen by subordinates as punitive. Again, meeting objectives was reinforced as the name of the game.

Paperwork. Personnel specialists developed a variety of forms, procedures, and instructions for managing by objectives. The visible, tangible, additional paperwork coming out of the personnel department caused the system to be seen as "another personnel program" instead of as a tool for managing the business.

The measurement of performance provided information useful in identifying individual development needs, making compensation decisions, and assessing potential for promotion. Personnel specialists seized the opportunity to "simplify" the paperwork by combining these personnel functions with management by objectives. Some tried to accomplish all the paperwork at the annual appraisal of performance. The paperwork revealed the "system." It didn't take long for employees to discover how the system worked and to find ways to beat it. Then the inventors of the system added forms and procedures and instructions. It became a game in which everyone lost. The experimentation in combining paperwork and trying to accomplish several separate functions all at once was a major cause of the failure in managing by objectives during this period.

Installation by edict. Enthusiasm for the relatively new concept of managing by objectives led some top executives to want their entire organization to begin using the program immediately. A common approach was a letter to all employees announcing the program and the starting date. Crash training sessions in writing objectives helped produce the necessary initial drafts of objectives. The internal bandwagon began to roll, each department wanting to be credited with being the first to implement the program.

No one really knew at that time what it took to have a successful installation or how long it would take to achieve it. Each organization that tried to install MBO did its best to succeed. But when the system itself was at fault, no amount of effort could make it succeed. So, when the burst of enthusiasm had passed, and the great expectations of the program were not realized, superiors and subordinates allowed the program to quietly disappear. In many cases, it remained only as a sheaf of paper in the drawer, updated annually.

Stage III: The Emergence of the Traditional Approach

In spite of the "mechanical failures" that occurred and the "design errors" that crept in during the experimentation stage, MBO was firmly established as an important management tool by the mid-1970s. Enough companies had experimented with it, enough writers had extolled its virtues, and enough experience had been accumulated to know some of the benefits, pitfalls, obstacles, and effort involved.

Where the MBO approach had been tried and had failed, for whatever reasons, the formal, companywide effort endorsed by top management disappeared. The term MBO was no longer used. Talk about the MBO effort that didn't work was seldom heard because of the scars left behind. However, objectives were still used, just as they had been before Drucker's pronouncements. And bits and pieces of the MBO effort could be detected, though they went by different names from those connected with the ill-fated MBO program.

Successful MBO installations meant top management still endorsed the program, objectives were written annually, and participants had adjusted themselves to the demands of the program. Success was defined by those companies as whatever they were doing with MBO; it was not necessarily that the MBO program was a major contribution to the success of the business.

Traditional MBO, descriptive of what most companies were doing, can be summarized as follows:

1. Objectives were set annually for parts of the job, not the entire job. From two to eight objectives were normal. There was no at-

tempt to define how much of the job was covered by the objectives, but some form of weighting objectives was common.

2. Objectives were set where measurement was easy and data were available, regardless of the importance of the results to the success of the business. Subjective measures were avoided, again regardless of the importance of the objectives.

3. Meeting or modestly exceeding each objective became the major concern of individual participants. The rule was learned quickly: Don't risk it; set objectives you know you can reach; it doesn't pay to fall even a bit short or to succeed by too large a margin.

4. Action plans were required for each objective. Written at the same time as the objectives, usually on the same piece of paper, these plans received undue attention as measures of performance.

5. Reviews of progress toward objectives during the year seldom took place. The end-of-year review of results versus objectives was part of an overall appraisal of performance, potential, development needs, and compensation. The "annual doomsday appraisal" was continued. Objectives added to its punitive impact.

6. Paperwork requirements imposed on MBO participants were accepted as part of the system. Participants worked out various ways to beat the system.

7. On a day-to-day basis, there was merely token use of the MBO program at all levels. Complacency replaced enthusiasm. Compliance was perfunctory. Participants got used to "submitting their MBOs" over a period of years without paying attention to the potential benefits. The program they had filled their need to be able to say they had an objectives program. That the program was of no real help, or that it was in some ways counterproductive, was considered to be the problem of personnel and top management.

8. Teamwork was a minor issue. The procedures suggested did not stress teamwork or provide appropriate reinforcement when it occurred.

9. MBO programs were installed, operated, and updated by copying others. Some tailoring of what was borrowed was common. All too often, it was a case of "monkey see, monkey do." Lack of experience with MBO made it difficult to recognize its myriad potential problems and pitfalls. What a major competitor did, or what a neighboring organization considered successful, or what appeared in some trade journal was accepted as proof that the practice was sound,

practical, effective, productive. Problems were accepted as necessary, matters to be put up with. Companies were apathetic about developing a system that would provide all the potential benefits listed in the literature.

Although no two MBO programs were identical, the general points should be useful in comparing traditional MBO with the better way of using objectives suggested in this volume.

Stage IV: The Search for a Better Way

Organizations of every size and kind were using objectives programs by the late 1970s. Each year, more and more managers were learning something about MBO. The more they learned, the more they questioned whether it was something they should try (if they weren't doing it already) or whether they could improve the approach they were already using.

Among the reasons for the continuing interest in MBO, the following stand out: (1) Managing a business is becoming more complex, and this trend is not likely to change. Technical advances, automation, data processing, government controls, and the expectations of the workforce all add to the complexities. (2) With the growing complexity of business, a firm sense of direction in the overall organization as well as in each department and each individual is becoming increasingly important to business results and morale. (3) The planning and control processes common to business, such as budgets, forecasts, and strategic plans, don't provide all that's needed by individuals to manage their specific job responsibilities. (4) Behavioral research encourages approaches that call for greater involvement of the individual in all management processes; involvement leads to development, commitment, teamwork, motivation.

The reason key executives turn to MBO for help with their management problems, or seek to upgrade their MBO approach, is usually a mixture of believing there is great value in having an MBO system that works and feeling there is something missing in their current approach, that some parts of their existing system are not working well, that while they may have important objectives in writing, they are not actually managing their business effectively.

The developmental stage was ushered in by managers who were used to some form of traditional MBO, who were enthusiastic about the potential benefits, and who were looking for a better way of doing it. Here are some examples of situations that led key managers to seek a better way of using objectives. In each case, the organization had been using objectives but not with a fully functioning systems approach such as that suggested in this book.

Case 1: A Deliberate Effort
to Get All the Potential Benefits of MBO

The president of a retail chain had experienced the "fizzle and flop" of an MBO effort in a former organization. He found the theory exciting, but he saw the great initial effort collapse within four months. He puzzled over what went wrong, and how to make an MBO program work. After his disappointing experience, he identified in broad terms what he was looking for:

1. A theoretically sound system that would permit the realization of all the potential benefits suggested in the literature.
2. A system that focused on business results, not on justification for compensation decisions.
3. A system practical enough that managers would be willing to live with it over the long haul.
4. A system that didn't call for a single burst of enthusiasm by anyone (a reflection of his great desire to avoid a "fizzle and flop" experience).
5. A system that could be installed in deliberate steps over a reasonably short period of time.

He knew it wouldn't be easy to come up with such a system, but he was willing to hunt for someone who could help him install the kind of system he was hoping for, and then to do what was necessary to support the installation.

Case 2: Crisis Conditions Require
Rapid Establishment of Two-Way Communications

A new man had just been appointed to take over as plant manager at a facility with a host of problems. As he saw the situation, top management was desperate. Privately he was told he had just 90 days to move in and accomplish a turnaround in several critical areas of plant operations. He knew very little about this particular plant or its personnel, but he had experience in plant engineering and as assistant manager at another plant.

Under these crisis conditions, he needed a means of quickly establishing two-way communications with his key personnel. He wanted them to learn what had to be accomplished from his point of view. He needed to learn who did what, and how each key individual functioned in the plant organization. In a previous work assignment, the managers had used three to five objectives. Now he saw the need for defining all major responsibilities and having objectives covering the entire job. Teaching, learning, and coordinating efforts as a team were his major concerns as he sought to achieve the required operations turnaround.

Case 3: Inflexibility and Tunnel Vision Resented

As a long-time employee of the organization, an executive had grown accustomed to a limited number of high-priority objectives dealing with profits, sales volume, and manufacturing costs. But she resented the inflexibility of the system that measured success or failure on the basis of locked-in objectives set the first of the year. And she felt too little attention was paid to building the organization as far as people and teamwork were concerned. With the autonomy granted her when she was appointed division president, she set out to find and install a system different in the following respects from the one used in the other divisions:

1. Objectives would be changed whenever it became sensible to change them in light of new priorities, changing circumstances, and available resources. Superior-subordinate agreement to the changes would be the only requirement.
2. The seeking of new business opportunities would be stressed throughout the year. Objectives would be added as needed.
3. The need to make trade-offs at critical decision points would be recognized and supported by top management when performance was evaluated against objectives.
4. Objectives would be set for each area of responsibility, including people and teamwork areas. Reinforcement for results in the people and teamwork areas would be as strong and consistent as for operating results.

Case 4: Company Success Not Assured by Meeting Objectives

A new CEO found that all senior managers were rated as top performers. This meant all were achieving their objectives. This didn't square with the fact that the organization was in severe financial distress. The CEO was puzzled as to how each individual could succeed while the organization failed. Discussing traditional MBO practices revealed some clues that were later confirmed as the real problem: Managers had learned (been taught by the practices of the organization) to set targets they knew they could reach. An elaborate system for documentation of excuses and justification of objectives had developed.

The CEO wanted to update the system to reduce the mechanics and paperwork and to increase the verbal communications related to objectives, priorities, performance standards, and accomplishments. The aim was to shift the focus to achieving significant contributions to company success, not merely meeting objectives.

Case 5: The Paradox of Freedom and Control

A rapidly expanding, high-technology organization was having trouble managing its growth. The top executives had the expertise, but were unwilling to "let go" as newcomers were added. So, lists of objectives grew to ridiculous lengths; executives frantically tried to manage all the pieces; subordinates felt like puppets dancing at the ends of the strings.

As subordinates, the executives all wanted freedom to use their expertise to get the job done. As bosses, they all wanted to retain control over results. Thus they were searching for a system that would provide the paradox of increased delegation and freedom for subordinates to innovate and experiment within the necessary parameters, and at the same time provide increased control to bosses so they would be willing to let go.

Case 6: The Hidden Costs of New Assignments

A major division of a large marketing organization studied turnover of personnel and the associated costs and concluded that recruiting and formal training costs were high but necessary. The largest hidden cost turned out to be associated with internal transfers and promotions—that is, the cost of gearing up employees to be fully productive in a new assignment where formal training was not provided. In addition, although difficult to measure, there was the cost of gearing up employees to handle new assignments within their present jobs.

The system this division was looking for had to accomplish the orientation of an employee to a new assignment in a matter of hours, not the weeks or months previously accepted as normal. The system had to take advantage of all that is known about motivation to learn, to take the initiative, and to use innovative approaches to achieving agreed-upon results.

Case 7: A Staid Organization with Many Old-Time Employees

A successful but staid manufacturing company was seeking a way to inject new vigor into its organization, especially its old-time employees. Promotion possibilities were close to zero. Many of the senior employees were at or near the top of their salary ranges. The challenge was to motivate employees to work enthusiastically and be creative under those conditions.

The president recognized the need for a system to encourage and reinforce success. She felt individual and team progress and accomplishments could be identified through objectives. She wanted to focus on the value of the accomplishments to the organization in order to encourage the setting of more challenging objectives. She felt this would lead to increased innovation. She hoped to find a management system that would "turn on" the organization without the usual rewards of pay and promotion.

Case 8: A Foundation Needed for a Total Organization Development Effort

A large manufacturing organization with plants at scattered locations wanted to build a common language, uniform management traditions, and teamwork on a global scale and at the same time increase the productivity and morale at individual locations. A variety of formal and informal MBO programs existed throughout the organization, but none were successful enough to be given consideration for the global effort. A new approach was needed.

The foundation of the total effort had to be a system that individuals at every location would be willing to use. Data were also needed for use as "before" and "after" measures of organization development. It was felt that data on a variety of management communication practices and conditions affecting productivity and motivation would encourage employees to join the organizationwide objectives effort. Finally, the organization wanted to provide skills training in conducting superior-subordinate job performance dialogues to support the proper use of objectives in the organization.

Case 9: Teaching and Learning in an Overseas Assignment

A manager assigned to an overseas subsidiary felt the need to bring effective management practices, as well as the latest industry technology, to his new position. He also recognized the need to learn the customs, management practices, and attitudes of subordinates throughout the organization in order to build effective work relationships in a minimum of time. He had been using objectives as a personal management tool for years but felt his approach lacked structure. He feared that in adding structure, the system would become rigid, impractical, paper-heavy. He wanted objectives to be the vehicle for increasing communications on every aspect of the business.

These examples show the current stage in the evolution in design and the variety of ways in which a management system built around the use of responsibilities and objectives can be used to grapple with management problems and take advantage of unique opportunities.

Where Does the Evolution Stand Today?

The design of management systems based on the use of responsibilities and objectives has been evolving for a quarter of a century. We are now in a developmental stage, with organizations of every size and kind examining their approaches. Many are finding ways to improve on their past practices, to realize more of the potential benefits. Their experience tells us to look first to the practicality of the system itself. Does the system actually help managers manage all the important responsibilities connected with their total job? Then look at how well the managers are using the system.

The essential features of the current developmental stage can be summed up as: more pressures of all kinds to manage better; more knowledge of the potential benefits of a management system built around the use of responsibilities and objectives; more searching for a practical system that will actually help a manager to manage better;

more willingness to do what is required to install and sustain such a system.

As the evolution goes on (with all the support and encouragement we can muster), who knows what new approaches will be developed and what additional benefits will be discovered? Meanwhile, a management system that is built around the use of responsibilities and objectives, but that is definitely not traditional MBO, is presented. How it works, and the necessary operating instructions, are included with each of its parts. It is hoped that with the perspective added by the evolution in design, the reader will recognize in each chapter what is new and unique that makes the system the "coming generation" in design.

4

The Coming Generation in Design

A system's design is not changed without reason. Changes should make the system better—sufficiently so to justify the change. Minor changes are frequently made to "debug" a system in operation. Infrequent, but of great importance, are the sweeping changes that produce a new "generation" of the system. The system presented here represents the coming generation in management systems design. The system has the same function as ever—achieving optimum business results and realizing human potential—but far more than minor debugging of traditional theories and practices is involved. Virtually every part of this management system differs significantly from the traditional one. All the differences together add up to a new generation in practical, systematic management. They represent a breakthrough in the quest for a better way of managing.

The primary use of the management system is for self-management, to help individuals manage their job responsibilities more effectively. Individual efforts have to be correlated, of course, to accomplish the objectives of the business. The management system facilitates the necessary communications with superiors, subordinates, and other associates in the business to achieve teamwork and to avoid gaps, overlaps, and misunderstandings in getting the work done.

While the primary use of the management system is for self-management, self-direction, and self-control in achieving business objectives, it is also designed for use with personnel processes, such as selection, development, career planning, job evaluation, appraisal of performance, appraisal of potential, and administration of compensation programs. Although these personnel processes are quite different from production, sales, and profits, they should be seen as integral parts of a smoothly functioning management system. The same is true for structural relationships, control mechanisms, and organizational improvement processes. Each part is designed to contribute to business results. Each is *important*.

Now comes a question of great significance. How will you know when the management system is being used as designed? Evidence that individuals are managing their job responsibilities can be examined. One interesting way of examining the evidence was suggested by a corporate lawyer. He posed this question to an associate in an operating department who firmly believed that a comprehensive approach to managing was practiced regularly in the organization: "Let's suppose you were arrested today, and accused of systematically and effectively managing your responsibilities. Would there be enough evidence to convict you?" From his desk drawer, the associate quickly produced his written objectives. "So far," the lawyer teased, "all you could possibly be convicted of is writing some objectives and putting them in your drawer. What the court wishes to see is evidence that those objectives represent the responsibilities of your entire job, and that you are actually using them in managing your job and accomplishing what's important to the business."

Systematic and *effective* as just used are key ideas linked together in the coming generation of management systems design. The systematic management of an entire job is quite different from the systematic management of part of a job. If a job isn't managed in its entirety, then some parts of the job are slighted as far as the management functions are concerned. Managing doesn't mean equal time, effort, and resources should be given to each responsibility or each objective, but it does mean that the amount of planning, organizing, directing, controlling, and innovating that go to each responsibility and each objective should be proportionate to its importance to the success of the organization.

However, managing the entire job using a systematic approach is not meaningful unless the effort yields accomplishments that are important to the business. In appraising performance, the effectiveness measure is the value of the accomplishments, not simply the fact that the objectives were met. Objectives are tools to use in managing and accomplishing what's important. Emphasizing the value of the accomplishments to the business is critical in changing from the traditional way of using objectives to a better way of using them.

Looking at the linkage of systematic management practices and effective performance from another angle, when individuals are rewarded on the basis of significant personal accomplishments only, teamwork is likely to suffer, and the balance among the myriad results necessary for business success is likely to be lost. Parts of any job might seem unglamorous, unappreciated, unimportant in comparison with other parts. But if those lowly parts of the job are not performed satisfactorily, the business might be jeopardized. When the efforts of each individual are closely correlated with the efforts of others, so that satisfactory results are achieved on all objectives, individual accomplishments are placed in proper perspective.

The ideal situation, then, is to have all employees approach work each day with a full understanding of their entire job to be managed as part of the overall work effort, with the tools to manage it, and asking this basic question: What can I do today so that at the end of the year I, my boss, and others will know that my job has been well managed, that we as a team have accomplished what's most important to the continued success of the business—that we set out to do it, and we actually did it? With this dual approach to work, priorities are constantly being examined so that the payoff from effort is optimized, and at the same time no part of the job is neglected.

Notice how often the word *important* is used in connection with managing responsibilities and accomplishing results. Job content is defined in terms of important responsibilities and important objectives. Priorities for action are based on importance of the results. Accomplishments are measured in terms of their importance to the organization. The coming generation in design is a system for managing all that has to be done—all the important bits and pieces of the job, not just a select few—with the emphasis on what's most important to the continued success of the business. Such a system meets both organizational and human needs.

Evidence of a Viable, Functioning Management System

The evidence that the system is functional, and that individuals are using it to manage their job responsibilities and accomplish what's important to the business, includes the following:

1. Each subordinate knows the current objectives, standards, and expectations of his or her superior and is informed of the needs of the business as changes occur. Transmitting this information is an ongoing process, not a one-time event. It takes place verbally and in writing, on a one-to-one basis and in group sessions.

2. The subordinate has a "living" document covering the content of the entire job. The document identifies the major areas of responsibility connected with the position, the most important controls to be used to manage each responsibility, and the most important end results to be achieved. The document is agreed upon with the superior and correlated with other documents in the organization so that it supports the overall mission of the organization. The document is "living" in the sense that it can be changed whenever there is reason to change it to benefit the business.

3. The subordinate has a system for tracking progress toward objectives. At least monthly, progress toward each objective and the need for change are evaluated by the employee. Action steps are taken as required.

4. The subordinate alerts his or her superior as soon as a potential problem with achieving an objective or an important opportunity to explore is recognized. This is a ground rule of "no surprises for the boss." Potential variances from desired results, and business opportunities worth considering, are identified in making the tracking system evaluations.

5. The subordinate does an appropriate amount of "homework" before seeking help from the superior in carrying out a job responsibility. This might be called a ground rule of "no delegating up." The superior requires evidence of homework in the form of problem identification, analysis, recommended action plans, and expected outcomes before reacting in the role of coach and counselor.

The homework-before-help ground rule applies to business opportunities as well as job performance problems. Homework in this case includes identifying the opportunity, the business potential, recommended action plans, and expected outcomes.

6. The subordinate develops action plans as needed to ensure the achievement of objectives. Effective action plans make clear what action steps are to be taken, who is to carry out the steps, when the steps will be taken and completed, and any constraints to be observed in the use of available resources.

7. The subordinate reports on his or her stewardship on all objectives at least quarterly to the superior, using the job content document and tracking system notations. The superior reacts to the report on each objective. In this process, priorities and standards are agreed upon, and necessary adjustments in action plans and objectives are made.

8. The subordinate participates in team reviews, covering matters of greatest importance to the business and items of concern to other team members. The team reviews (superior with immediate subordinates as a group) follow and supplement the superior-subordinate stewardship reviews.

9. The subordinate submits in writing a report of accomplishments at the end of the cycle (usually one year) and discusses it with the superior. The report is limited to important accomplishments. It shows, for each item, what was accomplished compared with the objective, the value or importance of the accomplishment to the business, and factors that helped or hindered. No alterations or rewrites of the report are allowed. The superior adds a commentary. The accomplishments report with its commentary becomes a permanent "highlights" record of the contributions of the individual to the success of the business during the period.

10. The individual is an active participant in the process when the boss sees the need for: (1) analysis and action planning to improve the individual's job performance, (2) identifying and correcting behavior of the individual that interferes with job performance, and (3) identifying and matching organizational requirements for personnel with the interests and aspirations of the individual, and then taking appropriate steps to prepare the individual for career opportunities.

11. Individuals participate in an ongoing organizational improvement process as a way of life for both subordinates and bosses. Subordinates supply candid data on practices and conditions in the

organization that affect their ability and willingness to do what is expected. Bosses use the data as reinforcement for current practices and conditions that are helpful and as direction and motivation to make changes where improvement is needed. Subordinates cooperate and collaborate with their bosses in implementing changes and evaluating results.

The Impact of a Viable Management System

The impact of the management system just described is felt throughout the organization. Roles change, old and rigid ideas give way to new ideas and flexibility, other management procedures and practices may be altered or perhaps even discarded.

The subordinate is cast in the role of operating manager—in a very real sense the chief operating officer with respect to his or her job—and is responsible for taking the initiative as much as possible in using the management system in managing his or her job responsibilities. The superior functions as adviser, coach, counselor, consultant. The functions of the two roles are summarized in Table 5.

Behavioral theory on leadership and motivation is built into the workings of the management system. Continuing education is encouraged, but it's not necessary to dwell on behavioral theory in order to get the system started or keep it going. Individuals can learn and increase their managerial effectiveness by experimenting with suggested management practices as parts of a total system.

Table 5. Roles of subordinate and superior.

Subordinate	Superior
Identifies responsibilities and develops objectives.	Reviews, advises as needed to correlate individual efforts, approves job content.
Develops initial action plans to achieve objectives, carries out plans, tracks progress, develops further plans.	Reviews plans on request, advises as needed, supports action plans.
Evaluates and reports progress and accomplishments.	Reviews progress, advises as needed, reinforces progress, teamwork, and accomplishments.

Flexibility in adapting leadership behavior to the needs of the followers and the situation is encouraged by the workings of the system. Flexibility is also encouraged with regard to the documents that define responsibilities and objectives. The documents will vary for each individual and each position. Some individuals set up and manage 50 or more objectives with ease; others with similar jobs choose to manage their responsibilities with half that number of objectives or less. Some objectives can be precisely stated and are easily measured; other objectives may involve inprecise measures and subjective judgments. Time spans for objectives achievement may vary from a week to a year or longer. The practical design of the system allows for flexibility in setting it up and using it.

When the system is installed organizationwide, existing management tools and longstanding practices may be affected. Budget preparation may need to be rescheduled to follow the establishment and correlation of objectives. The traditional annual doomsday appraisal by superiors is made obsolete. The compensation system must be examined to see if it will support or wreck the efforts to accomplish what's important to the business. The structural relationships may need to be changed to reflect changes in organizational objectives, obstacles to those objectives, and job content of individuals. The control mechanisms may need to be changed to set up and reinforce achievement motivation throughout the organization.

One manager, all alone, can benefit from use of the system. The benefits are such, however, that restricting its use is self-defeating. The benefits multiply as the system is implemented organizationwide.

The Benefits of the Improved Management System

When an organization updates its management system, it's natural to look for the potential benefits. All the potential benefits of the system have not yet been discovered, because perfection in the concepts and in their application is yet to be achieved. However, the potential benefits of the fully functioning system described here add up to significant contributions to better management. Here are the benefits most frequently mentioned by those who have used the system. Consider each one in light of its contribution to accomplishing what's important to the business.

1. Those who use the system know more precisely what is expected of them.
2. Subordinates have more freedom to accomplish what is expected of them, more opportunity to exercise self-direction and self-control.
3. Achievement motivation is nurtured at all levels.
4. Planning is improved and simplified through stress on important results; back-up action plans are developed only as needed to ensure the achievement of the results.
5. Bosses are more likely to work at their own objectives and to let go of work defined by their subordinates' objectives.
6. Subordinates are more responsive to changes in business priorities and standards of excellence.
7. Bosses have better control over the achievement of results, more confidence that effort and resources are being used to achieve objectives according to their importance to the success of the business.
8. Changes in job content, power to act, or structural relationships may be initiated at any time with minimal disruption of work flow and loss of productivity.
9. Superior-subordinate relationships are improved owing to less need for close supervision, and to making the role of the superior one of adviser, coach, counselor, and consultant.
10. Positive reinforcement and coaching are used extensively; traditional criticism is obsolete.
11. Development of managerial abilities is accelerated as a result of more coaching and counseling.
12. Subordinates know more precisely where they stand in the eyes of their superior on all major areas of job responsibility.
13. Subordinates know more precisely the basis on which their performance, potential, and developmental needs are appraised.
14. Teamwork is improved through identification of common objectives and through reinforcement of collaboration in achieving objectives.
15. Meeting objectives is desirable, but not enough; the name of the game is managing the entire job and accomplishng what's important to the success of the business.
16. Compensation is appropriately linked to contribution; rewards must be earned each year.

17. The incentive to "play games" is removed. Both superior and subordinate have reason to be honest in setting objectives, evaluating progress, and reporting accomplishments.
18. Identification, development, motivation, utilization, and retention of talent in the organization are fostered at all levels.
19. Organizational improvement efforts are established as a way of life throughout the organization.
20. The parts of the system work together and produce synergism in overall management performance.

Installing the System and Avoiding Breakdowns

Improving on existing practices requires changes in the way managers manage. Resistance to installation of the new system can be minimized by following this simple suggestion: Let the boss use it first and set the example. In this way the boss stays one step ahead of subordinates in learning how the system works, getting familiar with each of its parts, and trying out the operating instructions. The boss is in command of the system installation at lower levels in the organization. The boss decides when they start using it, and what help they get in learning to use it well. The boss also has a great opportunity to establish more effective communications, upgrade performance standards, redefine objectives and priorities, and make organizational improvement a way of life.

But system breakdowns are possible. All it takes is improper installation or neglect of one critical part, and the effectiveness of the whole system can be seriously impaired. Here are two suggestions for avoiding breakdowns:

Get the system installed and functioning throughout the organization as soon as is practicable. Dragging out the installation time indicates failure to realize the value of making the installation and getting it operating throughout the organization. A deliberate effort is required. It takes a commitment to provide essential orientation and skills training and to use each of the system's parts as designed.

Install and use the entire system. You wouldn't think of removing your automobile distributor as you prepared for a trip. You wouldn't think of disconnecting your computer before using it. You wouldn't think of leaving out the paper as you typed an important letter. Neither should you think of removing, disconnecting, or leaving out parts of the management system. It functions most effectively as a whole.

Traditional Practices Versus the Coming Generation in Design

Many ways of using objectives in managing had been conceived by the end of the experimentation stage of the late 1950s and the 1960s. Many of these experiments remain as part of traditional management practices. Many other ideas, some bordering on the ludicrous, were also conceived during those years and also remain with us.

Management programs are put together by well-meaning individuals doing the best they know how to do. Once in place, it's embarrassing to throw the programs out too quickly, as we have discussed previously, even when a better way is apparent. We owe much to the pioneers of management programs, but we're in a different world today, in a developmental stage in advanced management systems, and we have a responsibility to those who will follow to stay on the cutting edge of innovation. Traditional management systems are incapable of delivering the benefits described in the management literature as outcomes of the effective use of human resources. Many companies have found out the hard way that seemingly innocent practices can wreck a business.

There is a way that is better than traditional management systems. A new approach has been developed, tested, refined. It is flexible enough to fit any situation, yet structured enough to be useful organizationwide. A viable management system that is sensible and practical, that really works, has been outlined. In the following sections, more detail is provided on how to use the parts of such a system in managing what's important to your business.

II

THE MANAGEMENT SYSTEM AND INDIVIDUAL NEEDS

The system for managing what's important is designed to accomplish two indispensable business outcomes: (1) effective management of each individual's entire job, and (2) business success through individual (and team) efforts adding up to accomplishing what's important.

This section discusses the "how to" of making these outcomes a reality. The system does not represent perfection—achieving perfection is an eternal quest. But the system is a better way than the traditional approaches in wide use today. This claim calls for explaining what's new and better. It calls for definitions, guidelines, models, procedures, and operating instructions. And these how-to suggestions have to complement one another and form a cohesive management system that is founded in the soundest theory we have on the effective use of human resources.

So let's set the stage for the how-to chapters that follow by re-emphasizing: The system cannot function without appropriate attention both to the entire job and to significant individual contributions to business success.

It's not enough for an employee to systematically carry out the management processes of planning, organizing, directing, controlling, and innovating unless the outcomes of those efforts include accomplishments important to the success of the business.

It's not enough for an employee to accomplish one or even several important objectives if at the same time the employee fails to manage the remainder of his or her job responsibilities and fails to achieve satisfactory results in all aspects of the job.

The framework of a better way of managing makes it possible for all employees to manage their entire job well. This means allocating effort and resources to each area of responsibility, and each objective, in proportion to the importance of the results to the success of the business.

A new distinction between *managing* and *management* has been developed by a council of business, industry, and academic leaders for the Society for Advancement of Management:

> Managing—designing and maintaining an environment for effective and efficient use of resources and performance of individuals working together in groups toward accomplishment of preselected missions and objectives.

> Management is both a science and an art; as a science it is organized knowledge—concepts, theory, principles and techniques—underlying the practice of managing; as an art it is application of the organized knowledge to realities in a situation, usually with blend or compromise to obtain desired practical results.

The term *managing* applies to the doing, to the proper use of each of the management processes in relation to each area of responsibility for achieving business results. Managing the entire job begins with defining all major areas of responsibility for results and then deciding what needs to be accomplished. Each person in a business organization will have one or more areas of responsibility in each of three categories: work, people, and self-development. To manage all these segments of the total job requires a systematic approach.

Deciding what's important to the success of the business is a process, not a single event. Each of the following is involved in the process: the definition of areas of responsibility connected with a particular position; the selection of end results desired, correlated with the objectives of others; the periodic evaluation of progress by the individual; progress reviews, in which current priorities and standards are examined; and the evaluation of accomplishments as contributions to business success.

Accomplishing what's important to the success of the business involves all of these elements plus all of the other management system parts that play a role in the achievement of the desired business results. The effectiveness of managerial dialogues, the approaches to organizational behavior, control practices, career development systems, and organizational improvement processes either add to or detract from the impact of the management system as the way to accomplish what's important.

The management system itself has to be sound if it's to help the business succeed. The effectiveness of the management system depends on the practicality of the parts, how the parts fit together, and the willingness of individuals to use the system in managing. The basic requirements for success in managing a job, then, are knowing the right things to do, and systematically doing them. This includes an understanding of the models, the practices, and the procedures to follow and the willingness to use them. Willingness to use the system increases as managers learn how it works, can see that it's sensible and practical, and can see that potential benefits far outweigh the cost in time and effort. Given the chance, the system can shape attitudes toward experimentation, learning, cooperation, and collaboration.

This section focuses on how the system meets the needs of individuals in managing their jobs and accomplishing what's important. How the parts of the system work, and the operating instructions to make sure each part is fully used, are explained for the benefit of the management newcomers who seek to establish effective managerial practices. For more experienced managers, the parts and operating instructions permit comparisons to be made with their current managerial practices and offer the challenge to continually seek a better way of managing.

5

How to Use Job Content as the Key to Power and Results

One manager who is enthusiastic about having subordinates' efforts properly directed starts each staff meeting this way: "My job was created because my boss needed some help in doing his job. Now, any questions about why your jobs were created?"

Whenever it's important for certain results to be achieved, and the work involved is too much for one person to handle, changes need to be made. Adding personnel is perhaps the most common change. As soon as the team grows by the addition of a new member, some fundamental questions arise. What is the newcomer responsible for? How does the addition of a new member affect the job responsibilities of others on the team? What has to be correlated to avoid gaps, overlaps, and misunderstandings in job responsibilities, and to increase teamwork? What effect will these changes have on the motivation of the individuals involved? What about the development, use, and retention of talent in the organization? These issues are all related to job content.

A major management challenge is to set up the content of jobs and establish a work climate that encourages individuals to develop their talents and fulfill their personal objectives, and at the same time make significant contributions to the success of the business. A balance of results in a number of critical areas of responsibility, including both short- and long-term considerations, is required for business success. Job content can become the key to power and business results—the clout to make the right things happen.

Job Content: Responsibilities, Objectives, and Power

Job content has to do with the work itself. It involves the responsibilities to be managed, the results to be achieved, and the power to achieve them. Job *content* has to do with the motivators, the satisfiers: responsibility, achievement, recognition for achievement, psychological growth. Job *context* has to do with the environmental factors used to control job dissatisfaction: company policy and administration, supervision, compensation, interpersonal relations, and working conditions.

Defining job content should be viewed as an ongoing process. Jobs should be designed for growth; they should require the individuals to learn and do things they've never done before. And as knowledge and skills develop, new challenges need to be built into the job content. Job content must be flexible to meet the needs of the organization for business results, and the needs of the individual for psychological growth.

The whole job has to be defined if it's to be managed. A document outlining responsibilities and objectives provides a practical format for defining a whole job in such a way that it can be managed. A job content document that simplifies communications and minimizes paperwork is important to making the system viable.

Once a responsibility or an objective is agreed upon as part of the job content of a particular position, the matter of power is involved. With each responsibility, and with each objective, the individual is delegated certain authority and must exercise power in order to achieve the desired results. The effective way to use power in achieving work output was discussed in Chapter 2. Managing power and resolving power conflicts between superior and subordinate, and between or among groups, are discussed in Chapter 16.

The Influence of Job Content at Higher Levels

Knowing job content at higher levels provides a guide to defining job content at lower levels. When lower-level employees do not know higher-level job content, they have to make assumptions. If the assumptions are faulty, the results of their work are not likely to be seen by higher levels as productive contributions to the success of the business.

Knowing the responsibilities, objectives, priorities, and standards of those at higher levels takes more than reading a document. It involves explaining by the boss, and questioning by the subordinate, and discussing as much and as often as necessary for full communication and understanding. There are ample opportunities for communicating when the need and value of sharing the thinking at higher levels with those at lower levels is clear.

The Responsibility for Defining Job Content

Who actually defines job content, the superior or the subordinate? Experience tells us two things: Who writes down the words that define the job varies with the situation. And it really doesn't matter who first suggests a responsibility or an objective.

For newcomers to a job, the superior is heavily involved in spelling out job content. Discussions of job responsibilities, the bottom-line challenges to be faced, the obstacles to be overcome, the relationships, the high-priority projects, the available talent to be developed and utilized, the people problems, the opportunities for personal growth—these are all typical preliminaries to preparing a job content document for a new member of the team. For experienced professionals, the superior's involvement in spelling out job content may be limited to granting approval and making sure that correlation with the jobs of others is achieved. In some cases, the superior may need to scrutinize job content to make sure the professional still has room to grow, has new heights to reach, and is motivated to achieve.

It really doesn't matter who suggests an item first in preparing a job content document. What does matter is that it's understood and accepted by both superior and subordinate. Agreement is needed on the job responsibilities to be managed and on the end results that are of greatest value to the business. This is most apparent when an individual enters a new position. Of course, the importance of superior and subordinate discussions of job content never diminishes.

The process of defining job content is not easy. Fortunately, once job content is defined, keeping it updated is relatively easy. Striving for perfection in defining job content is a trap to be avoided. To avoid this trap, assume that there is no such thing as a "final" draft. Work on the draft until there is basic agreement that job content is defined well enough to begin using the document in managing. Time and effort are better spent in using the document, learning from the experience, and improving the document whenever possible.

The Process of Defining Job Content

There's a sequence of steps in defining what's important so it can be managed. And out of that managing, what's important to the success of the business is likely to be accomplished.

Step 1: Understand How Your Boss's Job Contributes to the Success of the Business

The first step is to gain an understanding of the responsibilities, objectives, priorities, and standards of your superior. To understand your superior's job means understanding how it contributes to the overall organization. These insights help you see where you fit in, how you can make your contribution.

Step 2: Identify the Major Areas of Responsibility of Your Job

The second step in defining job content is to identify the major areas of responsibility connected with the job. A responsibility is an area in which the individual is held accountable for achieving results. Each individual will have one or more responsibilities in each of three categories: work, people, and self-development. The category of work includes responsibilities such as financial results, growth, the various functional areas that apply (marketing, manufacturing, customer service, finance, administration, distribution, purchasing, research and development, personnel), business planning, and expense control. The category of people includes responsibilities such as the selection, training and development, motivation, utilization, and retention of talent in the organization. Responsibilities for teamwork within the organization, and relationships with both internal and external individuals and groups, are also part of this area. The category of self-development includes responsibilities such as improvement in job-related knowledge, skills, and attitudes.

Titles should be descriptive of the area of responsibility to be managed. A responsibility title is a general description (usually in one to four words) of one of the important parts of the job—an area in which certain results are critical to the survival and success of the business, thus an area in which it's worthwhile to invest time and resources to achieve the desired results. The responsibility title suggests accountability for results, not for activities. In effect, for each responsibility title, the individual is saying, "I have responsibility for results having to do with [title]." The "how much" and "when" connected with the results are deliberately not included in the responsibility title, so avoid the use of verbs ("increase," "reduce") and reference to progress, problems, dates, or specific end results.

In selecting responsibility titles, use language that will be readily understood in the organization. The same title may be used at several organizational levels. For example, "personal development" would be appropriate for everyone to use throughout the organization once it was selected as the most meaningful language to describe this particular responsibility common to each individual. Many jobs, however, have unique responsibilities that call for distinct titles. While it's risky to provide examples that might be copied without due thought, seeing how responsibility titles vary from job to job can be helpful. Consider the following examples of responsibilities found within one organization:

- President: financial performance; production; sales; product planning and distribution; marketing; engineering; finance; administration; safety; business planning and control; key personnel; industrial relations; relationships and teamwork; personal development.
- Vice President, Finance: controllership; financial analysis; annual budget; data processing; long-range planning; business planning and control; key personnel; industrial relations; relationships and teamwork; personal development.
- Vice President, Administration: legal affairs; industry and government relations; purchasing; traffic; communications; property management; business planning and control; advertising and public relations; special services; key personnel; relationships and teamwork; personal development.
- Vice President, Engineering: manufacturing; facilities design and construction; facility upgrading; engineering services; environmental controls; plant engineering and maintenance; energy utiliza-

tion; business planning and control; key personnel; relationships and teamwork; personal development.

- Manager of Operations: production; plant maintenance; engineering; administration; safety; customer service; business planning and control; key personnel; industrial relations; relationships and teamwork; personal development.
- Regional Sales Manager: sales; customer service; customer planning; field system; sales forecasting; pricing; business planning and control; key personnel; relationships and teamwork; personal development.
- Plant Manager: production; cost control, shipping and yard; maintenance and engineering; quality control; pollution control; purchasing; safety; business planning and control; key personnel; industrial relations; relationships and teamwork; personal development.
- Yard Superintendent: raw material; crushing; filling bins; switching; unloading; key personnel; relationships and teamwork; personal development.

Step 3: Select the Controls to Manage Each Responsibility

The third step in defining job content is to select the elements of a responsibility that will be most useful in managing. These elements (1) help define the area of responsibility, (2) link the responsibility (a general title) and the objectives (specific end results to be achieved), and (3) provide the most practical means of measuring results. They help in managing the responsibility. Therefore, broadly speaking, they are controls.

For example, one executive responsible for financial results selected the following controls to use in managing: return on investment; total revenue, actual versus budget; and pretax profit, this year versus last year. These controls indicate what this executive meant by responsibility for financial results. They link specific objectives with a specific area of responsibility. The controls spell out what is to be measured, and how it will be measured. They do not specify the end result desired. The objectives that the executive sets tell how much return on investment (12.5 percent), total revenue (meet budget), and pretax profit (10 percent increase) are desired.

In selecting the controls, ask yourself, "What will I use to monitor how well the responsibility is being managed?" "What will my superior want to consider in discussing and evaluating my performance on this responsibility?"

Controls should be selected primarily because of their usefulness and practicality in managing a responsibility. While controls are easiest to use when they are tangible, measurable, precisely stated, and readily available, it's not possible, nor is it necessary, for every control to meet all of those criteria. Problems arise when precise measurement and availability of information are overemphasized. Consider the following examples:

An executive responsible for financial results found there were 62 items on the monthly printout from the computer related to this area of responsibility. From a practical standpoint, that was an unmanageable number of controls. The executive determined that the responsibility could be managed by tracking four key items. When the data for one of these key items indicated a potential problem, he was able to refer to the large amount of detail that was available in making his analysis of the situation.

Another executive became frustrated when trying to select precise, measurable controls to help her manage her responsibility for her key people. When she sought help, she was asked to list the most important elements of the responsibility. These were readily identified as job performance, compensation, training and development, and replacement planning. Objectives related to each of these four elements were set. In discussing this responsibility area with her boss, the executive found these elements to be both useful and practical as links to the objectives. Together with the objectives they provided all the precision in measurement required to manage this responsibility.

Importance of the control in managing comes first; measurement and availability of data come second. Avoid selecting convenient, tangible, precise measures that are not important in managing the responsibility. Select important elements of the responsibility as controls, then decide how much precision in measurement is practical. An examination of the trade-offs of value and cost often reveals imprecise and/or subjective measures to be both useful and practical in managing what's important.

When useful and practical controls are not readily identified in setting up job content, you may need to create new controls. The challenge is to pick controls that provide the best linkage and the most useful measure for managing the responsibility without undue cost.

The proper selection of controls keeps a manager "honest" in managing a responsibility. Using more than one measuring device increases the control over results. For example, suppose our executive responsible for financial results had tried to use total revenue, actual vs. budget, as the only control. Total revenue might well exceed budget, yet the organization could be in financial trouble. But the executive also used return on investment and pretax profits as controls. Financial results could be considered well managed only when the total revenue *and* return on investment *and* pretax profit objectives were achieved at satisfactory levels.

Step 4: Set Objectives That Are
Important to the Success of the Business

The fourth step in defining job content is to set objectives in each area of responsibility that will contribute significantly to the success of the business. That means that your objectives should support the objectives set at higher levels in the organization.

Objectives are more useful if they are stated in terms of end results rather than activities or effort. Objectives are easier to use if they are precisely stated and measurable. However, important objectives should be used even if it is difficult to measure them. The procedures for using objectives in managing job responsibilities are set up to secure a common understanding of when a job is well managed, and the importance of what has been achieved.

Achieving an important objective is seldom due to the efforts of just one person. More likely, several individuals have contributed when an end result is achieved. Therefore, the same objective might be listed as part of the job content of more than one individual. An objective should appear on a job content document whenever it's important for the individual to contribute to the achievement of the result. Other parts of the management system can then make sure that the objective is reviewed regularly and managed according to the best judgment of those accountable for the result.

Objectives provide specific information that makes clear the "what" that may not be specified by the control. They add the "how much" or "when." Objectives stop short of spelling out the "why" and the "how." Understanding each objective requires "reading" the responsibility, control, and objective together. The responsibility title describes the broad area in which the individual is to produce results. The control describes what will be used to measure and manage the achievement of a specific result connected with the responsibility. The objective pinpoints the specific result desired. A useful job content document makes it possible to answer yes or no to this important question concerning a given objective: Did I (or he or she) achieve the specified result? As a general guideline, the fewest possible words to convey the intended meaning should be used. The simpler and clearer the objective, the easier it is to use it in tracking and reporting progress and reporting results.

The decision to put an objective on a job content document, to keep it there, or to drop it, is an ongoing challenge. It's a matter of how important it is to have it there. Consideration should be given to the importance to the individual, the superior, the subordinates, and others who may be affected by the objective. An objective should be on the document as long as any of the following conditions exist:

• The individual needs it to manage a responsibility. Being part of a job content, listed on the document, means it cannot be overlooked or ignored in tracking and reporting progress and accomplishments.

• The superior requires it. Being on the document ensures that the individual will be personally involved in managing the efforts to achieve the objective.

• One or more subordinates need the direction and motivation it provides for individual effort and teamwork.

• It will be helpful in informing others and gaining their cooperation.

An objective should be dropped from a job content document while the individual still has accountability for the result when both of the following conditions exist:

• The superior no longer requires the individual to track and report progress on the objective.

• The responsibility for the objective has been delegated to a lower level and it's being well managed, and the individual no longer needs to personally track progress on the objective in order to properly manage his or her responsibility.

Step 5: Test Each Objective, and the Sum of All Objectives,
for Achievement Motivation, Priorities, and Standards

The fifth step in defining job content is to test each objective and the sum of all objectives, for strength of motivation to achieve them, for priorities, and for standards. Research has shown that the strength of motivation to achieve a given result varies with the probability of success in achieving it. Motivation increases from low to high as the probability of success goes from zero to 50 percent, then drops back to the low point as the probability of success reaches 100 percent. Said another way, no chance of achieving an objective means little or no motivation to try; no chance of failure also means little or no motivation to achieve it. A 50-50 chance of success/failure means the strength of motivation to achieve the objective is at the maximum. Setting individual objectives that are too easy or too difficult is therefore self-defeating. The same is true with regard to the total of all objectives to be managed.

Priorities have to do with relative importance. "This" is more important than "that." Every objective on a job content document should be important, or it should not be there. But even in such a document, some objectives are more important than others. Understanding the priorities of an immediate superior is essential to understanding the priorities in one's own job. High priorities call for the investment of appropriate time, effort, and resources to accomplish what's desired. Based on what it will take to achieve the high-priority objectives, lesser priorities can be evaluated. The total job has to be doable. If any pulling back is needed in "how much" or "when," it should be on the items of lesser priority. Emphasis should be on what's most important to the success of the business.

Standards have to do with level of performance (how good is "good"? how high is "high"?). Objectives need to be evaluated in terms of the level of performance they reflect as seen by the immediate superior. Due to changing circumstances and needs, what was acceptable yesterday may no longer be good enough today. In such a case, upgraded objectives and increased effort will be required. If too much effort is being invested in relation to the value of the results to the business, downgraded objectives and less effort will be required to achieve the balance that shows the entire job is well managed.

Step 6: Achieve "Correlation" with Others in the Organization

The sixth step in defining job content is to achieve "correlation." What does "correlation" mean in a system using responsibilities and objectives as management tools? To achieve correlation means to achieve a reciprocal, supportive relationship. Each job content document needs to be correlated, or tied in with other documents in the organization to become a tool that helps the business succeed. The efforts of individuals need to be mutually supportive and must also support the overall mission or purpose of the organization. This means the job content document is intended as a dynamic tool that is created by an individual, modified to correlate with the efforts of others, and changed as often as required to meet the current needs of the business.

Correlation of objectives takes place first with the superior alone, then with other team members. Further correlation may be required as the review of job content documents takes place with subordinate levels. Also, interaction with other groups or individuals in the organization may reveal a need to resolve conflicts in objectives or ways in which teamwork can be increased. No proposed changes in a job content document may be considered final without the approval of the superior.

A superior/subordinate review of the subordinate's job content document should lead to these results:

1. A common understanding of the major areas of responsibility connected with the job, the most important controls to be used to manage each responsibility, and the most important objectives to be achieved.
2. The superior's satisfaction with the document, and the contributions to the success of the business reflected in the objectives.
3. The subordinate's commitment to manage each responsibility and achieve each objective.

A team review of job content documents (superior with immediate subordinates) should lead to these results:

1. A common understanding of the responsibilities and objectives of each team member.
2. Modifications of individual documents as required to correlate efforts of team members in support of the superior's objectives.
3. Increased commitment of each team member to achieve results critical to the success of the business.

Minor changes in job content to meet the changing needs of the business should be made on the document, with a date showing when the change was made. No other notations should be made on the document.

The Format of the Job Content Document

The format of the job content document (Figure 1) will allow you to quickly identify each important part of your total job. The format links your objectives to the major areas of responsibility of your job. As you go through the job content document, relate the objective to the control and to the responsibility by reading them as one sentence with three parts, as shown in the document.

The job content document shows the suggested method of identifying each responsibility (numbered, in caps, underlined) and each control and corresponding objective (designated with a capital letter). Use subnumbers as required when there is more than one objective related to a control.

Job Content—Cases and Comments

Case 1: The Failure to Use the Full Management System

An experienced plant manager had used seven critical operating objectives for years in running his plant. With his in-depth knowledge of plant operations, and his day-to-day follow-up on progress toward each of the seven objectives, he felt no need for any formal system. He had it all in his head.

When the new top management of the company began to implement a formal system as a better way of managing the entire job of each individual, he confidently went along. His job content document had 8 responsibilities and 26 objectives. He assumed he could manage his entire job the same way he had always done—in his head. He simply ignored the suggested procedures for tracking progress and results.

He soon ran into trouble. His new boss wanted to see evidence that he was on top of his entire job, not just seven important pieces, and that he was setting the proper example for his staff in managing. He overreacted to the request and prepared detailed action plans on each of his objectives, and required his staff to do the same. Several plant projects were delayed because of all the time put in on this busywork. The plant manager blamed the new management system

Figure 1. Format of the job content document.

JOB CONTENT

Position:_____   Date:_____

1. (A RESPONSIBILITY TO BE MANAGED)

    A. (One element of this responsibility   A. (One objective or end
       useful as a management control   result important to achieve
       and linkage to an objective)   in fulfilling this responsibility)

    B. (Another control)   B. (Another objective)

    C. (Another control)   C. (1) (Another objective)

                                             (2) (Another objective)

                                             (3) (Another objective)

2. (RESPONSIBILITY)

    A. (Control)   A. (Objective)

    B. (Control)   B. (1) (Objective)

                                             (2) (Objective)

3. (RESPONSIBILITY)

    A. (Control)   A. (Objective)

    B. (Control)   B. (Objective)

    C. (Control)   C. (Objective)

    D. (Control)   D. (Objective)

Figure 1. (Continued.) *Examples from various positions.*

JOB CONTENT

Position: President
1. FINANCIAL PERFORMANCE
   A. After-tax return on year-end total assets   A. 8.5
   B. After-tax profits as percent of net sales   B. 5.0
   C. Absolute after-tax dollar profit   C. $560

Position: Vice President Catalog Dept.
1. CATALOG MERCHANDISING
   A. Initial fill rate   A. 77%
   B. Cancellation rate   B. 9%
   C. Surplus generation   C. 14% of gross demand
   D. Policies and procedures   D. Complete documentation of integrated catalog process by year end

Position: Plant Personnel and Safety Manager
1. EMPLOYMENT
   A. Number of employees   A. Keep enough employees to cover job openings with 5% maximum overtime
   B. Quality of new hires   B. (1) Hire the best qualified applicant
                                            (2) Meet line supervisor's need
   C. Affirmative action   C. Implement program

Position: Regional Sales Manager
1. SALES
   A. Sales volume (tons)   A. (1) X Product 144,000
                                            (2) Y Product 108,000
                                            (3) Z Product 87,000
   B. Sales trends   B. Analyze monthly; take action as required
   C. Selling price   C. Meet or exceed updated forecasts
   D. Market share   D. (1) Monitor monthly by product; take action as required
                                            (2) Develop action plan on Y Product and begin implementation by 6/1

Position: Director, Quality Assurance
1. SCRAP CONTROL
   A. Scrap as percent of sales   A. Not to exceed 3%.
   B. Use of QC inspector   B. Tackle problem areas on timely basis
   C. Scrap conditions reporting   C. Report excessive conditions when discovered; shut down jobs when appropriate
   D. Scrap reduction   D. (1) Improve processes to reduce scrap by 12/31 (with engineering and manufacturing)
                                            (2) Make recommendations on incentive program by 7/1

for the delays and for the sagging morale of his plant staff. Then his boss overreacted, and the organization ended up losing an experienced plant manager.

On the bright side, other managers in the organization could see what happened. They learned the value of using the full management system in managing. The system soon became a way of life for the organization, including the plant.

Case 2: The Use of an Imprecise, Subjective Control

A group of engineering specialists in a high-technology industry was organized to develop three approaches to a product improvement. The most viable approach would be used for production. To achieve teamwork and results under enormous time pressures,,the top manager agreed to use the management system involving responsibilities and objectives as a better way of managing the project.

In defining job content for her position—and thus the project—specifically for her most important responsibility, she had trouble deciding what to measure, and how to measure it. She finally settled on what was admittedly an imprecise, subjective measure covering several criteria critical to the success of the project. At the postproject critique, the group was unanimous in wanting to continue using the management system, but they felt it would have been even more useful if that one most important control had been more precise. After three hours of wrestling with how to improve the control, they gave up. They agreed that it was anything but ideal, but it was the best they had, and that it would have been impossible to manage the project and achieve the results without it. That one control created more meaningful discussion than all the others combined. It forced creative thinking and in-depth analysis and evaluations, and was the critical benchmark for testing their final recommendations.

Case 3: Frustration with Too Few Objectives

Over the years, an executive had been exposed to several traditional MBO programs, each one requiring that the number of objectives for an individual be small, preferably between three and five. He had found it impossible to concentrate on a few major objectives and ignore the other results he was trying to achieve. And he was unable to consider all the lesser objectives as supportive of the major objectives. Often, there was no fit at all.

As he moved up the ladder, his frustration grew. Recognizing the political necessity to comply with division and corporate requirements, he openly complied with the program and privately developed his own list of objectives, usually numbering between 30 and 40.

When he became the top executive of the division, with general manager responsibilities, the official objectives program disappeared. Compliance with corporate requirements for division objectives was handled quietly. But his interest in managing the division effectively at all levels increased. When he learned from a colleague in another company that there was a better way to manage than traditional MBO, flexible enough to meet needs at every level, he was anxious to introduce it to his organization. At first, having a set of objectives covering his entire job was the major issue to him. He soon realized that an appropriate job content document was only a start in managing the entire job. He saw that subordinates' awareness and understanding of his job content and their own helped them in tracking and reporting their progress, in getting needed help to accomplish what was important to the business, and thus in realizing all the potential benefits of a viable management system.

Case 4: Frustration with Too Many Objectives

A new business, organized as a subsidiary, was growing rapidly. The CEO had hand-picked her staff. Each was an expert in some aspect of operations. The CEO recognized she had to manage a group of prima donnas and make them into a team. Enthusiastic about using objectives, she developed a list for each newcomer to ensure full productivity most rapidly. She felt she personally had to keep track of progress toward each objective. But before long she realized she couldn't turn the pages of her objectives book fast enough. She was trying to review progress toward over 800 objectives each month.

Out of frustration with trying to keep track of long lists of objectives—getting longer as each new employee was added—she asked for my help. First, as part of a better way of managing, she had to accept the idea that an effective management system leads to real delegation and increased freedom for subordinates in doing the work, as well as increased control by the superior over results. Then, a job content document was developed for the CEO position, which fit comfortably on three typed pages. Eleven major areas of responsibility and 37 objectives were identified. After struggling with over 800 objectives, 37 seemed too good to be true. But she wanted to go still further. After pondering the matter of delegation, she proposed having on her document just one responsibility area—financial performance—and a total of three objectives. This would set an example of simplicity for her staff.

I had to ask her some blunt questions: "You mean you intend to manage this entire subsidiary without your personal attention to any results other than those three related to profit?" Silence. "You think your boss, the group vice president, won't insist on discussing sales? Or the markets you're moving into? Or your personnel and organization structure as the business grows?" More silence. A frown was spreading over her face. "You choose to have nothing on your document that tells your people that you're concerned about them, their performance, their compensation, their development, their future, their working as a team?" The frown deepened. "And you want your people to know you refuse to set the example in working at your own self-development?" Finally, the CEO answered, "Oh, no!"

Somewhere between the extremes of too many or too few responsibilities and objectives is a manageable number that permits managing what's important. This CEO ended up using 37 objectives to make sure she was managing the 11 areas of responsibility that covered her entire job.

6

How to Manage
the Right Risks

Life is set up so we have to take chances at almost every turn. Things
don't always work out as we hope, but we go ahead and plan as if
they will. And things work out often enough that we keep making our
best judgments and taking chances.

Risk is involved in almost every aspect of managing a business.
Let's face it: Objectives, delegation of responsibility, priorities, activities that lead to improvements, achievements, personal development,
and teamwork—all involve risk. Risk is involved because these matters are linked to the future, and the future is unknown. For example,
objectives are commitments to take action to mold the future. Objectives are based on expectations, informed guesses, anticipations. Objectives try to balance results desired in the immediate future with results desired in the long term. Objectives identify what you want the
uncertain future to be.

If the risk inherent in planning ahead seems high, consider the
alternative. How much risk is there in doing nothing about the future? How much chance is there that nothing will change or that all
the changes will be exactly to your liking? How comfortable can you
be doing nothing, knowing you could have an impact on what the future will be like? Trying to eliminate risk and uncertainty in business
is useless. Even trying to minimize risk leads to rigidity and economic
stagnation. Risk is involved whenever there is a commitment of re-

sources to achieve results. By knowing what's important to the success of the business, risk taking can be encouraged.

A better way of managing what's important involves a systematic approach to achieving business results by taking the right risks. It's as important to decide when to change or abandon an objective as it is to set it up. A better way of managing calls for evaluating progress in light of the value of the desired results to the business and then taking appropriate action. Appropriate action may be to increase effort, apply more resources. Or it may be to reduce effort and resources, or abandon the objective, so that the effort and resources can then be channeled more productively.

Preventing Change and Creating Change

In handling their responsibilities, managers face the challenge of preventing change in some instances and creating change in others. Prevention of change has to do with meeting standards, norms, quotas, budgets, schedules, specifications. A manager works at preventing a failure to meet the standard. When we are adhering to the standard, meeting the objective, we say that everything is under control.

A potential problem in this kind of control is that we can become so preoccupied with meeting specific objectives that we become blind to their real value, or lack of it, to the business. For example, of what value is producing a product that meets specifications and schedules if customers buy a product from competition that outperforms it? If the product is not accepted in the marketplace, efforts to meet specs and schedules don't mean much. The emphasis must shift suddenly to efforts to create the changes that will make the product competitive.

The manager's efforts to prevent the wrong kind of change and the manager's efforts to create the right kind of change occur simultaneously. A manager works at causing a positive departure from the standard by doing things that will have an impact on the future, that is, by creating progress. Much energy is involved in making the future. Managers study and enter new markets, develop new products, build new plants, develop new ways to cut costs, reduce waste, organize more efficiently, move out of unprofitable markets, and eliminate obsolete products, processes, and routines. All of this is risky, but it's the kind of risk a progressive company thrives on. Opportunity to contribute to the success of the business by creating change is translated into objectives. Objectives require the commitment of resources and action steps to achieve them. Progress comes by creating change, by making the future what we want it to be.

Delegation, Trust, and Risk

Delegation involves trust and risk. Delegation of work means entrusting another person with the care and management of work to be done. The risk, of course, is that the person may not do what is needed and the hoped-for results may not be achieved. Delegation sets up a stewardship. The subordinate becomes the steward entrusted with the performance of specified work, the desired results of which are understood by both superior and subordinate. The superior must decide what parts of the job can be committed to the care of the subordinate, how to get the subordinate to accept the work willingly, and how to follow up on how well the assigned work is being done.

Delegation implies giving up personal control over specific results and the activities to achieve them. It's easy to rationalize holding on to time-consuming vocational hobbies, usually related to personal interests, prior successes, special training, and expertise. In delegation, the superior's hobbies may become the responsibilities of the subordinate. This shift of responsibility involves the willingness of the superior to relinquish personal control and to teach the subordinate whatever is necessary to manage and achieve the desired results. On the subordinate's part, there must be the willingness and ability to learn and to do what is required.

Delegation has to do with responsibility, authority, and accountability. In a business situation, a responsibility is an area in which the individual is answerable for achieving results. Authority is the right to make decisions and take actions for the organization. There are usually limits to authority, but within the specified limits, authority involves all the rights and powers needed to carry out assigned responsibilities. Authority may involve giving orders, spending money, hiring people, using materials and facilities, and in general committing the resources of the organization to achieve certain results. Accountability is the obligation to carry but responsibilities and to exercise authority. Accountability is the stewardship duty to answer for, and report upon, the discharge of responsibility and use of authority. Responsibility and authority can be delegated. Accountability cannot.

Delegation requires risk. Industrial psychologist Douglas McGregor recognized this fact when he wrote that without risk there is no delegation. Meaningful delegation is closely related to the principle of self-control. The principle of self-control includes the concept that members of management should have access to data for controlling their own jobs, but not for controlling their subordinates' jobs in the same way. In delegation, managers concern themselves with the results of their subordinates' activities, but not the details of their day-to-day performance. This requires managers to trust their subordinates, to have enough confidence in them to accept certain risks. Unless the manager takes these risks, there is no delegation.

This doesn't imply that there should be any restrictions on the amount of detailed data made available to managers in managing their own jobs. It does imply that when data are broken down in a way that reveals day-to-day performance of subordinates, they are no longer data for self-control. Data used in that way destroy the idea of delegation completely.

When McGregor wrote on this subject, the idea that delegation involves trust and risk and calls for managerial self-control seemed to him a radical concept. Ask yourself how common it is to find managers who violate this self-control principle today. How many managers accept the risks involved in delegation and practice this concept of self-control? In addition to using whatever information is important in controlling their own jobs, too many managers also request details about the day-to-day performance of subordinates.

Sometimes problems seem to force the taking of risks through delegation. An example from the Old Testament is found in Exodus 18. Moses, the leader of the Israelites, was the sole judge of any disputes that arose among the people. Moses's father-in-law, Jethro, saw that the way Moses was handling his responsibilities had created a bottleneck in decision making. Jethro said to him: "This thing is too heavy for thee; thou art not able to perform it thyself alone."

Jethro then offered some suggestions. One had to do with teaching the people, "the way wherein they must walk, and the work that they must do." A second was to set up an organization, appoint able men as supervisors, and let them share some of the workload. And of those judges, Jethro said: "And it shall be, that every great matter they shall bring unto thee, but every small matter they shall judge: so shall it be easier for thyself, and they shall bear the burden with thee."

Moses took the risk and followed Jethro's advice and it proved sound—the people were taught what was expected of them and none were asked to handle problems beyond their capability, Moses was "able to endure," and all the people went "to their place in peace."

A modern example of problems leading to taking risks is found in the success of the football team at Brigham Young University.

The Cougars are said to have the nation's greatest passing machine. Head coach Lavell Edwards, a former defensive coach and player, had been taught that the only time to pass was on third down with long yardage to go—that passing in any other situation was just too risky. However, when the Cougars had to rely on their running game, the results were close to disastrous. So, in spite of his own background, Edwards decided to develop a pass offense. That decision eventually led to recruiting Doug Scovil on his coaching staff.

It wasn't easy to lure Scovil from the San Francisco 49ers. Right away, Scovil made it clear that he didn't like the Cougars' playbook. "Well, get rid of it," said Edwards. "Change it. Put in your own stuff." Scovil did. He rewrote about 85 percent of the book.

Further insight into the delegation to Scovil is seen in the fact that unlike most head coaches, Edwards allows his expert assistant to call the plays. Scovil, in turn, has developed a system that teaches quarterbacks to read the defense and to be able to make on-the-field adjustments during the game.

Edwards, Scovil, and the quarterbacks know how to employ risk, and it has paid off. Under Edwards, BYU has won five conference championships, regularly makes the national top 20, and dominates the nation's offensive statistics.

There are no riskless decisions. Delegation involves risk in making decisions. A time-honored rule says that decision making should be pushed downward as far as possible. This means down to those who take action, taking into account practical limitations to the extent of this authority. Put another way: Once an assignment is made, give the individual the chance to carry it out. The concept of granting broad authority along with any specific limitations is expressed in the management charter of a division of a major organization: "All authority not expressly and in writing reserved to higher management is granted to lower management." Clearly, all managers in the division have the authority to make the decisions required to carry out their job responsibilities, and any limitations are to be spelled out.

The Right Risks

Selecting the right risks is part of the excitement of managing. In searching for them, we ask ourselves what we should do, how we should employ the resources of the organization so that meaningful accomplishments will be greatest and increased success will be most likely. It's a matter of: (1) separating important activities that can really make a difference to the business from the multitude of busywork or counterproductive activities, and (2) managing the time frame in which what's important is worked at.

In managing important job responsibilities, what is urgent must be handled on a different time frame than what is not urgent. When a task is important, whether it's urgent or not, the same management processes of planning, organizing, directing, controlling, and innovating are involved. The connections between importance and urgency in relation to a given task are presented in Table 6.

Important and urgent. When a task is both important and urgent, it calls for immediate application of effort and resources to carry it out. However, the amount of effort and resources have to be justified by the value of the outcomes to the business. Urgency does not equal panic. It means something requires immediate attention—perhaps because the matter is pressing, essential, critical, necessary, crucial,

Table 6. Relationship between importance and urgency.

	Important	Not Important
Urgent	Requires immediate application of effort and resources	Requires deliberate control of effort and resources
Not Urgent	Requires well-planned application of effort and resources	Requires preventive procedures

compulsory. Unless there is a systematic approach to managing the entire job, work can become a series of crisis situations, all both important and urgent. The ideal is to be ready for the important, urgent task, that is, to have the entire job so well managed that personal time and any required effort and resources of the organization are available to handle it.

Important but not urgent. A task that is important but not urgent calls for well-planned application of effort and resources to carry it out. The same kind of discipline—advance planning—is required when there is no immediate demand for attention as when the situation is urgent. Without a systematic approach to handling these tasks, they are likely to be ignored until they become reclassified as urgent. Urgency has to do with the time frame. When a task is important, not urgent simply means not urgent now; what is not urgent today will become urgent at some time in the future.

Urgent but not important. Urgency connected with a task that is not important calls for deliberate control of effort and resources. The urgent task usually gets immediate attention, regardless of its importance. There is a seductive appeal that is almost irresistible when your phone rings, or there is a knock at your door, or a letter requiring attention arrives. Whether or not the purpose behind the call, or visit, or letter is important to you, responding takes time and energy. We all have the same time limitations. The challenge is to control the events that siphon off our energy in unproductive endeavors so that we have more energy to accomplish what's important. Deliberate control over the tyranny of what is apparently urgent but is not important is a necessary minimum for effective management. The many excellent suggestions for time management found in the literature focus on how to deal with this issue.

Not urgent and not important. Tasks that are neither urgent nor important can creep into our thinking, planning, and doing. The brainstorming of ideas is one point of entry. Trying to impress the boss or others by movement and activity is another. Attempts to ride on the coattails of someone else is a third possibility. The most serious possibility is that we don't have a job that motivates us to make good use of our time, effort, and resources.

In the management system we're discussing, every key responsibility is managed, and effort to achieve every objective is judged on the basis of value to the business. Committing resources under this system produces the right risks. But risk has to be managed.

Managing Risk

Risk is required to establish a climate for achievement motivation. Individuals with a high need to achieve seek out moderately risky business environments, take calculated risks, set challenging targets for themselves. By creating the right kind of climate, managers can have an impact on the achievement motivation of their subordinates. The basic tool in creating this climate is the management control system—those processes and structures by which managers ensure that the available resources are put to work serving the objectives of the organization. The control system determines how risk is managed.

Delegation, self-control, and self-supervision all add up to relieving the boss of the need for day-to-day personal involvement in many of the activities necessary in running a business. It takes time and effort to set up the controls, but in return the boss gains freedom from detail. In accepting the delegation of responsibility and the concept of self-control, the subordinate gains freedom in doing the work, but along with it goes the responsibility for results, and the observance of the self-control ground rule, "homework before help" (explained in Chapter 8).

Self-control requires clearly spelled out responsibilities. It's also important to know what kind of help can be expected from other groups. The emphasis in future-oriented controls, sometimes called precontrols, is teamwork and team results.

Self-control requires information on how you're doing. You need to know what progress is being made. And you need to know it soon enough to take whatever action is required to achieve the expected results. When this information is set up properly, it becomes your ongoing control mechanism. Periodically, this information can be summarized as past-oriented controls or postcontrols, useful in learning from past experience and planning for the future.

Now, what about the "comfort index" of the boss while the subordinate is enjoying the freedom of self-control? The boss, after all, is still accountable for the results expected of the subordinate. Four factors assure appropriate control from the viewpoint of the boss.

- First, the boss is involved in the definition of job content for the subordinate. The boss has the final say on responsibilities, objectives, delegation of authority, and any limitations to be observed.
- Second, the boss is involved in selecting the critical controls used to manage each responsibility and in seeing that the information needed by the subordinate for self-control is available—when it's needed.
- Third, the boss is involved in the periodic reviews of the subordinate's progress. At these stewardship reviews, covering the entire job of the subordinate, the boss can go into as much depth as necessary on any responsibility or any objective. The outcome of these discussions—decisions and action plans—are subject to the approval of the boss.
- The fourth factor is the day-to-day ground rule of "no surprises for the boss." This rule is so basic that no effective superior-subordinate work relationship can exist without it. The subordinate is responsible for alerting the superior as soon as it's known that there's a potential problem with achieving an objective. Usually this means there is a variance between what was expected and what is happening, and the variance is large enough to cause concern about achieving the objective. Note the wording "potential problem"; the subordinate hasn't yet failed. This is an early warning system so that every effort can be made to avoid failure.

Under this ground rule, no subordinate has the freedom to fail to achieve an objective all alone, allowing no one else to try to help. The early warning allows whatever help is needed to be mobilized soon enough to influence the decisions that must be made. Coaching from the superior, assistance from others, and every available resource in the organization may be brought to bear in an effort to achieve the objective, if the importance of achieving the objective justifies it.

It's certainly possible for superior and subordinate to agree on a revised objective when the priorities of the business demand that available resources be used to achieve other important results. The rule makes sure the situation involving a potential performance problem is known to both superior and subordinate, and decisions on how to handle the problem are made in light of the available information, making sure the right risks are taken.

In summary, success in business comes from taking the right risks, committing resources in order to achieve important results. Instead of trying to eliminate or minimize risk, we manage it through our system of controls. As we learn to manage the right risks, we adopt the attitude expressed long ago by the Scottish writer Alexander Smith: "Everything is sweetened by risk."

Risks—Cases and Comments

Case 1: A "No Risk" Climate

In connection with the installation of a system for managing what's important in a multidivision organization, the risk involved in setting objectives was discussed. Over 400 managers were asked to judge the probability of success in achieving the objectives set throughout the organization in the past. Almost all the managers responded that the objectives set throughout the organization had a probability of success of 90 percent. In this same organization, the ground rule of no surprises for the boss had been firmly established for years. It was used in connection with "no fail" objectives. Together this added up to a virtually "no risk" climate.

In spite of in-depth discussions with the managers on the relationship of risk, strength of motivation, and achievement of business results important to the organization, managers continued to set no-fail objectives.

Privately, they admitted their fear of "sticking their necks out." They bought the theory of having objectives with a 50-50 chance of success, but no one wanted to be the first to put it into practice.

Traditions die hard. In this organization, the climate for risk in certain divisions and plant locations showed significant improvement after the first formal quarterly stewardship reviews took place. In other locations, it took the year-end reviews to convince the managers that the name of the game was now accomplishments important to the business—not merely meeting objectives.

Case 2: The Value of Accomplishments Made the Focal Point for Decisions

A retail business had a rather sophisticated management system. It was far better than average but still traditional MBO. Numerous precise measures were available for control purposes, and objectives were set annually for each key manager. One problem was the system's rigidity in a business subject to rapid changes in priorities due to merchandise innovations and style changes. The reason for the rigidity in using objectives was the top executive's feeling that there was too much risk involved in allowing objectives to be changed during the year. He feared that this might lead to the wholesale shifting of the targets to where the arrows hit. At the same time, he wanted effort and resources to be put where they would pay off the most.

After considering the trade-offs, he searched for, and found, a better way of managing. And with a viable system to stiffen his spine, he faced up to the risks involved in the big opportunities and used his budget accordingly. He made the value of an accomplishment to the organization the focal point of all management decision making. Objectives and priorities were no longer shackles but tools to obtain important results.

He was pleased to find that allowing changes in objectives and priorities in response to changes in the marketplace didn't lessen or weaken the use of objectives as a management tool. Instead, there was greater acceptance of them because they were now seen as useful and motivational rather than as restrictive and punitive.

Case 3: A New Approach to Time Management

All members of a department had attended the same seminar on time management. The training focused on setting and using priorities in managing events. After a year of using the suggested procedures, the department head felt real progress had been made in controlling work interruptions from both internal and external sources. But overall results were not what she had hoped for. Productivity had not increased measurably. Even though delegation had increased through pushing downward low-priority activities, morale was not high. In fact, many individuals in the department were feeling that work pressure was building steadily in spite of their efforts to work more effectively.

A better way of looking at time management was suggested as part of the installation of the new system for managing what's important. Department members were challenged to focus their energies on accomplishments important to the business. After the importance had been determined, they were to consider the time frame or urgency of taking various action steps. They were encouraged to use all the time-saving ideas that would help them focus on accomplishments they could all be proud of.

After several months of experience and year-end results to analyze, the department head reported these reactions from her people. First, they felt they were doing a better job of planning ahead. Second, as an outcome of planning ahead, the pressure-cooker climate had subsided. They found it easier to set priorities for day-to-day activities. Their view of the value of time management increased as emphasis on accomplishments replaced emphasis on time itself. Third, there was more teamwork as workers became more aware that significant business results could not be achieved by individuals working alone. Fourth, the emphasis on importance of what they were doing day after day led to the dropping of numerous traditional activities instead of passing them down the line. The department head's own reactions were summarized in two points: "We're all working easier, and getting more of what counts done."

7

How to Track Your Progress and Focus Your Efforts

Tracking or monitoring progress related to job responsibilities is part of the management process of controlling. Controlling involves setting up ways of measuring work in progress, comparing progress with established standards, interpreting results, and taking corrective action if necessary.

Ways of measuring work in progress are set up in the job content document. Tracking progress toward objectives involves comparing status-to-date with established standards. It is, first of all, a self-evaluation of progress. Based on the evaluation, action plans are implemented as necessary. At scheduled reviews, the boss's evaluation is added.

A viable tracking system is an indispensable part of an effective management system. It's the mechanism that links responsibilities and objectives with the action steps to achieve the objectives. It's the basis for taking action—the same action as previously planned, or different action based on revised plans.

The Benefits of a Better Way of Tracking

Those who choose to manage only part of their job by objectives may see no great value in having a formal tracking system. It's true that the status of three to five objectives is easier to keep in your head than the status of each important objective related to each major area of responsibility connected with the job. However, the benefits of a practical tracking system can be realized regardless of the job or the number of objectives being managed.

The benefits come from the unique tracking process itself, and its use in connection with the other parts of the overall management system. Some of the benefits are listed here so you can look for them as you continue your examination of how the system parts all fit together as a better way of managing. The principal benefits from this better way of tracking are:

1. It provides a mechanism for self-evaluation, self-direction, and self-control with regard to job responsibilities and objectives. It gives evidence you are taking steps to manage each of your responsibilities and all of your objectives.

2. It ensures that you consider, at least monthly, (1) progress toward each of your objectives, (2) the time, effort, and resources being utilized to secure the progress in light of the value or importance of the end results to the success of the business.

3. It serves as a springboard to communications on important matters. It helps ensure that there are no surprises for the boss. It's an early warning device leading to corrective action as required.

4. It provides a means for getting help as priorities change, obstacles loom, opportunities arise.

5. It clarifies communications. In connection with stewardship reviews, it provides your boss with "the bottom line" of your evaluation, allowing the dialogue to move directly to the heart of the issue. The tracking symbols clarify in advance the essence of what will be said in reporting progress. They also serve as a summary notation of the decision to continue present plans or to make changes in action plans to achieve specific objectives.

6. It saves time and effort. Making the tracking evaluations takes only a few minutes each month. But these evaluations pinpoint where your efforts will pay off the most. In job performance dialogues with your boss, communications are speeded up by the bottom-line tracking notations.

7. It requires you to share your evaluations of progress toward each of your objectives at least quarterly with your boss, and to find out how your boss evaluates your progress. This assures positive rein-

forcement when the job is being well managed, and coaching help from the boss when it's needed. It guarantees that you know where you stand in the eyes of your boss.

8. It gives evidence that you and your boss are working together to accomplish what's important.

Common Problems of Traditional Tracking

A tracking system provides the first solid piece of evidence that the entire job is being managed. There are four common tracking system problems to be avoided. One or more of them are usually associated with a traditional approach to managing by objectives.

Problem 1: No Formal Tracking System Used

No tracking of any kind is tantamount to no attempt to perform the control function. Objectives are then meaningless targets, useless as tools to help a business succeed. Tracking once or twice a year is very close to not tracking at all as far as its value in managing is concerned.

Without a formal tracking system, management decisions and actions are more likely to reflect current job pressures than sound judgments. Managing a business is a complex process, and so is managing an entire job well. The many facets of a job, and the trade-offs required in putting time, effort, and resources where the payoff will be greatest, call for a systematic approach—formal in that the tracking evaluations are recorded and frequent enough that corrective action can be taken as required to achieve the desired results.

When tracking is done exclusively in your head, it becomes tougher for you to keep on top of all the pieces of your job. Communication with your boss regarding your progress is more difficult and takes more time. It's less likely that your boss will be able to function effectively as your coach. The solution to Problem 1 is to have a formal tracking system and use it.

Problem 2: Numerical Data Copied

Those who attempt to track progress often equate tracking with having current numerical data—dollars, volumes, percentages, dates, increases, decreases. There are other kinds of important data, such as the opinions of the boss, but numerical data lend themselves more readily to the copying pitfall. Copying critical data from one form onto another is an attempt to single out data that are most needed from the total amount of data available. Copying data in connection with tracking progress is a waste of time and effort. It increases paperwork without a proportionate increase in benefits.

Worse, copying data onto a tracking sheet tends to focus attention on "the measurable" instead of on "the important." It tends to take the place of meaningful interpretation of the data, discussion, and action steps. The solution to Problem 2 is to have a tracking system that does not call for copying any data.

Problem 3: Data Not Evaluated

Data alone, whether expressed in figures, dates, or subjective statements, aren't of much use until they're interpreted or evaluated. Production to date of 100 units, sales to date of $100,000, completion of Step 3 on May 15, are examples of data only. Comparing data with objectives, these examples might be: Production to date is 100 units compared with our objective for the year of 500; sales to date are $100,000, up 12 percent over the same period last year; Step 3 was completed on May 15, two weeks behind schedule.

The question still remains: So what? Do the data suggest we forge ahead with our present plans or make some changes? Failure to evaluate data is an insidious pitfall because on the surface it might look like the data are being used to manage. The solution to Problem 3 is to evaluate all available data regarding an objective, and to summarize and record on a tracking worksheet, by use of a simple code, satisfaction with progress to date; that is, the decision to stay with present plans or to make changes in plans.

Problem 4: Objectives, Data, and Action Plans Put
on the Same Piece of Paper

Data related to objectives and action plans to achieve them should not be on the same piece of paper as the objectives. Such a practice involves unnecessary duplication of paperwork. In tracking progress toward an objective, all relevant data need to be considered, but they do not all have to be on the same piece of paper. As noted in Problem 2, copying numerical data from other forms is discouraged. What is needed is an evaluation of the data. The tracking evaluations provide the bottom line on progress to date. They sum up all the data and the analysis concerning each objective. The tracking system is a separate management tool that links objectives and action plans. Action plans are prepared as "insurance" that objectives are reached. Placing action plans on an objectives document leads to meaningless plans and duplication of paperwork. The solution to Problem 4 is to recognize objectives, tracking notations, and action plans as separate management tools, and to be practical in using each one.

Tracking: A Springboard to Action

The tracking system can be thought of as a control process that begins with an evaluation of progress to date and leads directly to management action. Tracking is a springboard to action.

Evaluating progress toward an objective involves consideration of actual progress to date compared to existing standards of excellence; your satisfaction with what is being done to achieve the objective; and whether the efforts and resources being used to achieve the objective match the importance of the results to the business.

In evaluating progress toward a specific objective, these kinds of questions are helpful:

• Is progress taking place as planned? If progress continues as it now appears likely, will the objective be achieved?

• Should I be content with what is being done to achieve this objective? Or should I plan to take some other action, do something differently, do something that is not now being done?

• Is there opportunity to make a more significant contribution to the success of the business by increasing (or decreasing) time, effort, and resources used in connection with this objective? In light of the current situation, should the objective be changed in any way for the sake of the business as a whole?

After evaluating the answers to these questions, you summarize your evaluation by selecting the appropriate tracking system symbol, which becomes your springboard to appropriate management action. You either make no changes in present plans, or you take some kind of action to better manage the objective.

The Frequency and Time Requirements of Tracking

A formal evaluation of progress to date toward each objective should be made at least monthly by the individual responsible for the objective. The nature of some business requires more frequent tracking of individual items, but for the entire job monthly tracking is usually both useful and adequate for purposes of managing, and practical in terms of the time it takes. The total time required to perform a formal monthly evaluation of the status of each objective using the suggested code should not exceed ten minutes. Most managers complete the tracking process for the entire job in five minutes.

The Format of the Tracking System

The tracking system is used in connection with the job content document, so the format for the required paperwork is designed to be compatible. The tracking system worksheet shown in Figure 2 has columns for making tracking system notations each month of the year and at each quarterly stewardship review.

The Tracking System Code

The following symbols are used to simplify the tracking of each objective.

+ *No change—continue with present plans.*

A plus sign means: the objective is being managed well; there is no need to change present plans; an acceptable level of performance can be expected by carrying out the present plan; priorities among objectives have been taken into account in making action plans; the current action plans represent the right amount of insurance that the objective will be achieved ("right amount" refers to the relationship between what is done to achieve the objective and the importance of the objective to the success of the business); appropriate amounts of time, effort, and resources are being used to achieve the desired results; there is no apparent opportunity to make a more significant contribution to the success of the business by either increased or decreased effort connected with the objective.

+ + *No change—continue with present plans. Progress to date better than expected.*

A double plus means progress is ahead of, or greater than, expectations; if progress continues as it now appears likely, the current objective will be exceeded; there is great satisfaction with

Figure 2. Format of the tracking system worksheet.

1st						2nd				3rd				4th
1	2	3	4	5	6		7	8	9		10	11	12	

progress to date, and your superior will consider this progress highly satisfactory; the objective is being well managed, and no changes in present plans are suggested. In this "well managed" sense, it means exactly the same as the plus symbol.

— *Action required—new plans to be made and implemented.*

A minus sign means you could do something to manage the objective better, and thus some kind of action is required; you really *need* to do something, or you feel you *could* do something different that would benefit the organization in some way; you are not satisfied with progress to date, or you feel your superior will not consider this progress satisfactory; a change of some kind is required in order to consider the objective well managed; business priorities or standards of excellence may need to be examined and action steps may need to be implemented; there's an opportunity to make a more significant contribution to the success of the business by increased or decreased time, effort, and resources being devoted to achieving the objective.

— — *Action required—action steps urgent, high priority.*

A double minus means you must do something immediately to better manage the objective; progress is not taking place as planned; if progress continues as it now appears likely, acceptable results will not be achieved; the importance of the desired results to the business warrants immediate attention; remedial action steps have high priority for time, effort, resources. There may be an opportunity to be seized; action steps are urgently needed; the importance of the opportunity to the business warrants an immediate increase in time, effort, or resources devoted to achieving the desired results. There may be a shifting of business priorities that call, for an immediate downgrading of time, effort, or resources devoted to achieving the objective; a change in action plans may be required in order to use the available resources for achieving other objectives of greater importance to the success of the business.

○ *Superior-subordinate discussion of a particular objective.*

A circle indicates a superior-subordinate discussion of a particular objective. Its placement indicates when the discussion took place. The discussion of a particualr objective may take place at any time between scheduled review periods. For example: A circle and a double minus in the October column of the tracking sheet means you had a discussion of this objective with your superior shortly after the October tracking evaluations were made. The discussion may take place at a scheduled progress review. An empty circle indicates further discussion is desired. After the discussion, the proper symbol to be placed in the circle is determined by the superior. For example: A circle with a plus inside it in a review column means the discussion took place at the review, but no changes were made in existing plans. A circle with a minus inside it in a review column means one or more action steps relating to the objective grew out of the discussion and were agreed upon.

- *Deliberate delay of action.*
  The large dot means there is a deliberate delay of action on the objective, and therefore an evaluation of progress is not meaningful until action begins. For example, if the first possible action steps are to begin in June, the dot is placed in each month through May. In June, an evaluation becomes meaningful.
* *Completion.*
  The asterisk means the objective has been completed or dropped. No further tracking is required.

The Use of Tracking Notations

The development of a year's tracking notations is represented in Figures 3 through 7. The tracking system worksheet and the job content document are used together. Both you and your boss should be involved in the management decisions reflected in these management tools and in using them as a basis for further management decisions and actions. You create and keep the master tracking sheets. The suggested code can be used to cover all situations. No other marks should be made on the tracking worksheet masters. Your boss should get a copy of your tracking worksheets in connection with each scheduled stewardship review. For most managers this means quarterly. Your boss can use the worksheet for notations to be used for follow-up until the next quarterly review.

Figure 3. Tracking system self-evaluation at the end of the first month.

Obj.	1	2	3	1st	4	5	6	2nd	7	8
1A	+									
B	+									
C	+ +									
2A	−									
B	+									
3A	⊘(− −)									
B	−									
C	•	•	•		•	•				
D	+									

Figure 4. Tracking worksheet at the beginning of the first quarterly steward-ship review.

Obj.	1	2	3	1st	4	5	6	2nd	7	8
1A	+	+	+							
B	+	+	+							
C	+ +	+	+							
2A	−	−	−							
B	+	⊘(−)	−							
3A	⊘(− −)	− −	− −							
B	−	−	−							
C	•	•	•		•	•				
D	+	−	+							

Figure 5. Tracking worksheet after the progress report has been made and items for further discussion have been identified.

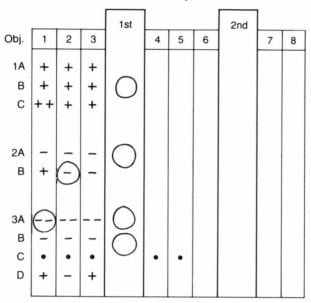

Figure 6. Tracking symbols added as a result of the in-depth discussion at the quarterly review.

Figure 7. Tracking notations at the end of the year.

Obj.	1	2	3	1st	4	5	6	2nd	7	8	9	3rd	10	11	12	4th
1A	+	+	+	(−)	+	+	+	(+)	+	+	+		+	+	+	(++)
B	+	+	+		−	−	−		+	+	+		+	+	+	
C	++	+	+		+	−	+		++	++	++		++	++	++	
2A	−	−	−	(−)	−	−	−	(−)	−	−	+	(+)	+	+	+	(++)
B	+	(−)	−		−	+	+		+	+	(−)		+	+	+	
3A	(−)	−	−	(−)(+)	−	−	−	(−)	+	+	+	(+)	+	+	+	(−)
B	−	−	−		+	+	+		+	+	+		+	+	+	
C	•	•	•		•	•	+		+	+	+		+	+	+	
D	+	−	+		+	+	+		−	−	+		+*	+	+	

The tracking system provides evidence of the efforts of you and your boss to manage your responsibilities. It documents the following kinds of information:

1. *Self-evaluation.* The tracking notations show your self-evaluation of progress toward each objective at least monthly. The symbols used to evaluate progress are (+), (+ +), (−), (− −). Your evaluation is the basis for continuing with your present plans to achieve each objective or for making plans for new or additional action steps.

2. *Discussions with your boss.* The tracking notations show which objectives, if any, were discussed in depth with your boss after each monthly self-evaluation of your progress or at scheduled stewardship reviews. Items circled in the monthly columns show your use of the "no surprises for the boss" rule and the extent to which you made use of your boss as a coach. Items with circles and appropriate symbols inside them in the quarterly review columns show the extent to which your boss gave you coaching help or special positive reinforcement.

3. *Agreement with your boss regarding current status.* The tracking record shows where you and your boss were in agreement as to your status on each objective, that is, agreement on the facts concerning progress to date and on current action plans to achieve each objective.

Agreement by the boss at the scheduled stewardship reviews is shown by no symbols of any kind in the review column—whether your latest self-evaluation was plus or minus. It means the boss agrees with your analysis of the situation, supports your action plans, and has no further suggestions to offer. It means positive reinforcement was given by the boss for how you are managing your job. Acceptance of your action plans by the boss can also be shown by a "plus" in a circle. For example, both you and your boss are dissatisfied with your progress to date but completely satisfied with the current action plans being implemented to correct the situation. The plus in the circle indicates acceptance of your current action plans and no suggestions for changes.

The tracking system documentation means your boss can't ignore his or her coaching responsibilities and then later blame you for failing to take corrective action. It keeps the boss "honest" in fulfilling the role of coach—reinforcing good performance and providing help when it's needed.

4. *Coaching by your boss.* Disagreement with you at the steward-

ship reviews requires the boss to function as a coach. In all cases where you and your boss see the situation differently, further discussion of the objective takes place. Typical outcomes of such discussions might be: (1) reinforcement for exceptional performance and results (+ +); (2) suggestions for action steps (−); (3) suggestions for urgent or high-priority action steps (− −). This documentation keeps you honest. You can't ignore your boss's feedback and coaching and then later blame your boss (1) for not giving you feedback and appropriate recognition for exceptional performance and results, (2) for not offering suggestions to help you achieve your objectives, (3) for not being specific about urgent or high-priority items.

5. *Agreement on action plans.* The tracking record shows each item where new or revised action plans were agreed upon following a superior-subordinate discussion. These items are shown as a circled minus or a circled double minus in either the monthly or quarterly review columns. Regarding notations in the monthly columns, interim discussions of a specific objective would include a review of action steps recommended by the subordinate. The boss would then have the opportunity to make suggestions before the plans were agreed upon and implemented. Chapter 8 has more on this subject. Regarding notations in the quarterly review columns, the boss has a variety of approaches to choose from to achieve the desired results. Chapters 8, 9, 10, 12, and 13 have more on this subject.

6. *Management of the entire job.* The tracking system notations are one piece of evidence that the job is being managed by the subordinate, with reinforcement and coaching from the boss.

In summary, the tracking system is a distinct management tool used for evaluating your job situation and for taking action. It provides an honest record of how the entire job was managed by you with the help of your boss, as you worked together to accomplish results important to the success of the business.

Tracking—Cases and Comments

Case 1: Newcomer Quickly Up to Full Productivity

The system for managing what's important had been introduced down to third-level management in a division of an organization. When the system was installed, Mr. A., a department manager, was spending over half his time in another city in an assignment he hoped would become full time in the near future. Three months later his wish came true and Mr. B. was promoted from a lower level and another department to Mr. A's position. Although a long-time employee of the division, Mr. B. knew very little about this particular job or about the management system recently introduced in the division.

As the external consultant assisting in the system installation, I wondered whether Mr. A. had attempted to use any parts of the management system for this purpose, even though he had been hoping he would be leaving it soon for his new assignment. Also, I felt sure Mr. B. would be eager for instruction and assistance to catch up with those who had been using the management system for the past three months. When I met with Mr. B., I mentioned the system's being extended throughout the division and offered my help. He had been on his new job two weeks and had received only a few hours' orientation from Mr. A. and his new boss. As I offered my assistance, I thought of the time it would take to help this one individual.

Mr. B. surprised me with his reply. He thanked me for the offer, but explained that he was using the system and everything was going very well. A little skeptical, I asked to see his objectives.

He opened a familiar-looking three-ring binder, and there, opposite the objectives, were tracking notations for each of three months, plus one quarterly review. He quickly instructed me in the meaning of the code symbols, pointing out that with his tracking system he knew exactly which objectives needed his attention. Then he showed me the action plans he was using, and proudly pointed out some small changes he had made that he felt would add to his efficiency in doing his job.

Mr. B. offered a sincere tribute to his predecessor: "Mr. A. knew his job. He explained his job content document to me. He explained the tracking system and why he had evaluated his progress as he had. He went over each of his action plans and explained what had to be done and why. He explained the routines for handling the office paperwork, and we chatted about the people in the department. Then he wished me lots of success and said to call him any time I had a question." Speaking of the value of the system, Mr. B. added: "I've never had it so good coming on to a new job. After only two weeks, I feel like I've been on the job six months. And my boss is the most surprised of all at how smoothly things are going. What I want to know is what about using the management system with my subordinates? Let's talk about that."

Case 2: Long-Time Professional Turned On

The system for managing what's important had been installed about six months earlier at a remote manufacturing facility as part of a companywide effort. During a routine visit to the plant, an operations executive from the main office had lunch with a department head and asked how the new management system was working out. The department head replied:

"Well, now, I've put in nearly 30 years at this plant, the last 12 on the same job, and I like to think I know what my job is, and that I'm right on top of it. So when the system was introduced, I figured it wouldn't do me any good. But I felt it might be of some value to the younger men and that I could put up with all the paperwork. Then I found out there was practically no paperwork. There were a few more responsibilities and objectives than I was used to, but they were set up so I could track them, and then I knew there was a chance to brag about, in writing, what I had done at the end of the year.

"I have no problems, so the first month, for my tracking evaluations, I put about half pluses and half double pluses. It took me 60 seconds to mark my worksheet and put it away in the drawer. The same thing the second month.

"The third month was different. One night I started thinking about the quarterly stewardship review coming up with my boss. It just didn't seem right to have nothing but plus signs down the whole tracking sheet. I know how I feel when someone brags about how perfect things have been since they took over their job. So I picked one important project I had Charlie working on with me—he's the best man I've got—and marked it with a minus. Then I picked three more items involving the other fellows, and marked them minus, just so I'd have something to talk about at the review.

"The next morning I sat down with Charlie, and we talked for an hour about things we might do to help push this big project along. We ended up deciding to do several things a little different than had been done before. We each made up our own little action plans and went right to work. In the next couple of days, I did much the same with my other minus items.

"The next week I sat down with my boss. The review went along moothly enough. My boss agreed with me on how things were going—no problems, as usual. He seemed so pleased at the little changes I was making that he came up with a couple of good suggestions too.

"So the next month I decided I would always have at least five items marked minus, so I'd always have at least five improvement projects going on. And I'm amazed at what it's doing for me. I'm like a kid with a new toy. It's the first time I've been excited about coming to work in ten years. Every day I'm doing more than putting in my time and making sure there are no problems. I'm having fun trying to make things better around here.

"And I've noticed my attitude toward my work is different. The tracking system gets me thinking about more than meeting quotas and budgets. I'm looking more and more at my own standards of how good a job we're doing and whether we're spending our time doing the things that count. I'm going to have some interesting things to say in my accomplishment highlights report at the end of the year— much more than just 'no problems.'

"Yes, you can tell anyone you want to about how the whole management system is working out for me, especially what the tracking system has done."

8

How to Benefit from "Homework Before Help"

There are two ground rules to be followed in the day-to-day managing of what's important. The first is "no surprises for the boss." The second is "homework before help." The no-surprises rule was discussed in Chapter 6 in connection with managing risk. The homework-before-help rule comes into play whenever the no-surprises rule calls for a subordinate to alert the superior to a potential problem or opportunity.

The relationship of the two rules is not difficult to understand. In the process of managing, you detect a potential problem or identify an opportunity worth investigating. You need to alert your boss according to the no-surprises rule. But both a potential problem and an opportunity to be seized always call for some kind of action. And before action steps can be taken, appropriate homework is required. So whenever the no-surprises rule applies, homework becomes the companion rule.

The reverse, however, is not always the case. There are times when coaching and counseling are needed without surprises of any kind being involved. The homework rule sets up an ideal situation for teaching and learning. It's a powerful learning experience for a subordinate to receive reinforcement for homework. And when the boss has suggestions to offer based on past experience and the vantage point of a higher position, that becomes a learning bonus. For the boss, developing the talents of subordinates and increasing managerial effectiveness by investing time and effort in coaching belongs in the category of taking the right risks.

When Homework Is Called For: Opportunities and Variances

The need for homework by the subordinate can occur at any time. Two situations make the need for homework obvious. One has to do with business opportunities to be seized, the other with variances from expected results.

First, and possibly more important if not more frequent, is homework related to business opportunities. The search for business opportunities must be continual. Homework encourages the subordinate to evaluate the opportunity. It also facilitates communication of basic information to others who may be able to contribute further information and aid in assessing the potential value of the opportunity to the business. And it makes it easier for the others who must be involved in decisions about priorities and allocation of resources.

Second is the homework related to the development of a variance from expected results. Variances are spotted early by regular tracking of progress toward objectives. When action steps are required, the homework process helps make sure the action steps have been thought out carefully.

What Homework Means

Doing homework does not mean any specific amount of time, effort, or paperwork. These depend on the needs of the situation. Opportunities with great potential and major problems may require a lot of time, effort, and paperwork. On the other hand, homework may be a brief mental exercise. In either case, there is a sequence of steps to be followed—one for opportunities and one for variances—in order to approach the new situation systematically. These steps have proved to be practical and useful for the busy manager. They quickly bring to the surface important issues, data, analysis, and recommendations.

Depending on the value and complexity of the situation, a more in-depth study may be justified before final decisions are reached.

Homework for a Business Opportunity

Homework in relation to a business opportunity includes the following steps:

1. *Identify the business opportunity.* Brief, simple terms are usually adequate for this step. The idea is to categorize the opportunity in a major area of responsibility so it can be considered in relation to other responsibilities. For example: (1) a new service for market A, (2) an improved method of handling process B, (3) a strategy for increasing market share of product C, (4) a method for reducing the cost of process D. This step pinpoints what you are talking about. It makes what follows easier to understand. It's the foundation for the steps that follow.

2. *Estimate the business potential.* How important could this opportunity be? How much could it be worth? What is the magnitude of the potential contribution to the business? Based on these initial estimates, what is realistic, what could actually be achieved? By when? For example: (1) There is an estimated market potential of $__, and we could reach $__ in three years and $__ in five years; (2) the installation would cost $__ and result in annual savings of $__, achieving payout in eight years; (3) the new procedure would provide the report to field management two days sooner with no increase in personnel costs. This step gives the bottom-line information. It explains why you are interested, why others should be interested. Estimates are often rough ones to begin with. If the opportunity appears worth it to the business, further research will refine the estimates.

3. *Consider several possible approaches to handling the opportunity.* Brainstorming several alternatives is a fundamental method of increasing the likelihood of the success of the approach selected. This step increases your confidence in your recommendations. It adds to the "comfort index" of your superior or others who might be involved in decisions that affect your recommendations.

4. *Select the approach to be recommended.* The selection from several alternatives will usually be a result of a cost-benefits analysis. This step reveals your grasp of the situation, tests your convictions from the previous steps, shows your courage to take calculated risks in

committing time, effort, and resources, and reveals your perception of the priorities involved.

5. *List the major freedoms and restraints to be observed (if any).* This step helps you and others involved to understand your recommendation and evaluate its impact on other parts of the business.

6. *Define the expected outcomes of carrying out your recommendations.* The outcomes should be defined in terms of objectives or targets to be achieved. If agreed upon, they are added to your job content document and become part of your job. Other outcomes, including negative side effects, if any, should also be identified. For example, a new and improved product representing a major marketing opportunity might siphon off current sales and change capital equipment requirements in manufacturing. New or revised objectives and action plans might be required throughout the organization. Step 6 is the basis for final decisions and commitments related to the business opportunity.

Homework for a Variance

Homework in relation to a variance includes the following steps:

1. *Identify the variance from expected results.* An undesirable variance means there is a situation that demands investigation. The tracking of progress toward a given result should be done frequently enough to serve as an early warning system. If caught soon enough, and if appropriate action steps are taken, a deviation may be corrected.

2. *Consider several possible causes of the variance.* The brainstorming technique is useful in this step. Considering various causes of a problem increases the likelihood of finding the most likely cause and subsequently taking appropriate action to correct it.

3. *Identify the most likely cause(s) of the variance.* Different causes usually lead to different action steps to correct the problem. Unless the action steps taken get at the actual cause(s) of the problem, they will be useless and possibly counterproductive. For example, the problem may be due to lack of know-how, lack of tools or facilities, lack of feedback, lack of appropriate reinforcement. Each would call for different action steps.

4. *Consider several possible action plans.* The action plans should be based on the most likely cause(s) of the problem. Brainstorming remedial approaches leads to a greater likelihood of getting a workable solution.

5. *Prepare a recommended plan of action.* Basically, a plan of action identifies the steps to be taken to achieve a desired result, who is to carry out the steps, and when. Chapter 9 discusses the preparation of action plans in more detail.

6. *Identify the outcomes expected from the action plan.* Corrective actions should result in reducing and then eliminating the variance. The costs of the remedial action steps should be considered. Time, effort, and resources have to be justified by the value to the company of correcting the variance. Negative side effects of the plan, if any, also need to be considered.

How Much Homework?

Homework should be approached as a self-management process. It's your job. You have the ball. Homework can help ensure that you're moving toward the right goal. So you should do as much as you have to in order to feel you are systematically managing the situation. Still, it's natural to ask how much time and effort should be put into doing homework.

One answer to that question has to do with the importance of achieving the objective. The more important the objective, the more time and effort are justified in analyzing the situation and planning action steps. A second answer has to do with the complexity of the problem or opportunity. However, the complexity of the situation should not be considered alone. Importance of the objective, plus complexity of the situation, justifies putting more time and effort into homework. A third consideration has to do with the difficulty of carrying out recommended action plans. Again, the combination of difficulties and the importance of achieving the objective is a guide to the amount of time and effort to be put into homework.

As a final consideration, doing the homework helps you see how much homework is needed. Going through each step in the process related to business opportunities leads you to define objectives and get a feel for the complexity of the venture and for some of the possible difficulties or obstacles to be overcome. That very process might suggest to you the need to go back and rethink each step, doing a more thorough analysis, and ending up with a more detailed plan of action. Or the process might show that the opportunity has less potential value than you originally thought. A small commitment of resources may be all that you can justify. Perhaps you'll decide to drop the idea in light of higher priorities for your time, effort, and resources.

When you've done your homework, you're ready to take action. Two options present themselves: Move ahead with your own plans, or take your homework to your boss and ask for reactions and help.

When to Go/Not to Go to Your Boss

The answer to this question of when to go to your boss with your homework is not a simple never or always. On the one hand, you were hired to do a job. So why not do it and not bother your boss? As long as you produce the results expected of you, what else matters? Aren't you too busy working to explain everything to your boss? And if your boss doesn't understand the details as well as you, you might get a monkey wrench thrown in your carefully laid plans, right? Besides, your boss has problems too, and you don't want to take up your boss's valuable time with your problems. And if you go too often, won't your boss begin to think you're unsure of yourself, or incapable of handling your job?

On the other hand, doesn't your boss have a right to know how you're spending your time and using the resources at your disposal? Your boss has delegated responsibility to you, but retains accountability for the outcomes, good or bad. Your boss has a boss and a responsibility to report on your progress and problems, so the more your boss knows, the better. And as your coach and counselor, isn't your boss concerned with your growth and development? And isn't it true that knowing more will make your boss a better coach?

These opposing positions point up the need for some guidelines. Never sharing your analysis of a situation and your best thinking of how to handle it, and going to your boss with everything, are extremes to be avoided. Go to your boss with your homework under either or both of the following conditions: (1) when you need to inform your boss; (2) when you need to learn from your boss.

The Need to Inform Your Boss

Information important to your boss should be relayed without delay as part of the no-surprises rule. Your analysis and recommendations for action should be considered part of the information important to your boss. Most commonly, a growing variance from expected results is a matter your boss needs to know about.

Sharing your homework with your boss is an excellent way of showing that you are managing your job well. It's a means of building your boss's confidence in your managerial abilities. It provides your boss with insight into your job performance problems and your management skills in tackling those problems.

The Need to Learn from Your Boss

Homework makes it possible for your boss to evaluate your approach to job performance situations. When your homework is appropriate in amount, and reflects practicality and good judgment, your boss can provide positive reinforcement. You need to know when your thinking is accepted by your boss.

Reviewing your homework allows your boss to identify any areas where coaching is needed. The following might suggest the need for coaching: coming to your boss with trivia, insignificant items indicating you need help with your priorities and an increased understanding of when to come for help; too much or too little homework in relation to the importance of the objective; evidence of insufficient job knowledge, lack of managerial skills, poor judgment.

A few "don'ts" say the same things another way. Don't bother your boss with trivia. Don't waste your boss's time when you're confident your action plans will correct the variance, and you will achieve your agreed-upon objective. Don't request a review of your homework when there is no need to inform your boss of a situation and your handling of it and you don't need to gain your boss's confidence or receive coaching.

After homework has been done and the decision to discuss your homework with your boss has been made, what should you expect from your boss? In what way can your boss help you?

What "Help from the Boss" Means

Help from the boss means:

1. To react to the homework of the subordinate by giving praise when there is evidence of appropriate homework, by giving praise when there is evidence that the objective is being well managed, and by giving help when it's needed.

2. To modify and/or approve the action plan recommended.

3. To support/assist implementation of the action plan.

4. To assist the subordinate in learning from the experience.

Benefits of Homework Before Help

When there is a firm rule that homework by the subordinate is required before the boss gives help, the subordinate, the boss, and the whole organization are affected in a positive way. The following benefits of this practice are mentioned most frequently:

1. The homework rule prevents "delegating up." Delegating up occurs when a subordinate is allowed to come to the boss with a problem and gets the boss to provide the solution. The subordinate says: "This is the problem, boss. What should I do?" And the boss replies: "Do this and do that."

Whenever a superior coaches without first requiring subordinates to do appropriate homework, subordinates' motivation to manage their job is reduced. In addition, none of the other benefits of homework before help are possible.

Homework is the opposite of delegating up. The subordinate says: "This is the problem, boss. Here is my analysis. Here is my recommendation." Using this approach, the boss functions appropriately as coach. And all the other benefits of homework before help are possible.

2. In reviewing homework, a superior gains insight into the practices and capabilities of subordinates in managing their job. Homework indicates whether subordinates have a systematic approach to identifying problems and opportunities, analyzing the situation, planning appropriate action, and using their superior as coach and counselor. This insight guides a superior in coaching and counseling with regard to subordinates' management skills.

3. A boss learns through reviewing and discussing the homework what subordinates know about the situation, the factors that affect the achievement of results, what resources are available, and what the priorities are. This information shows the breadth and depth of subordinates' job knowledge, and helps a boss pinpoint coaching and counseling needs connected with job performance.

4. Homework requires subordinates to carry out several man-

agement functions. Controlling, planning, and communicating are involved. Motivation to succeed on the job includes motivation to be well represented by your homework. Growth of subordinates comes out of this requirement of homework.

5. Subordinates get positive reinforcement when their homework is well done. A boss can give praise for homework appropriate to the importance of the objective. A boss can give praise when homework shows that time, effort, and resources are being used in the proper amounts to achieve the objective, and that the objective is being well managed. A boss can provide continuing support and encouragement in carrying out the agreed-upon action plans. As a result, subordinates' self-confidence grows.

6. Subordinates get help when the homework shows help is needed: A subordinate may not know the requirements for appropriate homework. The analysis may be shallow or missing key ingredients. The alternative courses of action may not have been adequately explored.

7. The process of reviewing and discussing homework builds superior-subordinate trust, which encourages openness and effective two-way communication.

8. When homework is followed by coaching, superior and subordinate learn from each other about the current job situation. Both are stimulated to act, the subordinate to carry out the agreed-upon plans and to learn from the experience, the superior to function more effectively in the coaching role.

9. The homework-help process reinforces achievement motivation and encourages achievement-oriented behavior.

10. Perhaps the greatest benefit of following the rules of no surprises and homework before help is this: When the management system is functioning, *there is no need for criticism.*

Don't mistake this for being "soft" in management discipline. Quite the contrary. Every individual is required to carry the full responsibility for his or her job. When there is a need to communicate important information, it must be done without delay. When coaching help is sought, appropriate homework is a prerequisite.

How can you criticize subordinates who do their best to manage well, who plan, track, report as agreed, and bring evidence of appropriate homework when asking for approval and support or further assistance? When you're doing your best, and your best is not good enough, you don't need criticism. You need help.

The system for managing what's important is set up for achieving business results, high morale, and building the organization for the future. The system is not designed to identify and punish failure. However, criticism is due when a subordinate accepts an assignment and then refuses to manage it, refuses to report problems, refuses to seek help when it's needed. Under such circumstances, an effective superior-subordinate work relationship is virtually impossible. If the subordinate is incapable or unwilling to change such behavior, then in the best interest of all parties the relationship should terminate. The subordinate should work elsewhere, preferably for a competitor.

Both superior and subordinate win when objectives are well managed on a day-to-day basis.

Homework Before Help—Case and Comments

Case 1: The Boss Who Always Said No

The subordinate had had the same boss in two different work situations over the past four years. Their relationship was strictly business but not unfriendly. The experience of the subordinate was that her boss always said no two or three times before saying yes. Every recommendation of the subordinate was challenged by the boss when they first discussed it. Being negative to ideas when they were first presented was accepted by the subordinate as the personality of the boss. "Back to the drawing board" was a way of life for the subordinate. After several discussions, the boss would end up granting approval. The subordinate noted privately that her original ideas were usually accepted with few, if any, changes.

The rule about homework before help came up in casual conversation with an associate in another department about the installation of a new management system in the division. The subordinate was not too hopeful, but the enthusiasm of her associate encouraged her to try it out on her boss. When the boss returned from a field trip, the subordinate had three items to present for approval. One involved permission to exceed a budget. The second was a scheduling change to correct a problem. The third was a request for permission to assemble a task force for a special project. The boss had no advance notice that any special homework had been done. The homework for each item was thorough but not overdone. The homework was outlined in writing to facilitate the review and discussion.

The first presentation was made, using the handwritten outlines. The boss said, "Go ahead on that one. What else have you got?" The second presentation was made. The boss asked several questions, made one minor suggestion, and gave approval. The third presentation was made. The boss picked up the phone and made sure a key individual would be cleared for the assignment, then confirmed dates for progress reports on the project. The meeting was over. The subordinate had anticipated it would take six to eight weeks, and six to eight meetings, to get the go-ahead on all three recommendations. It took less than 30 minutes.

The subordinate was stunned by what had happened. Getting the approval was important. More important, however, was how it had been achieved. She realized her boss was not negative toward ideas and recommendations. Her boss gave approval as soon as there was evidence the proposals were sound.

Happy epilogue. The boss discussed the concepts of no surprises and homework before help with the entire staff. They were accepted and established as firm rules for the department. As they became a way of life, staff members reported improved communications, time saved, and a huge increase in morale.

9

How to Use "Action Plan Insurance" to Accomplish What's Important

The management process of planning involves (1) the determination of a desired result and (2) a course of action to achieve the desired result.

An objective is a desired result. In defining a result you hope to achieve, you are carrying out the first part of the management process of planning. In preparing a job content document, you are establishing results to be achieved in each major area of responsibility connected with your job. Objectives are set to identify what you want the uncertain future to be. They are commitments to take action. Objectives commit available resources to achieve the desired results. But who does what, and when, to achieve an objective? That's the second part of the management process of planning.

Action plans outline the course to be followed to achieve the desired result. They indicate the steps to be taken, who is to carry out the steps, and when the steps are to be carried out and how long they will take.

When to Prepare an Action Plan

The guideline for when to prepare an action plan is simple: Prepare as needed to achieve the objective. The rule to "plan backwards" is a reminder to define the end result first, then the steps to achieve it. The obvious benefit of this is that action planning is purposeful, focused on a specific outcome. Reverse the rule and action steps become busywork leading nowhere in particular.

Planning is a mental activity. It doesn't always have to be spoken out loud or put into written form to be useful. Some of our daily planning is so simple we hardly know we're planning. In a business situation, however, it's not always that simple. With all you have to accomplish, and with all the details involved, written plans become an essential management tool—first for your own use, and then for communicating with others who need to know your thinking.

Action Plans to "Insure" the Achievement of an Objective

An action plan provides "insurance" that an objective will be reached. The more complete and detailed the action plan, the more insurance that the objective will be reached, and visa versa. However, it's possible to be overinsured or underinsured for a given objective.

To be deliberately underinsured indicates indifference toward achieving the objective. You choose to have inadequate control over the outcome desired. You've decided to ignore the value of action plans as insurance or you don't know their potential value. You choose to "fly by the seat of your pants" rather than systematically pursue your objective. Your view of the work involved in achieving the desired end result is distorted.

Being underinsured can make you less effective in two ways. First, you may do too much to achieve an objective. You may use time, people, budget money, equipment, or facilities in ways that are not justified by the value of the end result. With no action plans, or inadequate plans, you may become anxious about the outcomes, and thus behave rashly or impulsively. Busywork may hide the need for focused effort, specific decisions, and actions leading directly to the desired outcome.

The second danger in being underinsured is that you may not do enough work to achieve the desired result. By the time a growing variance is discovered, valuable time has been lost. You must then increase your efforts to "put out the fire." "Firefighting" is often done at the expense of other matters that need attention, causing additional "fires." This is anything but a systematic way of managing a business.

On the other hand, to be deliberately "overinsured" indicates a disposition for detail. It warns others that activity and effort may be a substitute for direct moves to achieve the desired results. It shows rigidity rather than flexibility in your approach to work. It means you have a distorted view of the work involved in achieving the desired end result.

Being "overinsured" has some distinct drawbacks. Time and effort spent on planning that is not needed to achieve the desired result are wasted. There's a great temptation to detail every minute step when detailed planning receives more reinforcement than achieving the desired outcome. In the real world of work, conditions that existed when plans were initiated often have changed by the time the plans are to be implemented. Minor changes in the situation can necessitate major changes in minutely detailed plans. "Back to square one" is not a sign of effective managerial practice in making action plans.

Another drawback of being overinsured is that it can lead you to be overly restrictive in carrying out the work. Excessive detail discourages innovation, the search for a better way. It leads to blind conformity rather than practical searching and honest thinking about where you're headed and how you're going to get there. When delegation is involved, planning details should be left up to the subordinate as much as possible. In terms of building the individuals involved in carrying out the action steps, and thus building the organization for the future, too much detail is counterproductive.

The Right Amount of Insurance

The right amount of insurance depends on some combination of the following:

The importance of the objective. Greater detail is called for when achieving the end result is of great value to the business.

The complexity and/or difficulty of planning and controlling the action steps. Greater detail is called for when activities must be coordinated, when new or different approaches are being used, when measures of progress are more subjective than objective, when time pressures and budget limitations exist.

The ability of the individual to carry out the plan, evaluate progress, and take corrective action as necessary to meet the objective. Greater detail is called for when the individual's competence to achieve the desired result is in question. This may occur when the employee is new and inexperienced, when the employee's skills are unknown or untested, or when the project is unfamiliar, the approach to be taken is new, or there are stringent restraints involved.

Who Develops the Action Plans?

The individual responsible for achieving an objective is responsible for developing the action plans to achieve it. For many objectives, action plans can be handwritten notes for your own use only. Sometimes, however, action planning is a complex process. Action planning often becomes a two-step process when the objective is of great importance, the steps to achieve it are quite numerous, many people are involved, and the coordination process is difficult. First, there is the development of a master plan, an overall approach, without much detail. Second, with that guidance, all those involved work out the detailed action plans for their particular contribution to the desired outcome. All those responsible for an objective also have the responsibility to make proper use of the boss as a coach and counselor in developing and implementing action plans. (This point is made in various ways in connection with tracking in Chapter 7, homework in Chapter 8, and stewardship reviews in Chapter 10.)

Frequently an objective appears on more than one individual's job content document. This means two or more people share the responsibility for achieving the objective. Each has 100-percent responsibility for what he or she does to contribute to the final results. This includes the responsibility to work together, to see that the individual efforts are complementary, that teamwork is achieved. Therefore, the action plans prepared by each individual to achieve the objective need to be correlated to avoid duplication of effort and to increase the insurance that the objective is achieved.

Traditional Practices to Be Avoided

The following pitfalls are to be avoided in connection with action plans:

Duplication of plans in different planning documents. For some objectives, adequate action plans may already exist in the form of schedules, critical path plans, PERT charts, or formal programs. Duplication of plans is forced on many individuals through inadequate management planning and control systems that cause managers to be uncomfortable with their knowledge of what's happening.

Planning too much detail too early. A great amount of time and effort can be spent developing action plans that are never implemented. Why aren't they used, after all the effort? Because as the situation develops and facts come to light, the detailed plans often prove to be inappropriate. Planning in too much detail too soon is a form of overinsurance.

Failure to adjust action plans as conditions change. This pitfall can be illustrated with airline flight plans. A destination is known, the usual route is to be followed to get there. During the course of the flight, new information is received. A severe electrical storm has developed along the intended route. Does the pilot stick with the flight plan he filed, endangering all aboard? Of course not. In-flight changes are made. An amended plan is used to reach the destination safely. Similarly, as action steps are taken, new information is generated. The information may confirm that the next planned action steps are still appropriate, or that different action steps are required to handle the changed conditions and to continue moving toward the desired outcome.

Failure to communicate action plans and necessary changes in them to those affected by the plans. Business success is more likely when the efforts of team members are correlated. Just as the objectives of one individual may need to be tied in closely with the objectives of another, correlation of action plans may be needed. Savings of time, effort, and resources may result from communicating action plans to other concerned parties. In addition, communicating current action plans to those affected encourages teamwork, invites their suggestions, enlists their support, builds morale, and increases the likelihood that the objective will be achieved.

Action Plans and "Do" Lists

"Do" lists are different from action plans. Most mangers have learned the value of making a list of the things they must do, or ought to do, or want to do. The items on the list are not necessarily related in any way. For many managers, a "do" list is a simple device for keeping track of odds and ends ranging from important business commitments to personal chores.

There are several ways to add sophistication to the use of these lists. One is to assign a priority for action to each item, using symbols or numbers to set up a ranking of importance and urgency from high to low. The ranking serves as a guide in planning how to make the best use of your time throughout the day. Another way is to add reference dates, identifying important past or future dates in relation to the item. A third way is to set up a system of abbreviations or codes to represent the status of each item, such as "completed," "action steps started but not yet completed," "other party to take next step," "I am to take next step with other party."

The point is that a systematic approach in using a "do" list makes the list a valuable management tool. But remember that using "do" lists when action plans are needed is a gross misuse of an important management tool. Action plans have a different function.

An action plan is related to a specific objective. The plan defines the steps to be taken to achieve the desired result. Action plans use the building-block principle. One step leads to another step. The steps may be taken over a short or long time span. A daily "do" list may be developed from items on one or more action plans. But the reverse is not true. Action plans provide insurance that specific objectives are achieved. "Do" lists provide a means of organizing the various activities of a short time span, such as an hour, a day, or a week. Effective managers learn to use both "do" lists and action plans in carrying out their job responsibilities.

Format for Action Plans

The suggested format for simple action plans is shown in Figure 8. It does not require preprinted forms.

The following suggestions have proved helpful in using action plans to manage.

Key the action plan to the specific objective for which the insurance is created. For example, putting the number of the objective taken from your job content document on the upper-right-hand corner of a page is all that is needed to have a practical filing system for your action plans. Action plan 3B relates to achieving objective 3B on your job content document. Adding your name or position at the top of the page is suggested when a copy is to be given your boss or others.

Identify the objective you hope to achieve on the upper portion of the page. This helps you focus the action steps on a specific result. You may copy it directly from your job content document or use a key word or two to remind yourself of what end result your action plan relates to.

Figure 8. Format of the action plan worksheet.

Area of Responsibility	ACTION PLAN # _____
	Objective to Be Achieved
Element Used as Control and Linkage	

Action Steps to Be Taken to Achieve the Objective	Who will carry out the steps—if not yourself	When the action steps will be taken

List the action steps you plan to take. Number each step so your plan is easy to follow. List the steps in chronological order unless that is impractical. For each step, state briefly what action is planned, who is to do it if it's to be carried out by someone other than yourself, and when it's to be done, if timing considerations apply.

Types of Action Plans

Most simple action plans fall into one of three types: closed end, open end, or combination. In the closed-end action plan, the major steps to be taken to reach the desired result can be identified right from the beginning. It's just a matter of writing the steps down, deciding who will carry them out, and selecting appropriate dates. Figure 9 shows a closed-end action plan. The amount of detail in the plan reflects this manager's judgment of the right amount of "insurance" as she viewed the situation when she initially prepared the plan. In carrying out Step 1, she put together another closed-end action plan, the schedule of meetings to be held in the following month and the "must" items for the agendas. Figure 10 shows her additional action plan as 2C(1).

In the open-end action plan, the desired end result is known, but how best to achieve it is as yet unknown. So the action plan begins with an initial step or steps, and based on the outcomes of those initial step or steps, further steps are planned. Figure 11 shows an open-end action plan. The open-end action plan is also used frequently in connection with a suggestion from the boss. Writing the suggestion as an action step immediately after the suggestion is made, and tying it to a specific objective, prevents loss of the idea and sets the stage for follow-up actions. Figure 12 is an example of an agreement to consider alternatives and have a recommended plan of action by a certain date. By making the request, the boss knows action is then under way to increase the insurance that the objective is reached.

The third type of action plan is a combination of the first two. In some cases, major steps to achieve an objective can be identified, but necessary detail for some of those steps has to be determined as the work progresses. In other cases, the detail of what must be done to carry out a major step may be known, but the major step itself depends on the outcomes of previous steps. For example, the outcome of a certain step might lead to course A or course B, or to a decision to

Figure 9. Closed-end action plan.

Area of Responsibility	ACTION PLAN # _2 C_
2. Accounting	Objective to Be Achieved
Element Used as Control and Linkage	*Three agreed upon writ-*
C. Accounting Procedures	*ten procedures completed for each division by 6/1*

Action Steps to Be Taken to Achieve the Objective	Who will carry out the steps—if not yourself	When the action steps will be taken
1. *Timetable for working with divisions set up*		*By 2/1*
2. *Selection of highest-priority procedures with division accounting managers. Meetings to be scheduled during month*		*February*
3. *1st drafts for division review:* *To divisions* *Back from divisions*		*By 4/1* *By 4/15*
4. *2nd drafts for division review:* *To divisions* *Back from divisions*		*By 5/1* *By 5/15*
5. *Final drafts typed*		*By 5/20*
6. *Introduction of new/ revised procedures to employees concerned — completed*		*By 6/1*

Figure 10. Supplemental closed-end action plan.

Area of Responsibility	ACTION PLAN # *2 C (1)*
2. Accounting	Objective to Be Achieved
Element Used as Control and Linkage	*C. (February schedule of meetings to select highest priority procedures)*
C. Accounting Procedures	

Action Steps to Be Taken to Achieve the Objective	Who will carry out the steps—if not yourself	When the action steps will be taken
1. *Meetings scheduled with division accounting managers and "must" items for agenda:*		
Division A (their conference room)		*2/7*
		9 A.M
— New ledger accounts *— Handling returns*		
Division B (my office)		*2/10*
— Switchover to automated equipment		*2 P.M*
Division C (their conference room)		*2/14*
		9 A.M
— Switchover to automated equipment		
Division D (his office)		*2/16*
— New inventory items *— Obsolete inventory items*		*9 A.M*

Figure 11. Self-initiated open-end action plan.

Area of Responsibility	ACTION PLAN # *4 B*
4. Reporting	Objective to Be Achieved
Element Used as Control and Linkage	*C. Reports to meet*
B. Special Financial Reports	*criteria of accuracy, timeliness, usefullness*

Action Steps to Be Taken to Achieve the Objective	Who will carry out the steps—if not yourself	When the action steps will be taken
1. Set up meeting with staff to identify causes of delays in report preparation *— Meeting notice sent to staff* *— Meeting in Conference Room B*		*By 4/12* *4/19* *1:30 P.M.*

Figure 12. Boss-initiated open-end action plan.

Area of Responsibility	ACTION PLAN # 3 D
3. Production Volume	Objective to Be Achieved
Element Used as Control and Linkage	D. Meet production per plan (Plant A)
D. Actual Output vs. Plan	

Action Steps to Be Taken to Achieve the Objective	Who will carry out the steps—if not yourself	When the action steps will be taken
1. Prepare three alternative approaches to increasing production at Plant A! Be prepared to discuss each approach and make recommendations.		By 9/15

"cancel the project." Each outcome would require the subsequent action steps to be different.

Uses of Action Plans

Action plans can be useful in managing what's important in a variety of ways. The most common uses are:

1. *As insurance that your objectives will be achieved.* Action plans are an optional tool for self-management, self-direction, and self-control in achieving results expected of you.

2. *For correlating your activities with others.* Teamwork is essential to business success. Action plans facilitate communications by serving as a springboard to necessary dialogue with others. When two or more individuals have the same objective, action plans identify who is to do what to achieve the common end result. When it would be helpful in correlating efforts with others, action plans can include information on equipment, facilities, or other resources to be used.

3. *For making recommendations in connection with homework.* An action plan is part of homework, and it's your responsibility to do your homework before going to your boss for help.

4. *For making deliberate use of help.* When your coach makes a specific suggestion, you ought to use it, or at least try. Suggestions from your boss may come during day-to-day discussions of job-related matters or during scheduled stewardship reviews. Why not convert a specific suggestion from your boss immediately into an action plan? That shows your boss you heard the suggestion and are committed to take action. The suggestion may become the initial step in an open-ended plan. It may be a complete single-step plan of action. It may trigger your thinking to develop a more comprehensive plan. (The use of action plans in connection with dialogues with your boss is discussed further in Chapters 10, 11, 13, 14, and 15.)

5. *As reference material for reporting your accomplishments.* A discussion of reporting your accomplishments is found in Chapter 11. In explaining your most significant contributions to the success of the business, action plans can remind you of what it took to accomplish the end results—what helped, what hindered, and what effort and resources were involved.

6. *For teaching subordinates.* Action plans can be used as a teaching device in two ways. One is to teach what action planning is all about as a management tool, that is, what action plans are for, and how to

prepare and use them. The other way involves the technical aspects of the work itself. When a subordinate's homework on a problem indicates a lack of technical knowledge, the boss may choose to coach the subordinate in preparing an action plan by outlining a suggested series of steps to be taken to achieve the specific work objective.

Action Plans—The Boss's Viewpoint

The boss has several rights and privileges regarding the action plans of a subordinate. As long as the boss uses these rights and privileges to function more effectively as a coach to the subordinate, they are acceptable practices. When examining action plans and making suggestions are used as a means of controlling the subordinate's day-to-day activities, the boss effectively cancels any delegation of responsibility previously agreed upon. When the management system is working well, there will be times when each of the following interventions by the boss will be appropriate in building the trust relationship necessary for the sake of the business, and helpful in developing the talents of the subordinate.

The boss has a right to inspect a subordinate's action plans at any time. The boss may want reassurance in the form of written evidence that an objective is being well managed, may want to learn more about the subordinate's planning skills, or may be concerned about the subordinate's job knowledge.

The boss has a right to make suggestions regarding a subordinate's action plans. After reviewing the work plans of the subordinate, the boss has the responsibility, as the coach, to offer advice and counsel when it would be helpful.

The boss has a right to request that an action plan be prepared and reviewed before it is implemented. In addition to permitting a check on the appropriateness of the action plan, this request is often used to make sure that an action plan exists, that some insurance has been created.

The boss has a right to request a more detailed plan of action. This request may be due to any one or some combination of the three reasons for taking out more insurance, that is, the importance of the objective, the complexity and/or difficulty of planning and controlling the action steps, and the ability of the subordinate to carry out the plan, evaluate progress, and take corrective action as required.

The boss has the right to retain a copy of a subordinate's action plan. The boss may want the subordinate to know there is full support in carrying out the action steps, may have a concern of some sort and feel the need to follow up personally, or may have an active role to play in providing resources at critical points or in removing anticipated obstacles.

In summary, action plans can provide appropriate insurance that objectives are achieved. Use of written action plans is optional, depending on the need in a given situation. When used properly, action plans serve a variety of purposes, all adding up to a better way of managing what's important.

Action Plans—Cases and Comments

Case 1: Multiple Benefits Discovered

Jack had learned that his boss expected him to follow up on every suggestion he made. His boss had an excellent memory and a low tolerance for subordinates who forgot his suggestions. Since the boss followed up closely unless there was visible evidence that the suggestion had been heard and was being acted upon, Jack learned to make notes whenever he was with his boss. Then, back at his office, he went through his notes, picking out the suggestions for action. His notes became a combination of a "do" list, action plans, and factual information, some of it relevant to his job, some of it useless. He crossed things off his notes as they were handled or as he saw they were not important to keep. At times he had difficulty deciphering his notes. He often wished he had asked that "one more question" when the matter was being discussed. Later, he was embarrassed to go back to his boss to ask it.

As time went by, the stacks of notes grew. Periodically, Jack would be forced to wade through the notes, trying to remember the conversations. Then he would make up fresh sets of notes, copying the unfinished items onto a new list. He felt his system worked well enough. His boss was satisfied. He accepted the paperwork as coming with the job and the boss.

Then he participated in the installation of a better way for managing what's important. He learned about the use of action plans to save time, reduce paperwork, nail down suggestions, agree on action steps, satisfy the comfort index of his boss, reduce the effort he put into trivia, and focus more effort on achieving important objectives. Now when Jack meets with his boss, he keeps factual information notes as usual, but whenever his boss makes a suggestion involving an action to be taken, he writes it down immediately as part of a specific action plan related to a specific objective. When the meeting is over, the paperwork is completed.

Jack reports that his work relationship with his boss has greatly improved. His boss admits increased confidence that agreed-upon action steps will be taken as planned. Jack reports increased confidence in knowing his status with his work and his boss, plus a savings of one to two hours a week in paperwork.

Case 2: More Effective Coaching in Much Less Time

Linda had a staff of eight whose work was technical. Five of her subordinates were fairly new to their jobs and needed a lot of coaching. In addition, there was a need for close teamwork. Linda had long years of experience to draw on and she enjoyed the technical aspects of her work. She was willing to work long hours to help her subordinates. They took advantage of her willingness to help without doing their homework. Linda planned the action steps. Her subordinates carried out the plans.

Only in retrospect could she see she was allowing her people to delegate up. A better way of managing was introduced to the organization. The new system required her to reverse this habit and have subordinates come to her prepared to discuss their recommended action steps when they needed her help.

The proper use of action plans by her subordinates saved Linda one to two days each week. Discussing action plans with her subordinates was an enlightening, time-saving way of reviewing their thinking and their work activities. She found she could be more effective as a coach in much less time. The job got done, and her people were learning and developing faster than they had before. She now believes subordinates feel more responsiblity for results and freer in doing their work when they develop their own action plans. Linda gains confidence in their abilities as she reviews their plans and observes how they use any suggestions she offers. It's easier to coach and to offer encouragement and support than to do the work for them. Linda is learning that being an effective coach is very rewarding but in a different way from doing the technical work herself.

10

How to Benefit from Stewardship Reviews

The process of making your boss an effective coach and your biggest booster is fascinating. It involves all the concepts and practices included as a better way of managing. Matters critical in this regard are: (1) how you approach the task of defining job content for your position, (2) how you handle the ground rules of no surprises and homework before help; and (3) how you present information and respond to your boss's reactions to your efforts to manage your responsibilities and accomplish what's important to the business. Items 1 and 2 have already been discussed. Item 3 is the subject of this chapter and the one that follows.

Here we'll focus on a process that provides not only an exchange of information on a specific responsibility or objective but also perspective on the job as a whole. It goes beyond the scope of a problem or opportunity discussed in connection with homework and help. It includes positive reinforcement for every responsibility being well managed and for satisfactory progress toward each objective, as well as coaching when that is needed. Through use of this process, it's possible to have your boss enthused about you as an employee— enthused enough to be your biggest booster. All you're doing to merit such enthusiasm is brought to light through stewardship reviews.

Objectives of the Stewardship Review

A stewardship review implies that there is something to examine, discuss, evaluate, plan, act on. This "something" is job performance—how well responsibilities are being fulfilled. Objectives related to specific responsibilities make it easier to discuss progress. At a stewardship review, both superior and subordinate have copies of the subordinate's job content document and current tracking system notations. These tools make it possible to have a productive review in minimal time.

A stewardship review is a special kind of dialogue. The subordinate reports, the superior reacts. The dialogue continues until both parties are satisfied. If the dialogue has been successful, at its end both superior and subordinate have learned much, have helped each other, and feel positive about the experience.

A stewardship review is a formal, scheduled event, in that the content, structure, and outcomes desired are known in advance. Scheduling can be flexible enough to accommodate current work pressures. Necessary delays should not be allowed to extend to the point that the review doesn't take place at all. When that happens, not only are the benefits lost, but also the whole management system is in jeopardy.

If reviews of the entire job are actually helpful and generally wonderful, why aren't they a regular event for every superior-subordinate pair? Perhaps because they don't know how to have a helpful, motivational review of job performance they can honestly call successful. When you don't know how to conduct this kind of dialogue, the review is not likely to occur at all. Or it may occur once a year in the form of a so-called performance appraisal. Or, worse yet, it may lead to smothering a subordinate with close supervision.

When there is no overall performance review, subordinates have only their own beliefs and assumptions to go on for managing their jobs. Subordinates can make assumptions about the standards and priorities of the boss, but only the boss can give them accurate information on these things. Coaching on individual objectives may take place whenever help is needed, but without stewardship reviews, the perspective on the subordinate's whole job is missing.

Yearly reviews are better than nothing. At least there's a chance to see the big picture before charging ahead into the new year. Looking back offers a great learning opportunity. But you can't turn back the clock. If corrective action was needed nine months ago but was never taken, business results have suffered. If a golden opportunity loomed six months ago but was never seized, business results have suffered. Looking back on such incidents can turn an annual performance appraisal into a punitive session of "Why didn't you?" and "You should have"—the opposite of a helpful, motivational job performance review.

Smothering a subordinate with close supervision is nothing less than a tragedy. Yet many a manager does this in the name of conscientious attention to detail and firm managerial control. Lacking appropriate control mechanisms, and feeling the ever-present pressure from above for business results, managers do what they feel they have to do. The development of subordinates is often ignored, and managers may actually work at the level below what they're paid to do. Development requires subordinates to have full responsibility for what they do in managing and for the results they achieve. This cannot take place with the boss breathing down the subordinate's neck.

Reasons for Having Stewardship Reviews

Stewardship reviews are important to both subordinates and superiors in their one-to-one work relationships. Superior-subordinate reviews include exchange of useful information, evaluation of progress, reinforcement, and coaching. As a prelude to examining the process of conducting the reviews, let's consider a few of the many reasons for having reviews. As a result of a stewardship review:

1. The boss learns how the subordinate is managing each area of responsibility and each objective. This enables the boss to evaluate whether the subordinate's job is managed well, and then to take appropriate action.
2. The subordinate learns how the boss sees the situation for each area of responsibility and each objective. And the subordinate is helped in managing his or her job (with all that's implied by the term "managing") by the reactions of the boss to the subordinate's report.
3. The subordinate is motivated by the positive reinforcement he or she receives when the boss feels that an area of responsibility or an

objective is well managed and that progress is at a satisfactory
level.

4. The boss is able to control priorities, to see that time, effort, and
resources are allocated according to the value of achieving the objective to the business.

5. The boss is able to evaluate the "standards of excellence" of the
subordinate, to see that the quality of work is at an appropriate
level.

The Process of Conducting Stewardship Reviews

The simplest description of the process of conducting stewardship reviews is this: The subordinate reports, the superior reacts, and
action plans are agreed upon. The use of the sequence of events in the
review is the key to building motivation theory and effective coaching
practices into the review process itself.

Some managers prefer to have the tracking sheets in advance of
the review so they can do their preparatory thinking. This is especially common for new bosses, new subordinates, and new jobs. Most
managers find following the sequence of steps in the process to be
adequate without advance preparation on their part. The process has
two phases. In phase 1, the subordinate reports and the boss reacts. In
phase 2, further discussion of selected items leads to action plan decisions.

Phase 1: The Subordinate Reports, the Boss Reacts

The subordinate takes the initiative and tells the boss the current
status of each area of responsibility by reviewing progress toward
each objective, one at a time, covering each item on the job content
document. The tracking system notations provide the bottom-line
status of each objective. The subordinate provides the necessary information to support that bottom-line judgment. The report may include back-up data, reference to progress on action plans to achieve
the results desired, and any supplementary information that would
be helpful to the superior in understanding the current situation. For
each item, the subordinate reports progress to date ("Here are the
important facts you should know about") and degree of satisfaction
with progress to date ("Here's how I feel about the facts"). After the
subordinate reports on a given objective, the superior reacts to it before the subordinate moves on to the next item.

The boss looks at the tracking notations and knows, in advance, about what the subordinate will say. So the boss is able to listen carefully to see if there is agreement on the information that backs up the tracking evaluation. The boss evaluates the report on each item as follows:

1. *The report data.* Is there a lack of information? Is there misinformation? Can I accept the report and the evaluation of progress as is? Is there more I should know?

2. *Progress to date.* Is the progress satisfactory? Is it unsatisfactory? Do I have a concern that the objective will not be achieved?

3. *The subordinate's standards.* Are the subordinate's standards of work excellence acceptable to me? Is the work quality short of what I expect? Is the subordinate spending time, effort, and resources beyond what can be justified because of standards that are too high?

4. *Job priorities.* Are time, effort, and resources being used in relation to the importance of achieving the objective to the success of the business? Is there opportunity to make a more significant contribution to the success of the business by either increased or decreased effort connected with the item?

After the evaluation of each item, the boss (1) accepts the report as given, showing that acceptance by providing brief, positive reinforcement (in any appropriate form of praise, encouragement, support) or (2) asks for further discussion of the item later in the review ("I'd like to come back to this item and discuss it in more detail").

*Phase 2: Decisions for Action Are Made on Items
Selected for Further Discussion*

When the superior feels the need for further discussion of an item, a circle is drawn beside the item on the tracking sheet in the quarterly review column (see Figure 5, in Chapter 7). Why not discuss the item and decide on appropriate action steps immediately after the boss has heard the subordinate's report on it? This is exactly the procedure when the subordinate does homework and comes to the boss for help. But that is for a single item. In a stewardship review, the whole job is being considered. A common pitfall to avoid is getting sidetracked on one item and never getting the big picture of performance on the job as a whole. In addition, reinforcement for all the items on which progress to date is satisfactory allows an individual to feel secure enough to discuss and act on the items on which improvement is needed. It's the boss who requests further discussion of an item at a stewardship review. A subordinate with a problem should handle it at once with the boss, not waiting for a quarterly review. There should be no major problems, no big surprises for the boss, in the subordinate's report at a stewardship review.

Further discussion of an item at a stewardship review may lead to agreement that current plans are appropriate, and no changes in plans are needed. Or an action plan may be needed, or action steps may need to be added to an existing plan, to meet the needs of the situation. Here are some examples of how the boss might use these further discussions of selected items at a review:

• Your boss may simply wish additional information or evidence to substantiate your report. After receiving it, your boss may agree with your current plans and have no suggestions to offer. In this case, the two of you are in complete agreement on the status of the item and current action plans, so a plus sign will be placed in the circle, meaning no change in existing plans.

• Your boss may have a suggestion or two to offer. You may need to discuss the suggestions and incorporate them into your current plans or set up an action plan to begin implementing what the two of you agree is now appropriate. As explained in Chapter 7, whenever there is a change in action steps to be taken, the tracking symbol inserted in the circle will be a minus or a double minus.

• Your boss may disagree with your evaluation of your progress. The discussion will lead to a common understanding of the differences in your opinions. For instance, if you think you are managing an objective properly, and your boss disagrees, the outcome of your discussion will be a change of some kind in your action planning and show as a minus sign in the circle.

• Your boss may suggest you do homework on an item and come back on a given date to discuss your analysis and recommendations. This becomes a first step of an action plan. The tracking symbol will be a minus or a double minus, showing some change in action steps is planned.

Minimal Paperwork for the Boss

The boss should be functioning as a coach at a stewardship review. That includes listening to the subordinate, probing for further information as required, evaluating what is going on, and then taking appropriate action in the form of making requests, sharing experiences, and making suggestions. Other than when the boss is teaching the subordinate to do necessary paperwork as part of homework and action planning, paperwork for the boss at a review is kept at a minimum.

The boss's copy of the subordinate's tracking sheet is a handy place for notes during the review. Notes by the boss are not required, but most bosses find making notations for follow-up on certain items to be a useful practice. It's practical for the boss to use the open space on the tracking sheets for the purpose of miscellaneous notes, because the sheets will be updated at the next stewardship review. When the boss wants more than brief notes of the decisions made and action steps to be taken by the subordinate, the boss can ask for a copy of the subordinate's more detailed plan of action. And, of course, there may be reason for the boss to prepare an action plan for personal use in supporting the efforts of the subordinate.

The Time Required for Conducting Stewardship Reviews

The review process requires an investment of time in order for the benefits to be realized. Each responsibility and each objective is taken into consideration, and reinforcement or coaching is provided for each objective at a quarterly review. However, as superior and subordinate follow the process at the scheduled reviews that take place at least quarterly, the time for the subordinate to report on each objective and for the boss to react to each report should be drastically reduced.

For example, when progress is taking place as planned on each objective related to a given responsibility, and the subordinate doesn't have any new information worth reporting to the boss, the tracking sheet markings say all that needs to be said by the subordinate. And if the boss has no questions, agrees with the subordinate's evaluation, and has no suggestions to offer, then brief reinforcement from the boss is all that is required before going on to the next area of responsibility. The dialogue might be this simple:

SUBORDINATE: On this responsibility, I have nothing to report that would be new to you. We are on target on each objective, and I see no need for changes in our action plans. Do you have any questions or suggestions?

SUPERIOR: Not at this time. I appreciate the good work done here. I consider this responsibility well managed. Let's go on to your next responsibility area.

Suppose that everything is really terrific for a subordinate at a review. Progress toward each objective is right on target and both subordinate and superior know it. The subordinate has no new information for the boss. The boss has no questions to ask, no suggestions to offer the subordinate. The tracking system notations provide the needed report data. The boss reinforces the subordinate with appropriate pats on the back. In such an extreme case, the entire quarterly stewardship review could be concluded in five minutes. The point is that effective stewardship reviews are essential to managing human resources well; the suggested process makes the benefits possible in minimal time. Time spent on individual items should correspond to the value of that attention, which is based on the importance of the objective to the success of the business.

In the world of work, progress is seldom exactly as planned, and communications are seldom what they should be. Information needs to be shared. Suggestions need to be made and translated into the beginnings of action plans to achieve improvements. It takes time to communicate. But the price is small compared to the price of failure to communicate.

The reporting/reacting phase of a stewardship review usually takes from 10 to 20 minutes. After that phase is completed, the in-depth discussion of items of concern takes whatever time is required to communicate information and ideas and develop action plans.

To sum up, the least amount of time is required when progress is as planned; there is no information important enough to report to the boss; there are no questions by the boss; there are no suggestions from the boss; and reinforcement from the boss can be given appropriately in brief comments. The greatest amount of time is required when progress is not taking place as planned, and new action steps need to be formulated; status, plans, and/or other important information must be communicated to the boss; the boss has questions; the boss sees the need to function as coach to the subordinate (probing, suggesting, teaching); and the boss sees the need for communicating support, providing encouragement, and setting up the conditions that will motivate the subordinate to use the coaching provided.

Stewardship Reviews Involving Dotted-Line Relationships

In addition to superior-subordinate reviews involving just two individuals, there are times when the process can become more beneficial as a result of a third participant. The third party may be invited to participate in the review process when there are functional or dotted-line relationships to consider. For example, the third party in a stewardship review between a plant accountant and the plant manager might be the division accounting manager with functional responsibility for accounting throughout the division.

Stewardship reviews involving a third party are conducted in much the same way as one-to-one reviews. Of course, the superior has final say about a third party participating in the session. It's possible that confidential matters of no concern to the third party, or about the third party, would make that person's attendance inappropriate.

When a third party is present at a stewardship review, the third party (1) learns firsthand the status of each area of responsibility and each important objective as reported by the subordinate, and also as seen by the superior; (2) can add useful information and make comments helpful to superior and subordinate; (3) can reinforce what is said by the superior for the benefit of the subordinate; and (4) can ask pertinent questions, gain needed information, prepare personal action plans, and communicate the substance of those action plans at that time if it would be helpful.

When it's not practical to meet as a threesome, the third party can quickly see what took place by reviewing the tracking sheets. Subordinate evaluations, which items were singled out for further discussion, and where coaching help was given can be immediately identified.

The subordinate's action plans, developed at the review, provide more detailed information.

In summary, the superior-subordinate stewardship review is adaptable to include dotted-line relationships whenever this is desirable. Where the third party is not present at the review itself, the review process facilitates later communications and follow-up, so the review process becomes both helpful and motivational to all parties.

Team Reviews Follow Stewardship Reviews

Team reviews of progress are important in making teamwork a reality. When the boss and immediate subordinates have a scheduled quarterly review, the process includes the exchange of useful information, the appropriate use of peer pressure, reinforcement of individual efforts and teamwork, and coaching help. In a team review: (1) Team members learn about the activities of others that are of interest to the group and of importance to the business. (2) The boss communicates current business priorities and the required standards of excellence. Trade-offs to accommodate new priorities or standards may call for changes in objectives and/or action plans by one or more members of the team.

The Process for Handling Team Reviews

The process can be described most simply this way: Individuals report on selected items, other team members react in ways to be helpful and to promote teamwork. In preparation for a team progress review, the boss should be prepared to discuss current business priorities and standards and to relate them to long-term objectives. Items to be presented by a subordinate should be based on the importance of the items and their relevance to other team members. The boss should be prepared to function as the team coach on matters of common interest to the group. The boss is responsible for controlling the pace and emphasis of the review.

In thinking through what needs to be accomplished in a team review, and the best sequence of steps to follow, consider these points:

1. The boss has much to contribute to the value of the review and should set the stage for the contributions of other team members. In order to keep the reports of individuals in proper perspective, the boss should consider starting the team review by first summarizing the current business situation, and then reporting and encouraging discussion on any actual or potential changes in business priorities or performance standards that might significantly affect short- or long-term objectives of team members. Knowledge of potential changes helps team members be alert to events and anticipate appropriate action steps to be taken.

2. Each team member should be given the opportunity to contribute to the review. There are four kinds of contributions: individual reports, responses to the reports of others, identification of potential problems, and identification of important opportunities.

3. The boss is responsible for "wrapping it up." There may be loose ends to tie down as individual reports are made and discussed. For example: New insights growing out of the review may suggest fur-

ther adjustments in business priorities and standards. Objectives may need to be changed to maintain correlation among team members and with other parts of the organization. Action plans may need to be modified to support changed objectives or to meet changing circumstances. Follow-up plans may be needed for items not concluded during the review.

Stewardship Reviews—Cases and Comments

Case 1: The Employee Didn't Know
There Was a Problem Until He Was Fired

A middle manager had 13 years of service when he was fired. Policy required an exit interview with the president of the division.

The employee brought to the interview copies of his annual performance appraisals from over the years. He had been rated "above average" or "satisfactory" by each of the four supervisors he had reported to. In addition, he produced a record of his salary increases. Each year he had been granted the increases suggested by the salary administration guidelines for those with his performance rating, years of service, and promotability.

He told the president that nothing unusual or negative had been said to him about his job performance for years. In his opinion, recent discussions of his progress and performance had been no different from those held over the entire 13 years. In other words, he didn't know there was a problem until he was fired.

In discussing this situation with me later, the president admitted that the situation with the employee had been known to top management of the division for several years. Management assumed the employee was equally aware of the situation. The president asked me if there was a way to avoid that kind of communication problem and the subsequent awkward exit interviews. I said yes but remarked that avoiding awkward exit interviews was of minor importance compared to the cost of mismanagement over the years that leads to that kind of situation.

In discussing the subject with the president, it was agreed that it takes a cohesive management system to manage human resources well, including a method of keeping both superior and subordinate honest in evaluating progress, not allowing the superior to communicate one message about performance downward and an opposite message upward, a system that appropriately links together individual development, teamwork, performance, compensation, and career planning.

After learning more about a better way of managing and accomplishing what's important to the business, the president had this to say about the case: "It would have been impossible to have that employee failing on the job and him not know it, if we had had this system functioning. We could have saved ourselves a lot of money and considerable trauma. And we could have saved that employee for the company, if not in that particular job. We failed to manage the situation, and we deserve what happened. But that employee was an innocent victim."

Case 2: The Subordinates "Heard" Their Boss
for the First Time at a Stewardship Review

A plant manager had been on the job nine months. She had held various positions at the plant for several years prior to her promotion and had earned the highest respect of her associates who were now her subordinates. She had been appointed because business results had been down enough to cause concern for two years, and morale at the plant was at an all-time low. Performance and morale problems were laid to the autocratic management practices of the previous plant manager and others throughout the plant who followed his example. A turnaround in these practices was seen as essential by the new plant manager and her superiors at division headquarters.

Over the first six months on the new job, the plant manager made many suggestions to individuals on her staff. In some cases, she made the suggestions month after month in personal conversations, without any action being taken. And several items had been discussed virtually every month in operating committee meetings, but no action steps had followed. Her frustration stemmed from the need to turn business results around and from seeing no evidence that her nonautocratic management practices were getting the job done. One bright spot was that morale had been restored to a healthy level.

At this point, the system for managing what's important was introduced at the plant. The installation proceeded uneventfully. The first evidence that a substantial change was taking place showed up after the first quarterly stewardship reviews. When the plant manager, functioning as the coach, made a suggestion, it became the beginning of a written plan of action to achieve improved results and a commitment by the subordinate to implement the agreed-upon action steps.

After the stewardship reviews, the plant manager made this observation: "There's hardly a new idea I've given any of them during these reviews. I've said it before, over and over. But this is the first time I've felt they really heard me. This time every suggestion and worthy idea coming from me or a subordinate has been transformed into action plans. I've been struggling to get these improvements under way for nine months, and now I can see it's actually happening. I'm learning how to function as their coach, and they're learning to play in a new ball game."

11

How to Use Accomplishments as the Key to Future Performance

Do you want employees to accomplish what's important? Then reinforce accomplishments that are important. Do you want employees to meet all of their objectives? Then reinforce the meeting of objectives.

These two things may seem to be the same, but they're not. Traditional MBO has demonstrated that a business can literally be wrecked while all the key performers are meeting all of their objectives. There's a better way of managing that breeds success: Have a system that requires employees to manage all their responsibilities and that places special emphasis on achieving important results. Then reinforce the achievement of those results in every possible way.

Reinforcing the Accomplishment of What's Important

A year of anticipation and preparation precedes the fourth quarterly stewardship review. You know that at the end of the year, a full review of your performance on all aspects of your job is required. You also know that a highlights report must be submitted, in writing, stating the facts regarding your most significant contributions to the success of the business as a result of your efforts. You are expected to manage well—to plan ahead for what's important to do, to carry out your plans, to accomplish many important results, to know what you've accomplished, and to become more and more valuable as an employee.

When reinforcement is focused on managing and accomplishing what's important to the business, here's what happens:

1. It encourages you to establish your job content based on the needs of the business and the importance to the business.

2. It encourages you to make use of the available time, effort, and resources to achieve your objectives according to their value or importance to business success.

3. It encourages you to be alert throughout the year for business opportunities, and to adjust your job content to take advantage of the most promising opportunities.

4. It encourages you to think about what you want your major accomplishments to be, the value of these accomplishments, and what must be done to achieve them, and to use this thinking to guide your day-to-day efforts.

5. It encourages you to watch for changes in business priorities and standards, and to adjust your efforts accordingly.

Conducting End-of-Year Stewardship Reviews

There are just two essential steps, and four optional steps, for conducting the final stewardship review of the year. First, follow the suggested procedures for a quarterly stewardship review of each job responsibility and each objective, and of job performance as a whole. Second, at the conclusion of the stewardship review, have the subordinate submit, in final form, an accomplishment highlights report for the year. A discussion of the report should follow. The following steps are optional:

• The superior may make notes during the review to assist in the preparation of the commentary to be attached to the subordinate's accomplishment report.

• The superior may discuss with the subordinate items in the accomplishment report that might be overstated, understated, or inadequately explained. The specific purpose of this is to assist the subordinate in properly evaluating and explaining accomplishments in the future.

• A joint analysis of reasons for successes and disappointments may be used to assist the subordinate in learning from the experience of the past year.

- The final stewardship review for the year may be used to lead into a discussion of objectives for the coming year.

Conducting End-of-Year Team Reviews

The annual team review is similar to the quarterly team review, but instead of progress toward results, the emphasis is on actual results and on identifying priorities for the future. Looking back, the team review provides open recognition of individual and team accomplishments. Looking ahead, objectives for the coming year can be discussed, and individual efforts can be correlated.

Preparing Accomplishment Highlights—The Subordinate's Report

Subordinates have total responsibility for reporting their most important accomplishments for the year. The reports are submitted in final form at the one-to-one year-end stewardship reviews. The superior is not allowed to change one word. Further, the subordinates are not allowed to redo the reports after submitting them to the boss. There's good reason for these strict rules. If the boss can make changes, and a subordinate can submit drafts until one is "approved," then it's no longer the subordinate's report, it becomes the boss's.

These rules make possible an honest report. The incentive to understate or overstate the facts is removed. If you fail to record your major accomplishments after working so closely with your boss to achieve them, what is the boss to think? That you're unaware of what's going on? That you don't understand what has been achieved, and its value? If you don't say it in your report, you may never get proper credit yourself, which in turn tends to rob your superiors, who should receive credit along with you. If you overstate the facts, you're likely to be embarrassed by the commentary of your boss. Again, your boss may assume you are incapable of understanding the true facts in the situation, or you are deliberately trying to deceive. The only way to "win" is to say it like it is, fully and accurately.

Here are the suggested steps in preparing the final draft of your report of accomplishments:

STEP 1. Review all you've accomplished in fulfilling your responsibilities. Review your job content document and your tracking notations for each objective. If necessary, review the facts on which your tracking evaluations were based. If you have subordinates, review their accomplishment reports. Review whatever you have that gives evidence of what has been accomplished under your stewardship.

STEP 2. Prepare a list of your major areas of accomplishment. Select the results you are most proud of. Limit your list to the results you feel contributed the most to the success of the organization. Remember that listing insignificant items will not favorably represent you, your boss, or your organization.

STEP 3. Rank the items on your list, putting the most significant contribution first.

STEP 4. Describe each accomplishment. Prepare a brief statement describing each accomplishment on your list. Keep in mind that the report will be reviewed by higher levels of management. Use language that will be understood easily by them as well as by your immediate superior. Make your statements clear enough so that the reader—without having your job content document, or your tracking notations, or you or anyone else there to explain what is written—will understand what you feel is important to understand.

A "news report" style, rather than a "whodunit style," is suggested as the best way to achieve both clarity and brevity. A standard four-point format that makes it easy to write, and easy to read, is as follows: (1) Provide a headline to identify the subject. (2) State what you achieved in relation to your objective. For example: "We achieved our objective of _____." Or "We achieved _____ compared with our objective of _____." (3) Describe the value or importance of the accomplishment to the business. For example: "This contributed _____." Or "This will mean _____." (4) Explain what went into it; what was done to get the results; what it took to make it happen. For example: "This was accomplished as a result of doing the following: _____." "This was accomplished in spite of _____." "This was accomplished with the help of _____."

STEP 5. (Optional) Add a statement of factors over which you had little or no control that significantly affected the results expected of you.

STEP 6. Prepare the final draft. Edit your report as needed to achieve its purposes. It should fit on one or a maximum of two typewritten pages. This means more explanatory detail can be added when fewer accomplishments are reported, or less detail with a greater number of accomplishments described. The choice is up to you. Make the report exactly as you want it. Remember, it's in final form when your boss first sees it.

Your accomplishment report shows what has been achieved of consequence, that you understand its value, and that you deliberately took the action steps to bring about those results. It is a self-portrait reflecting your managerial effectiveness, your chance to "autograph your excellence" in a way that is appropriate. It gives purpose to employing the management processes on a continuing basis. From your boss's point of view, it is an integral part of the overall process of providing reinforcement for accomplishments as the key to future performance.

Preparing Accomplishment Highlights—The Boss's Commentary

A subordinate's accomplishment report has to be placed in perspective by the commentary of the immediate boss, the person in the best position to know the facts and judge the circumstances that influenced the outcomes. No one should accept the subordinate's report of accomplishments without the commentary of the boss. Together, the subordinate's report and the boss's commentary keep the permanent record "honest." Just as the subordinate has total responsibility for preparation of the accomplishment report, the superior has total responsibility for preparing the written commentary that becomes part of the permanent record of important accomplishments.

No restrictions on the superior are intended in making the following suggestions for preparation and use of the commentary:

STEP 1. Write a brief statement indicating the extent to which you agree or disagree with the report of accomplishments and explanations prepared by your subordinate. Most commonly, a superior is in general agreement with a subordinate's report and has additional inputs on specific items.

STEP 2. Add specific comments you feel would help other readers understand your subordinate's report and evaluate the stated accomplishments as contributions to the success of the business. Other readers will include your subordinate and your immediate superior, and might include others at higher levels of management, personnel specialists, and individuals interested in having your subordinate reassigned to become their subordinate. Comments need not be made on each reported accomplishment. Accomplishments that have been understated, overstated, or inaccurately stated need further clarification. Accomplishments that are truly exceptional deserve special reinforcement in the commentary.

STEP 3. Attach the commentary to the accomplishment report of the subordinate. The two must be used together, never separately. Together, they become a permanent, important part of the subordinate's personnel file.

The Format for Accomplishment Highlights

The format suggested for the subordinate's report of significant accomplishments and the boss's commentary is the essence of simplicity, as you can see in Figures 13 and 14. Another way of handling the format is to use one sheet of paper for the reports of the subordinate and the superior. The paper selected is usually of heavier stock, 17 inches by 11 inches, folded in half vertically to create four sides. Company identification and special printing may be used to emphasize the fact that it is a permanent, important record.

Use of Accomplishment Highlights

Accomplishment highlights are useful to subordinates, superiors, higher levels of management, and those involved in compensation and promotion decisions.

For subordinates. The highlights provide a permanent record rein-

Figure 13. Format of the accomplishment highlights report prepared by the subordinate.

ACCOMPLISHMENTS HIGHLIGHTS

Report of: _____ Period from: _____ to: _____

Position: _____ Superior: _____

Signature: _____ Date of Stewardship Review: _____

Figure 14. Format of the accomplishment highlights commentary prepared by the superior.

ACCOMPLISHMENTS HIGHLIGHTS

Commentary to be attached to report of: _____

Period from: _____ to: _____ Prepared by: _____

	Initials	Date
Copy of commentary received by subordinate		
Accomplishment highlights reviewed at next higher level		
Accomplishment highlights added to personnel file		

forcing their major accomplishments for the year. In addition, there may be some valuable lessons taught by means of the commentary if the reported accomplishments are not accepted by the superior. What the superior adds may be facts, evaluations, and insights. For the subordinate, this adds up to a combination of reinforcement for past performance and motivation for future performance.

For the superior. The highlights provide summaries of what the subordinates have achieved under the superior's supervision. It provides answers to questions such as: Did this subordinate understand and respond to the priorities of the job? Did he use the coaching that was given? What have I learned about her talents and drives? The boss can use such insights in planning for the development, motivation, utilization, and retention of talent in the organization.

For higher levels of management. First, review of the accomplishment highlights at the next higher level of management is a convenient way to learn what's going on in the organization; it shows the higher level what is seen as important at the lower level; it shows where time and resources were spent; it indicates to what extent teamwork is going on. Second, it enlarges the use of reinforcement as a means of focusing efforts on important accomplishments; that is, another level of management is alerted to opportunities for it to give praise and offer encouragement and support. Third, it emphasizes the value and importance of clear communications downward regarding higher-level objectives, priorities, standards, and changing business conditions. Fourth, it keeps the subordinate honest. Knowing the accomplishments will be reviewed by higher levels encourages thoughtful consideration of what is reported. Modesty and exaggeration both have serious drawbacks. Fifth, it keeps the boss honest. The boss has to keep alert to the use of the full system for managing what's important. The boss is involved as coach in every aspect of the system. The subordinate's report of accomplishments, and the added commentary, give evidence of the managerial effectiveness of the boss as well as of the subordinate. Sixth, it encourages management to set an example and support continued efforts to make effective use of human resources throughout the organization.

For those involved in compensation decisions. Accomplishment highlights provide an auditable reference document to back up salary recommendations and approvals.

For those involved in promotion decisions. Making decisions regarding an employee's career is discussed in Chapters 15, 16, and 18. Past accomplishments are one excellent input as to an individual's potential to succeed in another specific work assignment. The highlights provide clues to how well the various management processes were used and to how well the subordinate understood both what happened and what caused it to happen.

Summary: Linking Past and Future Performance

The year-end reviews put all that has gone into managing the business over the past year into perspective. They also set the stage for the coming year's activities. But once-a-year reviews also have to be placed in perspective. Managing a business takes effort each day, and systematic approaches are required to achieve effectiveness in managing. Let's summarize the paperwork and the dialogue requirements presented here, as a way to gain perspective on the mechanics of linking past and future performance.

Required Paperwork

1. *Job content document.* The document is prepared annually to fit the business cycle. Approved changes made during the year are handwritten on the document, and dated.

2. *Tracking system notations.* A self-evaluation of progress toward each objective is recorded at least monthly by the subordinate. An evaluation of progress by the superior is added at least quarterly.

3. *Accomplishment highlights.* A report is prepared annually by the subordinate. (The maximum length is two typed pages.) A commentary prepared by the superior is attached to the report.

Paperwork Prepared as Needed

1. *Action plans.* These are written when needed to "insure" the achievement of specific objectives.

2. *Other homework.* Written homework may be needed as a prerequisite to action planning and to coaching by the boss.

Required Dialogues

1. *Agreement on job content.* A dialogue is held at the beginning of the annual cycle and whenever changes in job content are needed.

2. *Scheduled reviews.* Stewardship reviews are held at least quarterly. Accomplishment highlights are added to the year-end stewardship review.

Dialogues as Needed

1. *To comply with the no-surprises ground rule.*
2. *To set up or receive coaching from the boss.*

Not much paperwork is required in the system presented here, but what is required must be done. A practical way of organizing the paperwork is, therefore, part of the overall system. Also, many managers have found brief information and instructions printed on the paperwork to be helpful. This is especially so for newcomers to the system. As an example, some organizations choose to combine page 1 of the job content document and the tracking system worksheet onto one piece of paper (17″ × 11″), folded in half vertically and punched to fit a conventional loose-leaf binder. The summary information and instructions are printed on the outer sides of the paper. Figure 15 shows the copy, on the outside. The inside has the job content typed on the left and the tracking worksheet on the right. Additional pages (8½″ × 11″) are inserted as required, with job content typed on one side and the tracking worksheet printed on the other side.

A standard loose-leaf binder with five dividers is suggested for organizing the paperwork. Summary information on the dividers tells how the system works and promotes proper use of each tool and the system as a whole. Figure 16 shows the copy for the dividers.

Accomplishment Highlights—Cases and Comments

Case 1: The Chairman Learns About His People

The chairman of the board of a large industrial organization first learned about the use of accomplishment highlights when he was seeking a better way of distributing incentive bonus monies. He had noted a direct, consistent relationship of bonus money to position level. That is, the president got the top award, a percentage of his base pay, his vice presidents received a uniform, smaller percentage, and so on for all included in the program. The chairman wanted a program that would distribute the money in the bonus budget according to contribution, not position. He wanted to see evidence of

Figure 15. Information and instructions included with the job content and tracking sheet forms.

JOB CONTENT

Position: _____

- Reports on Stewardship to _____

- Accountable for Stewardship reviews with

  _____

  _____

  _____

  _____

The Purpose of the Job Content Document
- To help you understand your total position responsibilities and how your stewardship contributes to the success of the business.

- To help you identify the important objectives or end results you should be working to achieve in cooperation with others.

- To provide a practical format for defining your stewardship in such a way that it can be managed.

Responsibilities Common in Each Stewardship
- Responsibility for the work itself, for getting the job done.

- Responsibility for building people, teamwork, and relationships important to business success.

- Responsibility for your personal development.

The Format of the Job Content Document
- The document is designed to help you manage each part of your total steward-ship. The format links your objectives to specific areas of responsibility.

- To read the document, relate the objective to the control and the responsibility by reading it as one sentence with three parts, as follows:

I am responsible for results
having to do with

RESPONSIBILITY;

one element of this responsibility useful as a control and linkage to the objective is	one objective or end result important to achieve in fulfilling this responsibility is

| CONTROL; | → | OBJECTIVE. |

Figure 15 (*Continued.*)

TRACKING

Purpose of the Tracking System
- To provide a mechanism for self-supervision, self-direction, and self-control with regard to stewardship responsibilities and objectives.
- To save you time in managing your own stewardship and in communicating with your leader(s) and others.
- To serve as a springboard to action steps on important matters.

How to "Track" Your Progress
- Once a month, evaluate your progress toward each objective. Ask yourself these kinds of questions:

    Is progress taking place as planned? If progress continues as it now appears likely, will the objective be achieved?

    Should I be content with what is being done to achieve this objective; or should I plan to take some other action, do something differently, do something that is not now being done, for the sake of the business as a whole?

- Summarize your evaluation by placing the appropriate tracking system symbol in the proper monthly column.

Tracking System Symbols

✝ A "plus" means you're managing the objective well and there is *no need to change your present plans.* Also, it means you expect to achieve an acceptable level of performance by carrying out your present plans.

++ A "double plus" means progress is greater than could be expected; the desired results will likely be exceeded.

— A "minus" means there is something you could do to manage the objective even better, therefore, *some kind of action is required.* It means you really *need* to do something, or you feel you *could* do something different that would benefit the business in some way.

— — A "double minus" means action steps are urgent, high priority.

◯ A "circle" indicates a special discussion of a particular objective. For example: ⊖ in the October column means you discussed this objective with your leader shortly after you did your tracking for October; ⊕ in a review column means the discussion took place at a quarterly review but no changes were made in your plans; ⊖ in a review column means new action plans were developed at the quarterly stewardship review.

● A large "dot" means there is a deliberate delay of action on the objective; therefore, an evaluation of progress is not meaningful until action begins. For example, if the first possible action steps are to begin in June, the "dot" is placed in each column through May. In June, an evaluation of progress becomes meaningful.

✳ An "asterisk" means the objective has been completed or dropped; no further tracking is required.

Figure 16. Organization of paperwork with divider sheets containing instructions.

A system for managing job responsibilities

and accomplishing what's important

Direction

• DIRECTION FROM LEADERS

• Job Content and Tracking System

• Action Plans

• Stewardship Reviews

• Accomplishment Highlights

Figure 16 (Continued.)

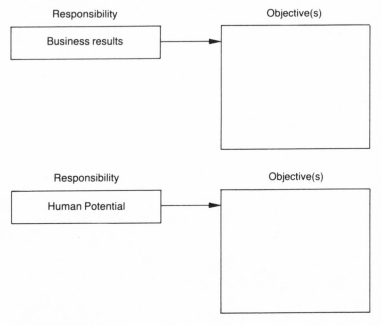

The Purpose of Direction from Leaders

- To provide guidance on matters important to us.
- To provide coaching and counseling as we need it.
- To correlate our efforts with the efforts of others.
- To provide encouragement and support to us in accomplishing what's important.

The foundation of all direction from our leaders is understanding their responsibilities and objectives.

Overall Direction to Our Individual and Collective Efforts

Everything we do should in some way contribute to realizing human potential and achieving optimum business results. Insert below selected objectives that provide overall direction throughout the organization.

Responsibility

Business results

Objective(s)

Responsibility

Human Potential

Objective(s)

Place in this Section

- The job content document of the leader you are directly accountable to in your present position.

- Optional: Selected objectives of others in the management of the organization.

Figure 16 (Continued.)

A system for managing job responsibilities
and accomplishing what's important

• Direction from Leaders

Tracking

• JOB CONTENT AND TRACKING SYSTEM

• Action Plans

• Stewardship Reviews

• Accomplishment Highlights

Figure 16 (Continued.)

The Purpose of the Management System

- To increase the effectiveness of our efforts.
- To accomplish results through others by appropriate leadership behavior.

The Parts of the System

- Direction from Leaders:

  To provide help and encouragement for our individual efforts.

- Job Content and Tracking System:

  To define areas of responsibility for results, and important objectives.
  To provide a means of keeping track of all important parts of our job.
  To serve as a tool to evaluate our progress as a springboard to action.
  To foster and facilitate communication with others.

- Fundamental Rules in an Effective Work Relationship:

  The "no surprises" rule requires us to alert our boss immediately when we are having a problem and may need help to achieve an objective.

  The "homework before help" rule requires us to think through a situation and have our own action plans prepared before we seek coaching and counseling from our boss.

- Action Plans:

  To provide "insurance" that an objective is accomplished.

- Stewardship Reviews:

  To report progress and results to date to the leader(s) we are accountable to.
  To receive positive reinforcement from our leader(s) for our progress and accomplishments.

  To receive coaching and counseling help from our leader(s) when it's needed.

- Accomplishment Highlights:

  To encourage that time, effort, and resources be spent in each area of responsibility and on each objective in relation to its importance to the business.

  To summarize the most important contributions from our stewardship efforts each year for our personal records and for use as part of our permanent personnel file.

Place in this Section

- Your own job content document and tracking system sheets.

(margin label:) Tracking

Figure 16 (Continued.)

A system for managing job responsibilities
and accomplishing what's important

- Direction from Leaders

- Job Content and Tracking System

Action Plans

- ACTION PLANS

- Stewardship Reviews

- Accomplishment Highlights

Figure 16 (Continued.)

The Purpose of Action Plans

- To provide "insurance" that we achieve objectives and fulfill responsibilities.
- To serve as reminders of things to be done, action steps to be taken, to achieve results.

How to Prepare an Action Plan

- Key the action plan to the specific objective for which the "insurance" is created. For example: Action Plan 3B relates to achieving objective 3B on your job content document.
- Identify the objective. This helps you focus the action steps on a specific result.
- List the action steps you plan to take. Number each step so your plan is easy to follow. List the steps in chronological order unless that is impractical. One step usually leads to another step. For each step, state briefly:

    What action is planned.

    Who is to do it, if it's to be carried out by someone other than yourself.

    When it's to be done, if timing considerations apply.

- File the action plan in this section in numerical sequence, using the action plan number.
- Add steps to your plan as you go along, using the building block principle. That is, as action steps are taken, evaluate your progress and then decide what steps to take next. When more detailed planning is called for to carry out a given step, consider setting up a separate action plan to identify the detail for that step.

Special Note: A Shared Objective Requires Correlated Action Plans

Frequently an objective appears on more than one job content document. This means that two or more people share the responsibility for achieving the objective. Each has 100% responsibility for what they do contributing to the final results. Therefore, the action plans prepared by each individual to achieve the objective need to be correlated to avoid duplication of effort and increase the "insurance" the objective is achieved.

Place in this Section

- Your own action plans.

Action Plans

Figure 16 (Continued.)

A system for managing job responsibilities

and accomplishing what's important

- Direction from Leaders

- Job Content and Tracking System

- Action Plans

- STEWARDSHIP REVIEWS

Reviews

- Accomplishment Highlights

Figure 16 (Continued.)

The Purpose of Stewardship Reviews

- To report progress to date to the leader(s) we are accountable to.
- To receive positive reinforcement from our leader(s) for our progress and accomplishments.
- To receive coaching and counseling from our leader(s) when needed.

The Sequence of Stewardship Reviews

- Schedule and hold stewardship reviews with those you are accountable for, in preparation for the review with your leader(s).
- Schedule and prepare for the review with your leader(s) by having your tracking notations current, and having action plans prepared as needed, based on your latest tracking evaluations.

The Process for Stewardship Reviews

Phase 1. The Subordinate Reports; the Leader Reacts

- The Stewardship Report:

  A brief, verbal report is given the leader regarding each objective, or at least each area of responsibility listed on the job content document.

  Only information that is new and essential for the leader to know is reported; the tracking notation serves as the report when there is no new, important information the leader should receive.

  The report covers the entire stewardship, one item at a time; the reaction from the leader on one item is required before proceeding to the next.

- The leader reacts to the report on each item in one of two ways:

  Accepts the report and provides brief, appropriate, positive reinforcement (agreement, encouragement, praise) of actual progress and the evaluation of that progress.

  Asks for further discussion of the item. A large circle is placed in the review column of the tracking sheet to identify the item for further discussion after progress is reported on all responsibilities and objectives.

Phase 2. Action Plan Decisions Are Made on Items Selected for Further Discussion

- Further discussion of an objective leads to a decision concerning future action steps, and the appropriate tracking symbol is placed in the blank circle. For example: a plus (+) means no change in present plans; a minus (−) means the discussion produced ideas or suggestions that call for action—that is, for new plans to be made and implemented.
- When there is to be a change in plans, action steps are agreed upon and added to existing plans, or new action plans are set up.

Place in this Section

- The job content documents and tracking sheets of those stewardships you are accountable for. The tracking sheets are to be updated at each review.

Reviews

Figure 16 (Continued.)

A system for managing job responsibilities
and accomplishing what's important

- Direction from Leaders

- Job Content and Tracking System

- Action Plans

- Stewardship Reviews

- ACCOMPLISHMENT HIGHLIGHTS

Accomplishments

Figure 16 (Continued.)

The Purpose of Accomplishment Highlights

- To encourage each of us to spend time and effort on each area of responsibility and each objective in relation to its importance to the success of the business.

- To summarize the most important contributions from our stewardship efforts each year for our personal records and for use as a permanent part of our personnel file.

How to Prepare Accomplishment Highlights

- You prepare a report of your most significant accomplishments

  Considering all your major accomplishments for the year, list them in order of importance. The number may vary from two or three to ten or more.

  For each accomplishment, write a headline descriptive of the subject matter and three paragraphs:

  1. What was accomplished compared with your objective.

  2. The value or importance of the accomplishment to the business.

  3. Factors that helped or hindered; what was done to achieve the results; evidence of cooperation and correlation of effort.

  Edit your report as required to fit on a maximum of two typewritten pages. Sign and date your report.

- Your boss prepares a commentary to be attached to your report

  Your boss reads your report of accomplishments and discusses it with you as required to gain full understanding of what you have written.

  Your boss then writes a commentary to add important information and to give additional insight into what was accomplished and its significance to the business.

Place in this Section:

- Your own notes and other material you will use in drafting and finalizing your report of your most significant accomplishments for the year.

Accomplishments

differentiation in performance. He wanted to know why A should receive a higher percentage award than B and why C should receive any award at all.

The existing incentive bonus program was revised to make the accomplishment highlights the reference document for all recommendations. The chairman was to give final approval on all awards. The revised incentive bonus program was explained to all participants at the end of the first quarter. The chairman reported that superior-subordinate communications on important matters quadrupled overnight.

At the end of the year, the preparation of reports and commentaries occupied much time. Each participant was striving for the "perfect" wording. Many requests were received asking that the two-page maximum for reporting accomplishments be raised to five or six pages, or have no limits at all. Others wanted a ceiling on the number of accomplishments to be included, such as three or five. The chairman held firm with the program design.

When all the incentive bonus recommendations were in, the chairman took them along with the accomplishment highlights for a long weekend of seclusion to study them. He admitted he was both delighted and surprised that he was able to approve all the recommendations. Further, he noted a significant spread from the largest to the smallest percentage awards in each level of management, and within each division of the company. Then the chairman surprised me by saying there was something that came out of the program even more important to him than an equitable distribution of the bonus money. It had to do with what he had learned from reviewing the accomplishment highlights. "I learned more about what's going on in the organization than I'd ever dreamed. It was like I was able to see inside the heads of my people. To see what was important to them. To get a feel for the depth and breadth of their understanding of how their work contributed to the whole. To see how they were getting along with their boss. To see evidence of the teamwork so essential to our success. It gave me renewed confidence that most of our key people are managing well, making things happen.

"And for those who didn't have much to be proud of, I think they got a message. For some, it will serve as a constant reminder that keeping their nose clean is not enough. We have both talent and experience in the group. It's a matter of using what we have. And for others, we may lose a few. The handwriting is on the wall. Those who are uncomfortable with this approach are the kind we can well afford to lose.

"One more thing. Even for those who were superb, next year is a new ball game. That message is clear also. No halo effect from year to year. Rewards for accomplishments must be earned each and every year."

At the end of the second year of using accomplishment highlights, the chairman summed up his experience in these words: "They provide me with my most significant learning activity of the year."

Case 2: A President Reinforces and Coaches

The president of a division with widely scattered plants and marketing offices recognized the value of having individuals manage themselves as much as possible, yet function as one team. The system for managing what's important was installed. At the end of the year, the president set up a schedule for the handling of accomplishment reviews. She wanted to be able to review the accomplishment highlights before the annual meetings with corporate management. In addition, she wanted the opportunity to communicate in a special way with the many individuals she seldom saw face to face.

The accomplishment highlights she reviewed covered all exempt employees through four management levels below her own, and for some departments five or six levels below were included. As she read each report, she looked for opportunities to provide reinforcement. Her handwritten comments in the margin included such notations as "Great"; "I've heard about this before. Thanks for the detail"; "Good work"; "Let's keep this up next year'; "Let's talk about this one. I think some others can benefit from what you've done"; "You and all your people are to be commended for this record." The president also took advantage of the opportunity to coach. "This is extremely important to me. Get together with the division manager on this one"; "What would happen if we doubled our efforts here?" "The teamwork you generated here was impressive. Be prepared to explain your approach to the staff next month." Since comments were not made on every accomplishment, or on every report, and they were restricted to accomplishments deemed exceptional or of special interest to the president, each comment had special meaning to the individuals involved.

The president then passed the accomplishment highlights back down the organization so all managers could see what she had written to their people. As a result of the president's personal attention to the accomplishments of the past year, the setting of objectives for the coming year took on new significance. Discussions of objectives for the new year revolved around importance to the business. And as soon as objectives were approved and correlated, initial drafts of accomplishment highlights began to take shape—individuals started to give serious thought to what they wanted to be able to report at the end of the new year as their most significant contributions and to what evidence they would be able to present that they made it happen.

III

THE MANAGEMENT SYSTEM AND SUPERIOR-SUBORDINATE NEEDS

Managers are required to have managerial dialogues. A dialogue is an exchange of viewpoints or information, a discussion, a personal meeting with two-way communication taking place. A *managerial* dialogue deals with the business and involves superior and subordinate. To have a viable management system, effective managerial dialogues are essential. This section deals with what has been learned from research and experience to achieve effective managerial dialogues. And going from concept to practice, it will provide you with models to use in applying the theory to on-the-job situations.

Effective managerial dialogues are helpful and motivational to both superiors and subordinates. They help subordinates to do what is expected in their current position, to prepare for future responsibilities, and to make career decisions. The help may come in a variety of ways from the boss: direction in establishing job content, suggestions related to needed action plans, inputs that provide perspective, additional relevant information, positive reinforcement for appropriate homework, guidance in self-development activities, and woven into each of these, encouragement and support. And the help should be given in such a way that the subordinate is motivated to use it properly in handling new assignments, making decisions, taking necessary actions, achieving expected results, and accomplishing what's important.

The boss should benefit from the dialogues also. New insights into the knowledge, understanding, interests, aspirations, motivations, and capabilities of the subordinate can come from empathic listening. From such insights the boss can more effectively coach and counsel the subordinate. As a boss accumulates success experiences in conducting managerial dialogues, there is bound to be increased self-confidence in using the models. This encourages continued use of the dialogue skills, thus sustaining the growth cycle.

There is another benefit for the boss. The outcomes of effective dialogues are linked directly or indirectly to achieving results important to the continued success of the business. Accomplishments of subordinates accumulate upward; that is, the success of a subordinate is also the success of the boss who delegates the responsibility, since the boss always retains accountability for results. Therefore, the success of subordinates can contribute significantly to the achievement of the boss's career aspirations.

The principal reasons for developing managerial dialogue skills are to get improved performance from subordinates and, in so doing, to build the organization for the future. Think of the subordinates who report directly to you, and mentally assess their level of performance. How many would you consider excellent? Satisfactory? Not Satisfactory? You can go through the same assessment process for subordinates at the level below those who report directly to you.

The number in each category, of course, is not the issue. The old adage still applies: A manager's job is not to get average performance from above-average subordinates but to get above-average performance from average subordinates. The challenge, then, is to upgrade those you now classify in the lower categories. Along with that, the challenge includes keeping all subordinates motivated to manage their entire jobs well and to accomplish what's most important to the success of the business. Effective managerial dialogue skills help a manager meet this challenge.

The first chapter in this section is devoted to applying behavioral research to managerial effectiveness. An understanding of the basic concepts can help a manager in using the models presented in the following chapters.

There are three kinds of dialogues, and thus dialogue skills, that most managers must have. The first involves talking with subordinates about some aspect of their job performance. The second deals with problem behavior of subordinates that affects job performance. And the third involves discussing subordinates' careers and preparing subordinates for the future (including future positions that they are interested in and/or new or enlarged responsibilities in their current positions).

A fourth kind of dialogue also has to do with career matters but is not a superior-subordinate dialogue in the same sense as the others. These are discussions that occur when a position is opening and the manager is responsible for making the selection from the available candidates and encouraging the candidate selected to accept the position. In this case, the candidates are not actual, but potential, subordinates to the manager. The selection of personnel is part of planning organizational behavior. Therefore, this type of dialogue is discussed in Chapter 16, in Section IV.

For each superior-subordinate dialogue skill, some guidelines are suggested, the steps in the process of conducting the dialogue are presented, and opportunities to apply the skill within the framework of the system for managing what's important are indicated.

12

How to Apply Behavioral Research to Managerial Effectiveness

Knowledge plus the ability to apply the knowledge in practical situations adds up to skill. In this chapter several fundamentals are reviewed to assist you in applying your managerial dialogue skills in particular situations. These skills may be crucial to your effectiveness as a manager.

Some of the fundamentals reviewed here are well known, with abundant literature on the subject. Others are relatively new, and research on them is continuing. All managers are encouraged to expand their knowledge in all areas that can lead to their increased effectiveness. As new insights are gained, improved approaches and models will be developed for managing, and new standards for defining what is considered effective will emerge.

The following topics will be discussed in this chapter: basic concepts of behavior, the process of learning, ability and willingness factors, the impact of expectations on performance, the use of praise as a motivator, and flexibility in leadership behavior.

Basic Concepts of Behavior

Why do people act the way they do? Why do people resist change, even when the change may benefit them? Why do individuals sometimes react exactly alike and other times react so differently? When things are perfectly clear to me, why aren't they clear to other intelligent individuals? How can I get people to respond to me the way I want them to?

Although human behavior is far too complex for a set of rigid rules underlying it to be found, there is a set of principles that can enlarge our understanding of behavior and improve our ability to anticipate and influence the actions of others. We need to develop the habit of looking for numerous causes, not a single cause, of any particular behavior. Also, we should assume that the way things appear to us may not be the way they appear to others. The following principles underlie all behavior:

1. Behavior depends on the person and the situation.
2. Behavior is influenced by a variety of human needs.
3. People behave in ways that make sense to them.
4. Behavior is influenced by how people see the situation.
5. Behavior is influenced by how people see themselves.

First, we'll consider each of these basic concepts. Next, we'll look at what's involved in changing the self-concept. And then we'll make some deductions about behavior that are important to the superior-subordinate work relationship.

Behavior Depends on the Person and the Situation

What individuals do is determined by their own capabilities and skills, by some aspect of the situation they are in, or in most cases by some combination of the two. In order to work effectively with others, then, you have to understand the individual and the situation, and how the situation affects the individual. For example, in one environment an individual may be bored, act irresponsibly, be uncreative, and direct his or her efforts toward objectives that don't contribute to the achievement of your objectives and those at higher levels. In another setting the same individual may exhibit enthusiasm for the work, eagerness to accept responsibility, an innovative approach to assignments, and evidence of teamwork. Just as one individual may respond differently in different situations, two or more individuals may respond differently in the same situation.

This principle suggests that the behavior of individuals can be changed by some combination of (1) changing the people themselves (through increasing their knowledge, through development of their skills) and (2) modifying the situation in which they work (through reorganization of the work, changed procedures, listening with empathy, involving them in planning and decision making). Changing the person and/or the situation involves the following principles of behavior also.

Behavior Is Influenced by a Variety of Human Needs

Human needs include the needs for air, food, physical activity, and rest; the need to be safe from physical pain and danger; the need for gainful and continuing employment; the needs for acceptance by others and a sense of belonging in the group; the need for the feeling of self-confidence and self-worth coming from the treatment and recognition received from others; the need for the feeling of accomplishment coming from the development and use of one's talents.

The behavior of some individuals, however, does not seem consistent with these statements of human needs. To understand this, we must look to the other principles. People are influenced by their previous experiences and their self-image. People's expectations lead them to do the very things that increase the chances that their expectations will be fulfilled.

People Behave in Ways That Make Sense to Them

People want to understand the situations they encounter. In order for words and events to make sense to people, they need to be put into perspective with other things the people believe or have experienced. Then the people behave according to the meaning the words, events, or situation has for them.

In the absence of information, people base their actions on assumptions. Such assumptions, of course, may be accurate or inaccurate. This points up the importance of adequate communication. When people have the information they need to understand the situation they are in, they don't have to speculate about what the situation "must be." Having the information, their efforts can be directed toward accomplishing what's expected of them. If you know what is to be accomplished and why it is important and you fail to communicate it to your subordinates, what are you teaching them? To be dependent on you rather than to act resourcefully.

Individuals forced to work for long periods under conditions of inadequate communication often conclude that they are incapable of acting independently, that there is no use trying to figure things out. For these individuals to take the initiative in their jobs would be for them to go against what makes sense to them. Their behavior does not mean they cannot demonstrate initiative. To change their behavior, the barriers to taking the initiative need to be removed. When it makes sense to take the initiative, they will do so.

Behavior Is Influenced by How People See the Situation

Previous experiences form the basis of a person's picture of reality. From their efforts to make sense of their experiences, individuals develop a point of view that is the basis for what they expect, assume, and hope to achieve. A success experience in one situation influences a person's expectations for success in another situation. And since each individual has unique experiences, which accumulate to form a unique point of view, reality looks different to each individual.

This principle points up the need to listen to individuals and to observe their behavior. If you as a manager know how your subordinates view a situation, you can understand the basis for their behavior. Comparing viewpoints (yours and theirs) against the facts of the situation can lead to modified behavior (yours and theirs) by changing how the facts are "seen."

Behavior Is Influenced by How People See Themselves

At the center of all reactions is a set of views called the self-concept or self-image. This is how people view themselves, their relations with others, and their relations with the world at large. Everything we say, hear, feel, do, or see is influenced by how we see ourselves. Selective seeing or listening, for example, is a function of self-concept. We quickly spot our own name among all the words on a page. We hear our own name amid the noise of a crowd. The self-concept acts like a filter, screening out what we don't want to see or hear and allowing what we do want to see or hear to pass through.

Our view of ourselves is constantly changing. We are not the same people we were five years ago. We're not even the same people we were yesterday. We're a day older. We've learned something new, however insignificant it might seem compared to our total experience. As a result, how we perceive events today is different from how we perceived events yesterday. Changes in our self-concept from day to day are reflected in our behavior. Changing the self-image, therefore, can have a powerful impact on behavior.

This principle points up the need for success experiences and reinforcement on the job. For example, how will a subordinate react to a tough, important assignment? A subordinate who feels confident of success would be likely to welcome the assignment. Reinforcement of progress and success from the boss would add to the self-image of the subordinate and influence the subordinate's reaction to further assignments. On the other hand, a lack of confidence might lead the subordinate to be overly cautious, to put off planning, decisions, and action steps, and to rationalize any lack of success. In this case, the coaching of the boss could influence the immediate outcome of the assignment and build the subordinate's self-image in approaching future assignments. In either case, the individual behaves in ways that protect and enhance the self-image.

Regarding the impact of reinforcement on the self-concept, the principle emphasizes the value of appropriate reinforcement for progress and accomplishments throughout the year. Building the self-concept of subordinates should be implicit in all development efforts.

Ponder this question: What might happen to the self-concept of subordinates who receive a series of easy assignments? What message might this convey to them about their abilities and standing in the organization?

Changing the self-concept. Changes in the self-concept are changes in perception, attitude, and understanding, not changes in knowledge, skill, or experience. This means basic change in the makeup of the person, not cosmetic or peripheral change. Changing our view of ourselves involves self-examination, which in turn provides direction and motivation to change. Change and growth rarely occur in clear-cut, logical steps. They tend to come in spurts or to take place gradually over a long period of time. Understanding the sequence of steps involved in changing the self-concept is especially useful in functioning as coach and counselor to subordinates. The steps include:

1. *Self-awareness.* In becoming aware of ourselves and our surroundings, we are constantly comparing and learning. Contrasts and comparisons with our previous experience and awareness of our and

others' standards in thinking and behavior prepare us for self-examination.

2. *Self-examination.* When we realize we "don't know" or when we realize we "wish we were different" in some respect, we are ready for looking at ourselves as we really are. Self-examination may be thrust on us by circumstances, or it may take place out of our need to be what we are capable of being. Self-examination leads to the feeling of "Oh, I see now," which must, consciously or unconsciously, precede change in behavior.

3. *New standards.* When we see ourselves in a particular way that we don't approve of, or gain insight into what we might become that is better than what we are, we change our standards, our expectations of ourselves. No one else imposes our standards on us. If we raise our sights, it is because we choose to raise our sights.

How do we develop new standards? How do we find out that we can be different? How do we decide our self-concept is inadequate? Unfortunately for those who like recipes or formulas, there are no simple answers. What can be done? In business, constructive coaching by the boss can lead to insight into our behavior. Anything that enables us to gain new insight—reading, meditating, observing, listening, researching, experimenting, participating in group activities— can lead to new standards.

4. *Self-development.* It has been said that all development is self-development. We take charge of our own development, if we want to grow. Nothing can be done to us to make us grow. We grow only as we choose to and as our own insight enables us to. When we develop insight into ourselves, we often feel the need to change, to do things differently.

5. *Ongoing self-realization.* Seeing ourselves as we are now is a necessary starting point for change, a basis on which to build. But we must also see what we can become, and grow into that kind of person. Beethoven continued to compose after he became deaf, and Milton didn't allow blindness to interfere with his writing. All individuals in a business organization cannot be expected to become world-famous for their accomplishments, but all individuals can choose to develop and realize more of their full potential.

Changing and building the self-concept of an individual in a business situation can be achieved by appropriate work assignments and effective coaching from the boss. A series of success experiences, under the guidance of an effective coach, provides a subordinate the opportunity to go through each of the steps involved in changing the self-concept.

Some Useful Deductions About Behavior

From the five principles of behavior, some deductions can be drawn that are important to effective superior-subordinate relationships:

• Understanding your own motivations helps reduce the barriers that prevent you from listening to, and understanding, the other person.

• Motivation is inherent within people. It's like the potential for growth. The challenge for the superior is not so much that of "motivating subordinates" as it is of unleashing and helping to guide the motivation already there.

• People respond to a situation as they see it. Help them to get a more accurate view of reality and you influence their behavior.

• The more you can help others feel comfortable in examining their own point of view, and how they arrived at it, the more you can help them to behave in a rational, flexible, creative way.

• People tend to change their viewpoint, and consequently their behavior, in the light of feedback or reactions of others to their behavior.

• What people can do should not be judged simply on the basis of what they are now doing. The effects of past learning and the potential of future learning need to be considered in judgments of potential.

The Process of Learning

After we are born, we learn to respond to the environment, to behave in certain ways in our own self-interest and for the benefit of others, to accept ideas as good or bad, true or false. Learning can be defined as the process of changing our behavior in response to our encounters with people, events, and things.

Our basic personalities are in large part learned. Fortunately, there is no time in life when people who truly want to change their personalities can't do so to a considerable degree. We can learn and change when we want to, and we do change, in small ways if not large ones throughout life. Important aspects of the process of learning include academic learning, academic wisdom, emotional learning, contrasts and comparisons, and learning and coaching.

Academic Learning

Academic learning involves mental effort. Learning algebra and learning how to read and write are examples of this type of learning. The person has to be motivated to acquire academic learning. It doesn't come easily or automatically. It comes by hard work.

The key problem for the teacher in academic learning is providing circumstances that are sufficiently stimulating, but not too demanding, for the learner. Striking the proper balance produces so much intrinsic motivation in the learner that the work of learning is continued. The more the teacher knows about what the learner can and can't do at a given point, the more likely it is that the teacher can set up the conditions that will promote academic learning. We can learn almost anything if we really want to learn it. For the coach and counselor in a business situation, the facts about academic learning should encourage us to be keen observers of the impact of our work assignments and of our coaching and counseling practices on our subordinates. Motivation is the important factor in academic learning.

Academic Wisdom

An important outgrowth of years of academic learning is academic wisdom. Academic wisdom is the capacity to make rapid and sound judgments in relatively new situations within our area of long-term experience.

Gaining academic wisdom takes more than time, and it does not come without effort. The first time we try to solve a problem of any kind, the learning comes very slowly. If the problem is difficult, it can be a terrible experience. But if we keep on working at the problem, eventually the difficulty disappears. We become more efficient at learning. Motivation increases because as we solve more problems their solution becomes easier and more rewarding. When first attempts at problem solving are difficult and nonreinforcing, a negative attitude may develop. But unless we persist in working on the problems, we never reach the point where solving them is easy and rewarding. When we persist, we gain experience that moves us closer to our maximum capability in academic wisdom.

The persistence of the automatically formed, high-level learning capability called academic wisdom is truly amazing. This and the other facts about academic wisdom need to be understood by those involved in filling positions and making decisions about early retirements. Otherwise, the organization might misplace or lose talent that could be important to the success of the business. Academic wisdom is an important asset in an organization and should be safeguarded and used with care.

Emotional Learning

Emotional learning is a continuous process that occurs without effort, without trying. It may even occur when we don't want it to, such as when we learn a new fear. Every time we interact with other people, emotional learning takes place; what we do affects them in some way, however small, and what they do affects us. When we deal with people and they approve of us, they will try, consciously or unconsciously, to be like us in terms of personality and knowledge. If, in their opinion, we do a good job at some task, they will be motivated to some degree to learn what we have learned and act as we act. In an effective job performance dialogue, for example, the emotional learning that takes place may have a greater impact on the subordinate's subsequent behavior than the academic learning coming from the boss's coaching and counseling.

Comparisons and Contrasts

We learn by making comparisons and contrasts, by measuring similarities and differences. To measure or evaluate something unfamiliar, we compare it with something familiar to us. Measurement is meaningful only when comparison or contrast with a known standard is possible. In business, data are meaningless until we compare them with some standard of measurement. Objectives have meaning because we compare actual results with desired results. In managerial dialogues, a subordinate's report of progress, plans, or accomplishment is based on various measurements. The superior's reaction to the report provides another measure that facilitates the learning process for the subordinate. The reader learns from this book by comparing and contrasting the concepts and models presented here with previous learning.

Learning and Coaching

Learning is accelerated through guided personal struggle. Learning can be painful, especially if old patterns of thought and action must be unlearned before new ones are mastered. In business, learning has to be active rather than passive. Knowing is not enough; what counts is *doing*.

We learn to do by the experience of doing. For example, individuals with superior knowledge of the principles of management may flounder in a management job. Theoretical knowledge may be of little value if it has never been put into practice.

Because learning to do comes from our own experiences, we can understand how properly motivated individuals can do outstanding work in spite of an ineffective boss. By examining and analyzing their own experiences so they have real meaning, the individuals can discover what is necessary to be successful. Those who refuse to make full use of their experiences in this way cannot grow under an ineffective boss. Of course, the person who examines and analyzes, but comes to the wrong conclusions, learns the wrong things.

This suggests that struggle guided by an effective coach is more likely to lead to worthwhile learning. The role of the coach is to encourage the learner to struggle, to examine experiences, to recognize and face up to problems. The coach steers the struggle through managerial dialogues, effective use of delegation, and new and challenging assignments. Effective coaches avoid the tempting but unproductive pleasure of showing off their own expertise. It's the learner who must struggle, if learning is to take place.

Learning can be aided by purposeful repetition. Coaching is not a once-and-for-all process. There are wide variations in the speeds with which people learn. Learning is habit formation, and habits are changed, not by some magical infusion of knowledge, but by struggle and by receiving reinforcement for one's efforts.

The main purpose of the coaching and the personal struggle is not to obtain an immediate result, as important as that may be. Rather, it's to help the learner develop the knowledge, skills, and attitudes needed to cope with the ever-changing situations in the dynamic world of business.

In summary, learning of some kind goes on continually for each of us. Job content should be the greatest motivation for learning in the business world. Next to the job itself, which is set up with the guidance and approval of the boss, the boss should have the greatest impact on the learner through effective coaching and counseling.

Ability and Willingness Factors

In a work situation, when a variance begins to develop between actual performance and what was expected, try to determine whether it is due to ability factors or willingness factors or both. Remedial action can't be effective unless it corrects the cause(s) of the problem or variance. Quite different action steps may be needed to correct an ability problem than would be needed to correct a willingness problem.

A better understanding of the impact of ability and willingness factors on business results can be gained from considering their components. In looking for the causes of a variance, each of the following should be considered. Some items apply to everyone; others are important only in connection with a particular type of work.

The Ability to Work

Everyone who comes to work brings certain abilities. These abilities, of course, are not fixed and unchangeable. But the physical and mental abilities that employees bring with them, coupled with other on-the-job factors over which they have little or no control, affect their job performance.

Physical abilities include general state of health, biological functioning, and the strength and stamina to tackle a job vigorously and keep at it, to perform well during long periods of pressure and overwork, and to recover quickly from fatigue.

Mental abilities include intellectual abilities, aptitudes, and knowledge and skill. Intellectual abilities involve learning, thinking, and analyzing and solving problems. These abilities apply to dealing with tangible, mechanical things, social situations and getting along with other people, and new, possibly abstract ideas. If it's true that most of us use from 4 to 10 percent of our intellectual capacity, then training, coaching, and the creation of an environment conducive to learning offer a continuing challenge to managers in business organizations.

Aptitudes refer to the potential for learning and performing certain kinds of work. But undeveloped and unused potential is of no value. Only when aptitudes have become knowledge and skill and are applied to achieve important results do they have real meaning for personal and organizational success.

Knowledge and skill are requirements for doing what is expected on a job. Individuals may have the intellectual abilities and aptitudes for performing a particular job, but their potential may need to be developed. They may need further education and training to add to their prior experiences in order to acquire the specific knowledge and skills required for the job.

On-the-job factors affecting ability to work include work environment, availability of work, equipment and supplies, and performance of others in a work-flow situation or when teamwork is critical.

Changes in the Ability to Work

It was once generally accepted that an individual's intelligence could not be changed and that aptitudes could not be added. Today there is increasing consensus that through education, training, and experience, both intelligence and aptitudes can be developed. Another factor to consider is the changes brought about by the process of aging, which have an important positive (or negative) effect on ability to work.

Examined experience is what has been learned from all aspects of life, including work. More than age or length of service is involved in gaining examined experience. Learning from past successes and disappointments involves analyzing these experiences as a basis for dealing realistically with future problems and challenges. Coaches can encourage continued education, provide training, and assist subordinates in examining their experiences and learning from them.

The Willingness to Work

Individuals may have the physical abilities, intelligence, aptitudes, knowledge, and skills necessary for success on a job and yet perform at substandard levels. The many possible reasons for their poor performance can be summarized by what the individuals are willing to do or not do. These willingness factors include attitude, motivation, and level of emotional maturity.

An attitude is a way of looking at a given situation, idea, object, or person. It's also a tendency or readiness to act in a certain way. Attitudes are mental habits that, like other habits, are affected by past experiences. Attitude is not inherited, it is learned. It is based not on the present situation but on a complex set of circumstances growing out of the experiences of a lifetime. It controls to a significant extent the effort individuals make in doing their work. A negative attitude toward work has much the same effect as trying to drive a car with the brakes on. A positive attitude toward work leads to the behavior that produces desired business results.

Changes in attitudes are possible. Superiors have a responsibility to influence the formation of the attitudes of their subordinates that affect business results. This responsibility cannot be delegated, should not be avoided, and requires constant attention. Knowing that attitudes are caused, you can work on causing positive ones while conducting managerial dialogues.

A changed attitude can lead to changed behavior. But, telling people to change an attitude usually doesn't work, even if they would like to change. However, changed behavior can lead to a changed attitude. And it's easier to change behavior.

The outcomes of managerial dialogues often include action plans—specific steps to be taken to achieve a particular objective. In taking the steps (behaviors), new experiences are accumulated that alter attitudes.

The drive we feel to achieve a particular outcome or to satisfy a particular need is called motivaton. Our motivation to achieve on the job influences what kind of job we do. Motivation moves us to action, helps us to persevere, and affects the degree to which we succeed. Insights into motivation can increase managerial effectiveness.

Personal needs that a job can satisfy play an important role in determining an individual's willingness to work. The needs vary from individual to individual. And even for the same individual, they vary in relative strength and at different times. Basic needs that relate to a person's job are economic and personal security and psychological growth. The best way to assure both economic and personal security is to perform well on the job. Motivation to grow psychologically is closely related to maintaining personal and economic security. Psychological growth means to add more knowledge to what one already knows; to combine new knowledge with previous learning so as to understand the enlarged picture; to think creatively; to surmount uncertainty, change and the complexities of life, people, and work; to think and act more independently; to be able to accept and carry out higher-level tasks. Thus motivation to grow psychologically on the job is motivation to perform the job well.

Jobs can have opportunities for psychological growth built in to them. "Challenging" and "responsible" jobs often contain the elements for growth. Job content should set the stage for psychological growth, and leader behavior should reinforce the growth. The return in human satisfaction for the workers, and in business results for the organization, is greatest when the work is meaningful and therefore has opportunities for psychological growth.

Several factors related to growth on the job influence the motivation to work. The factors involve the work itself, responsibility, achievement, recognition, and advancement. The boss may exert influence and control over these factors as they relate to the subordinate. Enjoying the work fosters psychological growth that, in turn, increases satisfaction and motivation to work. The challenge for management is to match the interests, aspirations, and qualifications of the individual with the requirements for success on the job. (This subject is dealt with in more detail in Chapters 15 and 16.)

Great satisfaction is gained from having a responsible position and handling it well. Responsibility, in an amount that challenges the individual to grow psychologically, is the foundation of work motivation. It provides opportunity for achievement, recognition, satisfaction, and where possible, advancement.

Superiors have at their disposal this powerful motivator: delegation of responsibility and authority. The use of this motivator should be continual, feeding responsibility and authority to subordinates as they demonstrate ability and the willingness to accept the responsibility. Appropriate reinforcement for a job well done may include the opportunity to tackle a higher-level task, which represents a higher level of growth.

Achievement as a source of job satisfaction is the most frequently mentioned of the motivators, but its effect is of short duration. Seeing the results of a piece of work puts a conclusion on the work. A problem solved is no longer a problem. A completed job is over and done with, and the natural reaction is to ask what's next. Thus the opportunity to achieve must be given over and over again to each subordinate. In performing the work, subordinates can seek the personal satisfaction that comes from accomplishing results in which they can take pride. When the assignment also requires growth, that growth is an additional achievement and a powerful motivator for continued achievement.

Another powerful motivator is recognition for the accomplishment of assigned tasks, especially recognition from someone respected by the achiever. Many forms of recognition can be given in a work situation. Perhaps the most powerful form is to entrust the individual with more important responsibilities. This doesn't mean loading on more work. It means a continuing recognition of the capabilities of the individual, of the untapped potential, through assignments that require new knowledge, and use of the knowledge in making decisions and taking actions as part of accomplishing the task.

Advancement as used here means opportunities to perform work that is of greater scope or significance to the success of the business. Advancement, like challenging work assignments, should provide for and encourage psychological growth.

The five motivational factors that have to do with growth on the job are interrelated. Individuals are given responsibilities. This provides the opportunity for achievement. Individuals gain satisfaction from their achievements, and this satisfaction is enhanced by recognition from others whose opinions they respect. The achievements are rewarded by subsequent assignments involving greater responsibilities. As a result of successive achievements, the opportunity to advance to new and higher levels of responsibility is made available. All of these factors call for psychological growth on the job. Together they contribute to enjoyment of the work, and they encourage the continued willingness to work. This, in turn, builds personal and economic security. Under the guidance of an effective coach, it can be a continuing growth cycle.

Behavior and performance on the job come from ability to do the work and from attitudes and motivations connected with the work. In addition, people's behavior is influenced by their level of emotional maturity. Some individuals seem to lack emotional maturity. As adults, they continue to exhibit behaviors considered normal only for a child. However, all people show signs of immaturity at times, so evaluations of emotional maturity should not be based on single incidents.

Signs of emotional maturity include emotional stability and toleration of people and situations. Emotionally stable people tend to think things out rather thoroughly. They seek and accept responsibilities that they feel they can handle or that they want to learn to handle. Toleration of people and situations includes handling the inevitable frustrations of life without giving up or blowing up. Emotionally mature people are able to accept those who do not eat, dress, look, talk, act, or believe as they do. Such individuals carry out unpleasant assigned tasks without self-pity. They can cope with being treated unfairly. They try to understand the words and actions of others. They are concerned with doing things of value to others, and they apply their talents and available resources as best they can.

Managerial dialogues afford an excellent way to evaluate ability and willingness to work. In day-to-day working relationships, a boss can observe an individual's actions and reactions. This is the key to understanding the individual. The dialogues, both in one-to-one and group situations, make it possible to observe and understand subordinates and subsequently to coach them to increase their effectiveness on the job.

The Impact of Expectations on Performance

The powerful influence of the expectations of the boss on the performance of the subordinate should be understood by every individual functioning as a coach and counselor in a business situation. The research findings on this subject include the following points.

Bosses tend to treat subordinates according to what they actually expect of them. It's virtually impossible for the expectations of the boss to be hidden from a subordinate. The message of what is expected is usually communicated unconsciously. It's not just what the boss says, it's also the boss's behavior that is critical in communicating expectations. For instance, a boss who becomes "cold" and gives "the silent treatment" to a subordinate conveys a negative feeling, communicates low expectations, and fosters poor performance. Positive feelings need to be transmitted with equal or greater clarity.

Subordinates tend to perform according to what they believe is expected of them. Expectations are defined in the job content document. The discussions that take place when the subordinate seeks help or reports progress and results at stewardship reviews provide further clarification of what is expected.

Some bosses are able to create high performance expectations that subordinates fulfill. Other bosses create low performance expectations that subordinates fulfill. In order for subordinates to be motivated to reach high levels of productivity, they must consider the boss's high expectations to be achievable and important. When a boss sets expectations too low, lack of confidence in the subordinate's ability and also a lesser importance of the objective are communicated.

A boss's self-concept about his or her ability to train subordinates and influence the development of their talents is the foundation for building realistically high performance expectations. A heartwarming example is found in the story of James Sweeney, a teacher of industrial management and psychiatry at Tulane University, and George Johnson, a janitor at the university's computer facility. Sweeney believed that he could teach even a poorly educated person to operate a computer, and he chose Johnson to prove his conviction. Johnson performed his janitorial duties half the day, and Sweeney taught him about computers the other half of the day.

A university official believed a certain IQ score would be required to be a computer operator, so Johnson was tested. His score indicated that he was incapable of learning to use a typewriter and therefore that learning to operate a computer was out of the question. But Sweeney was not stopped by this. He believed so strongly in his ability to teach that he threatened to leave his post if his experiment was stopped.

Sweeney got his way, and Johnson learned to operate the computer, then was given charge of the main computer room, and was made responsible for training newcomers to program and operate the computer.

The self-concept of subordinates is influenced by their career record. Younger people are more malleable, and older people are more resistant to the influence of the boss because of the "reality" of their past performance. Many coaches have to deal with subordinates of both kinds.

Younger employees are more strongly influenced by managerial expectations. The early years in a business organization are therefore critical in establishing high standards and positive job attitudes. Designing job content of subordinates so that the motivation to work is at a maximum becomes a continuing challenge for the boss. Building on the self-concept of younger employees is a matter of creating a record of success experiences.

For older subordinates, the record is already there. For those with outstanding records, the challenge for the boss is to design jobs that will use and build on their talents. For those with mediocre records, the challenge for the boss is greatest. Bosses can approach this challenge optimistically by remembering that (1) everyone has untapped potential; (2) older employees may have valuable academic wisdom in their area of expertise; (3) learning is more a matter of motivation than age; (4) the self-concept can be changed; and (5) bosses can build the self-concept of subordinates by helping to create a series of success experiences on the job.

The boss has a major impact on the performance of subordinates. The boss can learn to communicate realistically high expectations to subordinates and influence the development of their capabilities and self-confidence. The system for managing what's important provides the theory and the practice for the boss to use in realizing human potential.

The Use of Praise as a Motivator

Praise is perhaps the most widely used and accepted of all human relations techniques. In business, it seems everyone believes in its value as a motivational tool. Praise can be defined as a complimentary evaluation of an object, act, event, or person that stops right there. For example: "Good work, that's a fine job." "You're doing great." "That presentation of yours was outstanding." These statements require no response. They tend to end the conversation rather than extend it.

From what was discussed earlier in this chapter, praise would have to be seen in relation to a particular situation in order to analyze its impact as a motivator. Recognizing the complexities of human behavior, let's look at some of the problems of trying to use praise as a motivator.

Problems with Using Praise

The belief that praise is pleasing to people has resulted in it becoming a piece of psychological candy. The "sandwich technique" and the "other shoe" approaches are common examples of sugarcoating blame with praise. The boss says, "That's a good job, but. . . ." When the shoe of praise has been dropped, we automatically brace ourselves for the shoe of criticism to fall. Most of us have been conditioned to these approaches from early childhood. Henry Ward Beecher said, "The meanest, most contemptible kind of praise is that which first speaks well of a man, and then qualifies it with a 'but.' "

One way people respond to praise is with defensiveness because praise is stressful. A very common response is a vague denial such as: "I was lucky." "It's nice to hear you say that, anyway." "I really can't take that much credit." Praise a subordinate for his or her role in a project and watch the role be played down. These are efforts to cope with the stress caused by praise.

Praise has many of the same problems as negative evaluations. The person who gives praise is clearly sitting in judgment, just the same as in a negative evaluation. When we are evaluated negatively, the chances are great that someone will try to get us to change, and this "request" (or requirement) is very threatening psychologically. The most threatening aspect of praise is the challenge, both external and internal, to live up to what the praise implies. If we accept the praise, we may feel we are under obligation to behave accordingly in the future. Living up to our abilities is one of the most difficult challenges we face, so it's quite natural to be defensive about it.

Functions of Praise

Praise has become a tool of common conversation. People have learned to expect praise. Fishing for compliments is done subtly, and sometimes openly, because we want to be assured of our value. And giving praise is easy. It is a way out of the burden of more meaningful conversation. Giving praise is a way of establishing status: The person giving the praise assumes the right to judge or evaluate another person. Praise is useful in controlling the closeness of our interpersonal relationships. When we listen and share our feelings with others, we grow close. When we choose not to be close to someone, we can make use of praise.

Praise can be used to signal that a conversation is about to end. On the phone, and in personal interviews, the conversation often ends with a complimentary evaluation. "I've enjoyed talking with you" may be a nice way of saying, "I've finished talking with you." In all of these situations, praise is useful in helping us control our relationships.

Turning Praise into a Motivational Tool

When a positive evaluation is changed in such a way that it extends the conversation instead of ending it, it becomes much more than praise, and it leads to different results. Turning praise into a motivational tool can be accomplished by following these suggestions: Extend the conversation. Listen with empathy. Try to be helpful.

1. *Extend the conversation.* A question such as, "How did you get them to go along with your idea so quickly?" or a statement like, "Tell me what's behind these great results," is more than a positive evaluation, for it calls for a response and therefore extends the conversation.

Asking someone to talk about a subject he or she is knowledgeable, or perhaps expert, on is not likely to cause defensiveness. Instead, it offers positive reinforcement to the individual. One of the best ways to reinforce good performance is to ask the individual to explain more about an accomplishment and some of the factors that contributed to it. This can be done privately and/or in front of peers or others interested in the accomplishment itself or how it was achieved.

2. *Listen with empathy.* Listening with empathy means we try to understand both the words and feelings being communicated. It implies no judgment, no agreement or disagreement. It implies that words and feelings are accepted as being valid for the speaker, if not for the listener. Listening accurately takes a great deal of effort. And if we do hear and understand, we run the risk of changing our own point of view. Empathic listening allows the listener to look deeply inside the speaker. With this kind of insight, effective coaching is more likely to follow.

3. *Try to be helpful.* Extending a conversation and listening with empathy set the stage for effective coaching and counseling. One of the most important aspects of a helpful relationship is honesty. This doesn't meant brutal frankness, but a sharing of feelings, attitudes, and experiences. The amount of sharing, and the emotional closeness that inevitably follows, will depend on the situation, the history of the relationship, and the attitudes and motivations that underlie the extended conversation.

When we want to develop people's talents, we may need to make them feel the responsibility of freedom, and a sense of equality, closeness, and reassurance. When the self-image is adequately protected, and the need for defensiveness is at a minimum, individuals are more likely to be motivated to hear and act on suggestions for improvement.

There are daily opportunities to experiment with the effects of praise. By answering these questions, you can tell something about whether your praise is a positive evaluation only or whether it has some motivational impact: Does the individual appear to want to continue the conversation or to terminate it? Does the individual open up, or appear to be somewhat uncomfortable and defensive? Does the individual appear to be more enthusiastic about learning and more willing to do the work expected, or less enthusiastic about the work and less willing to do it?

Flexibility in Leadership Behavior

Leadership is the process of influencing the activities of others to achieve specific results in a given situation. The leadership process is a function of the leader, the followers, and other variables in the situation. Leadership is taking place any time one individual is attempting to influence the behavior of another individual, regardless of the reason.

Leadership in Management

Management can be defined as a special kind of leadership focused on achieving organizational objectives. Conceptual, interpersonal, and technical skills are needed for carrying out the process of management. Leadership is most closely related to the interpersonal skill area. John D. Rockefeller summed up the importance of interpersonal skills when he said: "I will pay more for the ability to deal with people than any other ability under the sun."

Traditional Leadership Models

Many studies on leadership behavior have been conducted. No single leadership style has been shown to be effective in all situations. Three basic approaches to leading people are referred to frequently in the literature. No leader has to choose one and only one of these approaches for all time. In the course of managing, all three are likely to be used.

For instance, a manager who *suggests* to her subordinates that they figure out ways to handle special requests more smoothly in the future, *directs* her secretary to bring her a certain report, and *consults* with subordinates on the best way to push a special project to completion has used all three approaches. Each approach has its advantages and disadvantages. Effective leaders are able to adapt their behavior or leadership style to meet the needs of the followers and the demands of the situation.

Leadership and the Johari Window

The Johari Window is a well-known framework for thinking about how we see ourselves and how others see us. The accompanying diagram is adapted from the Johari Window for application to leadership effectiveness in a given situation. The four areas of the window can be described as follows:

Area A (clear): Known to leader and known to followers. The leader understands the impact his or her attitudes and behaviors are having on the followers. The followers understand what the leader is trying to accomplish.

Area B (shadowy): Known to leader and unknown to followers. What is unknown to the followers may be due to (1) the unwillingness of the leader to share relevant information with the followers or (2) the followers' not understanding the verbal and nonverbal messages of the leader.

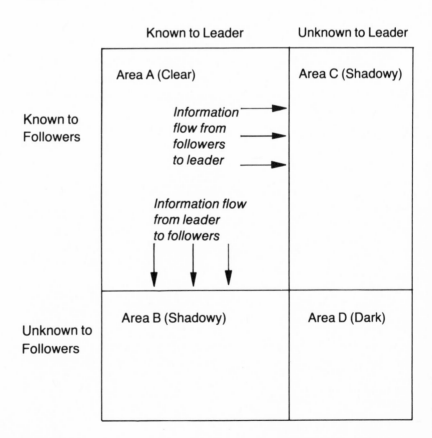

Area C (shadowy): Unknown to leader and known to followers. What is unknown to the leader may be due to (1) the unwillingness of followers to share relevant information with the leader or (2) the leader's not understanding the verbal and nonverbal messages of the followers.

Area D (dark): Unknown to leader and unknown to followers. What is beneath the surface in the leader's subconscious, unknown to the leader and the followers, has an impact on the behavior of the leader in trying to influence the behavior of the followers.

Leadership effectiveness in a given situation can be related to the size of the clear area of the window as compared to the size of the shadowy and dark areas. The larger the clear area, the more effective the leader. The clear area grows depending on the giving and receiving of relevant information between leader and followers.

Relevant used in connection with sharing information means appropriate, necessary, helpful, and important to the success of the business. In the business world, there is neither the time nor the necessity to share and process information that is not relevant in a particular situation.

Giving and receiving relevant information between leader and followers expands the clear area and diminishes the other areas. When followers are willing to be open and give relevant feedback to the leader on the effect of his or her leadership practices, and the leader is willing and able to understand the feedback, the clear area A expands and replaces some of the shadowy area C. When the leader is willing to be open and give relevant information to the followers concerning the leader's thinking and the needs of the business, and the followers are willing and able to understand the information, the clear area A expands and replaces some of the shadowy area B.

When there is an exchange of relevant information between leader and followers in a specific organizational setting, the effectiveness of the leader is maximized. The leader is the boss, coach, and counselor; the followers are the subordinates. Relevant information flow in both directions is the purpose of managerial dialogues.

Conditions That Contribute to Effective Leadership

An effective leader, functioning as the coach in the superior-subordinate work relationship, sets up the conditions that give subordinates confidence that their personal needs can be satisfied by accomplishing what's expected. Then an effective leader sets up the conditions that encourage subordinates to develop their potential.

In the organizational relationship common to most businesses, the subordinates' feeling of security is dependent on the judgment and decisions of the boss. To contribute to this sense of security, the boss should create the following conditions:

1. *A climate of acceptance and approval.* This climate is created by what the boss does, the manner in which it is done, and the behaviors that demonstrate the boss's underlying attitude toward the subordinates. The climate is relatively independent of standards of excellence demanded on the job or the strictness of discipline.

2. *Knowledge of what is expected.* This involves (1) the sharing of higher-level objectives and management philosophy, (2) joint agreement on the subordinate's job content, as it is set up initially and as it evolves to meet changing priorities and standards, and as the talents of the subordinate are developed.

3. *Feedback concerning performance.* Subordinates need to know how performance and progress are seen by their boss. General statements covering the entire job are inadequate. Specific feedback on individual areas of responsibilities and objectives is required. The feedback on individual items should be provided as soon as such feedback is meaningful. At least quarterly, feedback covering the entire job is needed.

4. *Knowledge of procedures, regulations, policies.* This knowledge should cover work operations and also the personal demands and peculiarities of the immediate boss. These bits of knowledge help the subordinates understand the environment and thus to live with it.

5. *Advance information on changes that affect the subordinate(s).* Unanticipated changes undermine a feeling of security on the job. Adequate warning of changes and the reasons for them reduce fear and resistance to change.

6. *Appropriate backing and support.* This implies backing when the subordinate takes action in accordance with agreed-upon parameters and agreed-upon objectives. It also implies strict disciplinary action when commitments are not kept, when established rules are flouted without valid reason.

When security in the superior-subordinate relationship has been achieved, the reaching for independence, self-development, and self-realization becomes more active. The subordinates will seek ways of obtaining more satisfaction from the work itself. To contribute to the realization of the subordinates' potential, the boss should create the following conditions:

1. *Opportunity to participate in the discussion of actions involving the subordinate.* Participation cannot be meaningful unless the conditions of security are met. In an atmosphere of security, subordinates feel free to express opinions and make suggestions, knowing they will be considered. Opportunity to participate, to have ownership in the final outcomes of the work, is one of the most important conditions of growth and development.

2. *Opportunity to contribute to the solution of difficult problems and to respond to important business challenges.* These opportunities are built into job content. Subordinates who feel secure can be encouraged to accept difficult and important challenges. And the boss is usually surprised at the talent that is demonstrated when the mechanisms of genuine collaboration are established and functioning in the organization.

3. *Opportunity to assume increased responsibility.* The desire for increased responsibility has to go hand in hand with the ability to handle it. When a certain level of security in relation to superiors is achieved, increased responsibility can be given. Where it is given gradually, so there is a succession of success experiences and subordinates are not made insecure again by an overload, subordinates will accept increasing responsibility. This concept also involves the security of the boss—the willingness to run the risk of delegation and have capable and developing subordinates.

4. *Opportunity to be reviewed at higher levels.* In cases of sincere differences on important matters, or a personality clash with the boss, subordinates need their "day in court." A mechanism for making clear one's position to the boss's boss is essential. Accomplishment highlights (discussed in Chapter 11) is a mechanism that protects the interests of both boss and subordinate on a long-term basis. On a short-term basis, the job content document, tracking system notations, homework, and action plans can be used as evidence of how well subordinates are managing their job responsibilities and focusing their effort and resources on accomplishing what's important. These documents are seldom used for the purpose of protecting either the subordinate or the boss, but it's important to have the mechanism in

place. An effective boss will set up a three-way discussion whenever it's needed or requested by a subordinate, and will create a climate in which subordinates feel free to go directly to the boss's boss on sensitive matters.

In summary, an effective boss sets up the conditions necessary for a healthy superior-subordinate work relationship. Effective managerial dialogues are built on the existence of these conditions. How the boss handles a particular situation will depend on the situation itself and the subordinates involved.

The essence of good leadership is flexibility. This implies knowledge of alternatives. Keeping abreast of behavioral research findings can provide useful insights that accelerate learning and growth for those willing to experiment on the job in the quest for a better way.

Once the concept of flexibility in leadership behavior is understood, it becomes evident that two factors are critical in applying the concept. One has to do with a boss's ability to diagnose a given environment so that the most effective behavior can be determined. This means the boss needs to understand the variables in the situation, and know the attitudes, interests, needs, and goals of the subordinates, individually and as a group. The second has to do with a boss's willingness to give and receive relevant information and to use the behavior most effective in meeting the needs of the subordinate and the demands of the situation.

13

How to Conduct Effective Job Performance Dialogues

Effective job performance dialogues are helpful and motivational in managing the entire job and accomplishing what's important to the business. The following guidelines and process for conducting job performance dialogues will facilitate achievement of these goals. Many of the guidelines have already been mentioned in relation to other parts of the system for managing what's important. Here they are all presented together for your convenience in using them.

Guidelines for Job Performance Dialogues

The guidelines for conducting effective job performance dialogues were developed from the responses of many successful managers who were asked to describe the practices of the "best boss" they ever had. The responses make it clear that the best bosses have effective managerial communication practices and they function in the role of a coach in relation to their subordinates.

Effective managerial communication practices can be described individually and by groupings. Each practice or activity should be carried out to achieve desired business results and to stimulate subordinates to improve their performance. Each practice or activity calls for managerial dialogues—two-way discussions—in which the subordinate is the active player-manager responsible for specific results and the boss is the coach and counselor responsible for developing and using the talents of the player to achieve and maintain the expected results.

In analyzing a performance problem, the cause of the problem may be found to be related to superior-subordinate communication practices rather than to the ability or willingness of the subordinate to do the work or to external factors over which there is little or no control. The guidelines apply to problems arising from any cause. When a discussion of job performance takes place, the guidelines should be used. Once the true cause(s) of a problem are identified, appropriate action plans can be formulated.

The guidelines for conducting helpful and motivational job performance dialogues are:

1. Maintain two-way communication.
2. Explain the needs of the business.
3. Define what is expected.
4. Delegate effectively.
5. Provide feedback on progress.
6. Provide help when it's needed.
7. Assist in the learning/growth process.
8. Make use of career aspirations.
9. Make use of group discussions.
10. Provide reinforcement of results.

These guidelines are useful in developing performance dialogue skills. Every performance dialogue involves two or more of these guidelines.

1. Maintain two-way communication. This may be the most important guideline, for without healthy two-way communications it's not likely that any of the other guidelines will be effectively implemented. Being available to communicate on important matters, showing interest in what is said, listening with empathy, and encouraging subordinates to speak up, especially when they disagree with you, are ways to maintain two-way communications and thus set the climate for effective job performance dialogues.

2. Explain the needs of the business. Explaining the needs of the business is an ongoing process, not a one-time event.

First, explain to your subordinates your own business objectives and commitments. Invite full discussion so there is in-depth understanding. Second, discuss important changes in the needs of the business whenever they occur; also have a scheduled time to review progress toward objectives, and put fresh emphasis where it's needed. Third, make sure that any discussion of current short-term business objectives includes consideration of long-term objectives as well, and vice versa. Fourth, help your subordinates understand your standards and expectations for meeting the needs of the business, so they will put their time and effort where they will pay off, and spend less time and effort on tasks that are less important to the success of the business.

3. *Define what is expected.* Developing a common understanding of what's expected of an individual in a position is the foundation for effective job performance dialogues. The ideal toward which to work is to have the subordinate take the initiative in defining desired results and getting the superior's approval.

When results are defined in specific terms, they provide a better basis for both doing the work and talking about it. Establishing priorities, setting high standards, and encouraging appropriate risk taking in setting targets should take into account the accompanying motivational benefits.

Defining what's expected is a dynamic process. It requires setting targets in advance. But much more than that, as targets change, as priorities shift, as standards need to be upgraded, a fresh definition of what's expected needs to be agreed on.

4. *Delegate effectively.* Effective delegation includes: specifying the results expected in giving an assignment, not the activities to be carried out to achieve the results; following up on important results, not on activities and details; insisting on reviewing the independent thinking of your subordinate on problems and important decisions before sharing your own thinking; clarifying the freedoms and restraints to be observed by your subordinate in making decisions and taking actions.

Delegation involves a combination of freedom and controls. Subordinates should have all the freedom they can handle in order to develop and use their talents for the benefit of the business. The control element ensures that the expected results are forthcoming or that appropriate action steps will be taken.

5. *Provide feedback on progress.* A boss should see that feedback on

important results is provided to subordinates. Feedback to a subordinate can come from a variety of inputs: written reports, verbal feedback, personal observations. The feedback provides positive reinforcement when progress is satisfactory, and spurs remedial action when progress is not what is expected.

Periodic discussions about progress to date should be set up to meet the needs of the situation. Feedback from the boss is most effective when it comes after the subordinates have expressed their own evaluation of progress. The boss should be frank and open when giving feedback on progress to subordinates.

6. *Provide help when it's needed.* If the job is appropriately challenging for the employee, there will be times when assistance of some kind is needed. The ground rules of homework before help (see Chapter 8) calls for the boss to coach and counsel subordinates, not do their work. Help is given by reinforcing sound homework and aiding the subordinate in learning, growing, and improving.

7. *Assist in the learning/growth process.* It's quite possible to have experiences without gaining much of value from them. In a business situation, it's important for superiors and subordinates to learn and grow, not just get older. The process of learning and growing is aided by discussing important accomplishments and the possible reasons for the successes. Equally important is understanding why results have not been fully satisfactory. Joint efforts in analyzing past experiences and planning future experiences should be a regular management practice aimed at developing the talents of subordinates.

8. *Make use of career aspirations.* Knowing the career aspirations of a subordinate can be of great help in job performance dialogues. Whenever the immediate situation can be related to future opportunities, the subordinate is likely to listen more carefully to suggestions and opinions and to act on them. Using career aspirations in conducting performance dialogues is a way of linking together personal and organizational objectives.

9. *Make use of group discussions.* Peer pressure for performance is a powerful motivator. So is the positive reinforcement that comes from reporting accomplishments in front of peers. So is being a member of a team that is accomplishing important results.

A boss can use group discussions to complement individual discussions: to gain a greater commitment to achieve the results, to give group members the chance to report progress and accomplishments in front of their peers, and to exchange experiences and share ideas on how to solve problems and improve performance. Group discussions help keep members concerned about team results and place individual efforts in proper perspective.

10. Provide reinforcement of results. Reinforcement of results has to do with the motivation to achieve. Consistent reinforcement of results is the most powerful tool available to a manager. Giving the right kind of praise and recognition to a subordinate for appropriate or outstanding performance should occur without exception. Giving undue praise and recognition for mediocre performance encourages mediocrity.

Failure to take appropriate action when a subordinate's performance is unsatisfactory teaches the subordinate that rewards are not related to performance. Under such circumstances, it's difficult to have a job performance dialogue that motivates a subordinate to learn, to grow, to improve.

Compensation decisions should be related to how well subordinates manage their entire job and to the importance of their accomplishments to the success of the business. When subordinates understand that compensation decisions are made on that basis, they are more likely to see job performance dialogues as helpful and motivational.

The Process of Conducting Effective Performance Dialogues

In Chapter 8 the discussion of a job performance problem or opportunity was presented from the viewpoint of the subordinate. Here, conducting a job performance dialogue is presented from the viewpoint of the boss—the coach and counselor. The process presented here has application to coaching and counseling in relation to a subordinate's homework, but it goes beyond that. A boss does not always wait to be asked for help. A boss should set up the situation to provide help whenever there is a need for it.

Conducting effective performance dialogues requires skill. Every manager conducts performance dialogues frequently, but practice alone doesn't ensure the development of skill. Practice is helpful when guidelines are understood and there is a model to follow so that a critique of what takes place is possible.

The process has five major ingredients, each of which is disarmingly simple. The difficulty comes in following the process and at the same time applying the guidelines. The ingredients of the process are:

1. Prepare for the job performance dialogue.
2. Maintain a helpful, motivational climate.
3. Focus on a specific result.
4. Explore causes/opportunities.
5. Agree on an action plan.

1. Prepare for the performance dialogue. A discussion of performance with a subordinate may be scheduled ahead of time or it may occur at any time when the need arises. The importance of the dialogue outcomes to the success of the business may range from small to great. Therefore, the time and effort spent by the boss in preparing for the dialogue will vary.

In preparing for a job performance dialogue, ask yourself these questions:

- What specific result will you focus on in the dialogue?
- Does the subordinate understand his or her responsibility to achieve the result under agreed-upon terms and conditions?
- Why are you concerned at this time? Is there a variance between what has happened and what was expected? Is there some new opportunity to be seized?
- For variances: What are the possible causes? The most likely cause(s)? The possible action steps? The recommended action steps?
- For opportunities: What is the potential? The possible approaches? The recommended approach? The freedoms and restraints to be observed?
- What must you do to have the outcomes of the dialogue be seen as helpful and motivational by the subordinate?

2. Maintain a helpful, motivational climate. Build into the dialogue what you know about motivation. Improvement requires change, and change requires motivation. In planning for the dialogue, in conducting it, and in subsequent follow-up actions, the basic concepts of motivation should be applied. What you say and do should help your subordinate to accomplish what's expected and to learn and grow from the experience.

The three most important suggestions for maintaining a helpful, motivational climate in a job performance dialogue are:

Let your subordinate do it. Encourage your subordinates to take the initiative whenever possible. When necessary, set up the situation so they can take the initiative. As soon as possible, and at every opportunity, give them the ball. Let them run with it as far as possible.

Reinforce your subordinate's contributions. Give some sign of agreement, approval, or acceptance of the ideas, suggestions, or thinking of your subordinates at every opportunity. Verbally, through body language, and by what you do, let your subordinates know when you're satisfied or pleased with the progress of the dialogue. This doesn't mean reinforcing everything a subordinate says. Be honest. Reinforce everything you can in good conscience reinforce. When you disagree with a subordinate, or feel you have something to contribute, handle it as a coach or counselor would.

Be a coach and counselor to your subordinate. When it would be helpful to share your experience, make a suggestion, contribute an idea, offer a critique, react to a recommendation, by all means do so. But do it at the proper time; be sure your assistance does not come prematurely. After your subordinates have done all they can do, you should step in and give assistance. By observing what your subordinates say and do, you can be more effective in your role as coach and counselor.

3. Focus on a specific result. The value of defining expected results in advance becomes obvious in a job performance dialogue. Comparing actual with expected results provides the measure called a *variance*. A boss and a subordinate should be able to discuss a variance from desired results with a great deal of objectivity. Both should have previously agreed it was important to try to achieve the result. When a variance develops, both should be concerned about it. Focusing on the result and the variance reduces the defensive or negative reactions that occur when a performance dialogue becomes personal. Predictably, a person who is attacked will become defensive.

Sometimes a job performance dialogue is centered on an opportunity rather than a variance. The focus should still be on a specific result. The difference is that you're looking ahead, setting new targets. Once the targets are established, there's a basis for identifying a variance that may develop.

The reason for focusing on specific results is so your subordinate will know what you're really concerned about. The way to get down to specifics is to identify the results you want to talk about. Use the available data. Give as many examples as are needed. Cite incidents to illustrate your points. Don't beat around the bush.

When you focus on results, it's easier to be specific. When you focus on specific results, it's easier to avoid personal attacks and defensive reactions. When you and your subordinate can address a specific problem or opportunity without defensiveness, you're conducting an effective performance dialogue.

4. Explore causes/opportunities. This part of a job performance dialogue is frequently ignored. When a variance is detected, many bosses demand a plan of action immediately. However, it is far more productive to first search for the real cause of the variance. This turns the job performance dialogue into a joint problem-solving process. In exploring for causes, consider:

The objective itself. Was adequate information available in setting up the objective? Was the objective reasonable? Is the objective reasonable today?

The subordinate's efforts. What has the subordinate done with the factors under his or her control? Has the subordinate allocated time, effort, and resources in accordance with the importance of the result to the success of the business?

The influence of the boss. Has the boss provided necessary support, cleared barriers, opened doors, kept commitments, provided coaching and counseling help when they were needed?

External circumstances. Are factors over which neither the boss nor the subordinate has control contributing to the variance?

It's helpful to list as many possible causes of a variance as come to mind. It's suggested that the boss write the list, getting the subordinate to supply the items for it as much as possible. This allows the boss to control the process, to see that as many possible causes are considered as sensible use of time permits, and to be sure that the most likely cause(s) reflects the best thinking of both participants. The effort in exploring causes of a variance helps pinpoint possible actions to take.

When an opportunity is identified, it should be explored thoroughly; if it's to be pursued, objectives and action plans should be developed; if necessary, other objectives and plans may have to be changed to accommodate changed priorities.

The reminder to explore business opportunities as well as business problems is made because this need is so often neglected throughout the year until new objectives are required for the coming year. All too often, it's neglected then as well.

5. Agree on an action plan. An action plan increases the likelihood that steps will be taken to secure improved performance or to seize an opportunity. The exploration of causes or opportunities is naturally followed by decisions on appropriate action steps. The action steps should correct the major causes of the variance or pursue the opportunity. Consideration of alternative courses of action is recommended before deciding on a specific action plan. Freedoms and restraints to be observed in implementing the action plan need to be identified and agreed upon. The plan should include who is to do what, and when, as well as provisions for monitoring progress and taking further action as required.

Written action plans are an aid to self-discipline. Plans document the commitment to action. When the boss chooses to coach and counsel the subordinate in the proper preparation of an action plan, or senses the need to control the content of an action plan, the boss should do the writing of the steps agreed upon during the dialogue. The subordinate, of course, retains the written plan at the conclusion of the dialogue.

Self-Critique of a Job Performance Dialogue: Checklist

1. *Preparation*
   Specific guidelines used well? Ignored? Misused?
   Specific process suggestions used well? Ignored? Misused?
2. *Dialogue Climate*
   Subordinate initiative encouraged? Discouraged?
   Subordinate contributions reinforced? Ignored?
   Coaching/counseling help provided? At proper time?
3. *Dialogue Focus*
   Specific result identified?
   Focus on variance/opportunity? Personal attack?
4. *Causes/Opportunities*
   Possible causes explored? Most likely cause(s) identified?
   Possible opportunities explored? New targets, possible approaches, freedoms and restraints identified?

5. *Action Plans*
   Plans developed jointly? Not at all?
   Plans in writing? Verbal only?

Applications of the Model for Job Performance Dialogues

The model for conducting job performance dialogues can be adapted to fit a variety of situations. Opportunities to use the process occur in day-to-day work relationships, whether initiated by the superior or the subordinate. They also occur in connection with stewardship reviews, with those items selected for further discussion.

The process may be used in: (1) joint analysis and action planning on a specific job performance situation, initiated by the boss (all five major ingredients of the process are used formally); (2) coaching and counseling by the boss based on homework initiated by the subordinate (a review of the subordinate's homework identifies which parts of the process have in effect been completed and which parts remain to be carried out to achieve the desired outcomes); (3) specific suggestions, ideas, reactions, or experiences offered by the boss and intended to be helpful to the subordinate (the entire process is mentally reviewed by the boss, but practicality dictates simply making one or more points that can be of immediate use to the subordinate); and (4) some combination of the first three items.

In summary, a job performance dialogue is more likely to be helpful and motivational if the process and the guidelines suggested here are followed. Keep in mind that the process and guidelines are offered to encourage you to increase your present level of managerial effectiveness. Review the suggestions in preparing for a job performance discussion. Review them again after the dialogue as you critique your own effectiveness. Doing this over a period of time will lead to both increased managerial dialogue skill and increased managerial confidence in using your skills to develop and use the talents of your subordinates and to achieve the business results expected of you.

14

How to Handle
Behavior Problems
of Subordinates

Problem behavior is any kind of behavior that adversely affects job performance. It may directly affect a subordinate's work, or the work of others. It may affect the attitudes and morale of others and thus indirectly affect business results.

Behavior dialogues are called for under varying circumstances. A subordinate may not realize the behavior is inappropriate. If this is so, the boss has to provide this information, and then carry out the process to achieve the necessary behavior change. When the subordinate already knows the behavior is inappropriate, but doesn't recognize or accept the need to change, the boss has a slightly different task: to clarify current standards and the need for a change, and then to carry out the process to achieve the change. In either case, the same guidelines apply and the basic ingredients in the process are the same.

Guidelines for Behavior Dialogues

The guidelines for conducting dialogues that motivate subordinates to change their behavior are:

1. Improvement is possible.
2. Openness is based on trust.
3. The teaching/learning process is an investment.

4. Accept the person while you reject the behavior.
5. Listening involves words and feelings.
6. Expect initial reactions to be defensive.
7. Professional help may be necessary.

These guidelines are useful in developing and using behavior dialogue skills. Every behavior dialogue involves some of these guidelines.

1. Improvement is possible. Belief in the ability of individuals to change, to grow, to improve is fundamental in conducting effective behavior dialogues. All training and development activities are based on concepts of human potential; with appropriate instruction and the necessary motivation to use the help that's available, improvement is possible.

Unless there is optimism on the part of the boss that the subordinate can change and improve, what's the purpose of a behavior dialogue? Subordinates sense it when a boss has no confidence in their ability or their willingness to change an inappropriate behavior. They also sense it when there's an optimistic attitude that change and improvement will result from a discussion dealing with a behavior problem. Since we can't hide our attitudes from our subordinates, this guideline suggests we examine our own beliefs about the possibility of improvement before we embark on the counseling process.

2. Openness is based on trust. A dialogue is not truly a dialogue if the participants are not open and honest with each other. The degree to which subordinates achieve openness depends on the degree to which they trust the boss. Past experiences may have taught the subordinates that authority figures, such as bosses, aren't truly interested in their feelings and their future; that being open with bosses isn't safe; that the most important thing is to please the boss, to be liked and accepted, to avoid criticism, so they must hide their real feelings. Trust has to be earned. It takes time for one person to develop trust in another person. The subordinate learns day by day to trust or distrust the boss. When subordinates sense in their boss genuine interest in them, desire to understand them, willingness to accept them as individuals, belief in their potential to learn and grow, and desire to help them succeed in their work and achieve their aspirations, then fears give way to trust and that climate of trust encourages openness in communication.

3. The teaching/learning process is an investment. A behavior dialogue is a teaching/learning process. The process represents an investment in the individual being counseled. The investment is made in the interest of both the individual and the organization. In the case of problem behavior, the time investment will be less if the behavior is readily accepted as inappropriate; the change required isn't too difficult and/or doesn't call for strong self-discipline; the problem involves surface habits rather than deep-seated emotional patterns.

An emotional investment may be required of the boss. A confrontation with a subordinate on a behavior problem may produce hostility or emotional reactions. Fearing such emotional strain, bosses often postpone behavior dialogues. Handled properly, the confrontation usually turns out to be much less painful than anticipated, and the investment is considered a wise one. Sometimes, a boss has to choose whether to invest in changing the problem behavior or to learn to live with it. Living with it means the individual is not helped, and the organization suffers.

A behavior dialogue should lead a subordinate to see a particular situation clearly, realistically, objectively. The price of continuing inappropriate behavior needs to be seen by subordinates in terms of their hopes, expectations, and aspirations. The impact of the teaching/learning process should extend beyond an immediate problem. The process should help subordinates in future situations.

4. Accept the person while you reject the behavior. People behave in ways that protect and build their self-image. When people feel accepted, understood, and respected as individuals, their self-image is protected. With that kind of security, people are able to discuss a behavior problem with less defensiveness. Empathy for the subordinate and the situation should not cause behavior standards to be lowered. Behavior standards should be set to contribute to the achievement of business results.

Another way of stating this guideline would be: "You're a valued associate in this organization, but this particular behavior is inappropriate and unacceptable." This guideline points out an interesting paradox. The more people feel accepted, the more likely they are to change. Acceptance as a person reduces defensiveness and enables a more realistic look at the situation. The behavior dialogue process is designed to help a person see the situation clearly and be motivated to act constructively on it.

5. Listening involves words and feelings. Listening and really hearing what is said is difficult. Words are one thing. Feelings are another. Listening involves "hearing" both the words and the feelings behind the words. Listening between the lines, and listening for what is not said, are expressions used to describe listening for feelings, listening for what is *meant.* Expressing feelings is one of the most difficult tasks people face. It is even more difficult when people are under stress or when they are emotionally upset.

What subordinates really mean becomes clearer as matters are "talked out." Encourage subordinates to verbalize their feelings. In talking matters out, subordinates are likely to see more clearly their own feelings and become more objective in dealing with them. The boss can help by identifying the feelings expressed by the subordinate to be sure that the listening is accurate. For example, "Are you saying that you feel that . . ." can clarify a point and encourage continued dialogue.

It's possible that what subordinates say about particular behavior problems may be merely a camouflage for some other problem the individual can't or won't talk about. Behavior dialogues should be restricted to behavior problems that adversely affect job performance. It's up to the boss to control the dialogue in this respect.

6. Expect initial reactions to be defensive. A behavior dialogue usually takes place because a behavior problem is serious enough to be worth the investment of time and effort to correct. This means the behavior dialogue usually begins with a certain amount of stress. The subordinate is under pressure. The issue in a behavior dialogue is bound to be personal. The subordinate is exhibiting behavior that is a problem for the organization. The self-image of the subordinate is involved.

Expect reactions in the early stages of a behavior dialogue to be defensive due to the stress, pressure, and possible impact on the self-image of the subordinate. The way you handle these initial reactions of the subordinate is critical to the outcomes of the behavior dialogue. Use the other guidelines, and follow the suggested steps for conducting the dialogue, to help you retain control over the process in spite of any defensiveness or negative reactions that may develop.

7. Professional help may be necessary. A boss shouldn't take responsibility for solving behavior problems of subordinates. People really have to solve their own problems. In cases where they can't deal with their own problems objectively because their emotions get in the way, they need help. Bosses are in a unique position to help subordinates deal with behavior problems that affect job performance. Showing interest and concern for subordinates with all of their problems is appropriate, but some situations call for professional help beyond the skills or direct concern of most managers. For example: Personal problems that don't affect job performance shouldn't be of direct concern to the boss. However, the boss can encourage the individual to get help from someone with special skills in dealing with similar problems (family counselors, the clergy, social workers, psychologists). Chronic behavior problems call for referral to someone skilled in dealing with complex behavior at a professional level (social workers, psychologists, psychiatrists). Individuals who exhibit extreme emotions, or have difficulty in discussing a behavior problem in a coherent and consistent manner, should receive professional help (social workers, psychologists, psychiatrists).

The Process of Conducting Effective Behavior Dialogues

An effective behavior dialogue results in changed behavior on the part of the subordinate. To have an effective dialogue, the boss must provide helpful inputs and do so in such a way that the subordinate is motivated to change the inappropriate behavior.

Conducting effective behavior dialogues is a skill. Every manager may one day be faced with the need for such skill. The following process is similar in some ways to the process suggested for other managerial dialogues, and in some ways it's quite different. Recognizing these similarities and differences will help in the learning of this skill.

The process is suggested, along with the guidelines, to help you analyze what you do that is effective and what you do that is not effective. It includes the following:

1. Prepare for the behavior dialogue.
2. Maintain a helpful, motivational climate.
3. Focus on a specific behavior to be changed.
4. Identify reasons to change (from the subordinate's viewpoint).
5. Explain the necessity of change.
6. Agree on an action plan.

1. Prepare for the behavior dialogue. Preparation is a matter of homework by the boss. There are four areas to explore: What specific behavior do you want to see changed? Why do you want to see the behavior changed? (This question tests your convictions that a change is actually necessary.) What possible benefits will your subordinate realize by making the change? (Consider these from your subordinate's viewpoint. Will the potential benefits provide the motivation to change?) And last, what specific action steps will set the change process in motion?

2. *Maintain a helpful, motivational climate.* The suggestions for maintaining a helpful, motivational climate in a behavior dialogue are the same as for a job performance dialogue. Briefly they are: *Let your subordinate do it.* Set up the situation so your subordinate can take the initiative. As soon as possible, and at every opportunity, let your subordinate run with the ball. *Reinforce your subordinate's contributions.* Give evidence of agreement, approval, acceptance at every opportunity. *Be a coach and counselor to your subordinate.* When it would be helpful to provide information, to share your experiences, or to give suggestions, do it. But do it at the proper time; be sure your assistance does not come prematurely.

3. *Focus on a specific behavior to be changed.* Make sure your subordinate understands that you want to discuss a specific behavior to be changed and the need to get personal. Concern for your subordinate, as well as for organizational results, is your responsibility as the boss. There is no way to deal with a subordinate's behavior problem without getting personal. Explain in specific terms the behavior you want to talk about. Use as many examples as necessary. Get a reaction from your subordinate to make sure your concerns are understood. Don't move on to the next step until your subordinate understands what specific behavior you're concerned about and that there is a need for the behavior change.

4. *Identify reasons to change (from your subordinate's viewpoint).* Have your subordinate take the initiative in suggesting possible benefits to be gained from changing the inappropriate behavior. If the subordinate fails to recognize and suggest items that you identified in doing your homework, you can suggest them at this time. You know why you want the changed behavior. Now you're helping your subordinate think through the benefits of change.

Inappropriate behavior may have an impact on your subordinate in a number of ways. Keep these in mind as you develop a list of reasons to change the behavior:

Aspirations. A behavior problem may disqualify an individual for promotion to a desired position, or at least reduce the person's
chances of being selected for it.

Needs. The needs for acceptance and achievement are powerful forces.
Inappropriate behavior may prevent the fulfillment of many
human needs.

Rewards. Behavior problems may result in the withholding of various
rewards available in the organization.

The stronger the motivation to change, the more likely the
change will be made promptly. It may be a good idea for you to write
down the possible benefits from a change as they are suggested, as a
means of emphasizing why it's in your subordinate's best interest to
change the behavior you are concerned about.

5. *Explain the necessity of change.* By this time in the process, your
subordinate may have accepted the need for changed behavior. If this
is so, simply reinforce your position that a change is a necessity and
that you wish to help your subordinate plan for and accomplish the
change. If acceptance of the need for a change isn't evident, you'll
have to be firm and direct in stating the need and add your offer of
help.

It's important that this step be handled at this point in the process. Implement it after the behavior problem has been identified and
the benefits to be gained from a change have been explored, but before action plans are discussed. This step aids the transition from
talking about the problem to a serious consideration of what is to be
done about it.

6. *Agree on an action plan.* An action plan increases the likelihood
that steps will be taken to change the inappropriate behavior. Written action plans provide a means of self-discipline. Plans document
the commitment to action. It's suggested the boss do the writing of
whatever action plans are formulated. This allows the boss to more
easily control the dialogue and counsel the subordinate.

As previously suggested, get your subordinate to take the initiative in suggesting action steps. Ask for one small step to be taken immediately. This helps you see the subordinate's thinking, and the extent of acceptance that a behavior problem exists that must be
corrected. You'll likely want to ask for at least one or more action
steps to be taken in the next week or so. You'll want to include provi-

sion for follow-up as part of the agreed-upon action plan. Plans should be quite specific about what will be done and when it will be done.

Self-Critique of a Behavior Dialogue: Checklist

1. *Preparation*
   Specific guidelines used well? Ignored? Misused?
   Specific process suggestions used well? Ignored? Misused?
2. *Dialogue Climate*
   Subordinate initiative encouraged? Discouraged?
   Subordinate contributions reinforced? Ignored?
   Coaching/counseling help provided? At proper time?
3. *Dialogue Focus*
   Purpose of dialogue and need to get personal explained? Avoided?
   Specific behavior problem identified? General statements or hints only?
   Subordinate's understanding of the problem confirmed by the subordinate's reaction? No reaction obtained?
4. *Reasons to Change (from Subordinate's Viewpoint)*
   Impact of behavior on aspirations, human needs, organizational rewards considered? Not considered?
   Possible benefits of behavior change listed? In writing?
5. *Necessity of Change*
   Necessity of change in behavior affirmed? Not mentioned?
   Offer made to help subordinate plan for and accomplish the change? No offer made?
6. *Action Plans*
   Plans developed jointly? Not at all?
   Plans specific? General?
   Plans in writing? Verbal only?

Applications of the Model for Behavior Dialogues

The model for conducting a behavior dialogue is used in the following three situations, each related to job performance and business success:

1. The boss identifies the behavior problem as warranting a behavior dialogue. The behavior problem may impair the subordinate's

job performance or it may affect the performance of others in the organization, or both. The behavior problem may be identified initially by personal observations of the boss, or from inputs from others inside or outside the organization—peers, superiors, subordinates, associates, suppliers, clients, customers—people whose reactions to the behavior affect business results. Whatever the source initially, the boss has to make the judgment, on the basis of the available evidence, that the behavior dialogue is justified.

2. The behavior problem is identified during a joint analysis of the causes of a performance problem. In this situation the boss may choose to handle the behavior dialogue as one distinct part of a performance dialogue or to set up a separate time to conduct the behavior dialogue.

3. The behavior problem is identified during a career dialogue involving qualifications of the individual compared to critical requirements for success in a given position. In this situation the boss may choose to handle the behavior dialogue as one distinct part of helping the subordinate prepare for a desired position or to set up a separate time to conduct the behavior dialogue, but for the same reasons of preparing for the future.

The behavior dialogue process and the guidelines are offered here to encourage you to increase your present level of managerial effectiveness. The model will be useful to you in conducting a behavior dialogue whenever it will benefit a subordinate and contribute to the success of the business.

15

How to Conduct
Effective Career Dialogues

Looking ahead, the possibility of promotions or transfers to new positions exists for many individuals, especially in large organizations. For most individuals in any organization, it's likely that the future will bring new kinds of assignments within their current position that call for certain knowledge, skills, abilities, and experience. Whatever subordinates' future occupational situations will be, career dialogues are the vehicle for discussing subordinates' aspirations, organizational needs, subordinates' qualifications in comparison with the requirements for success in a particular position, and the competition. Out of such discussions, realistic plans can be formulated by subordinates with regard to their careers.

Guidelines for Career Dialogues

The guidelines for conducting helpful and motivational career dialogues are:

1. A career dialogue is an investment in the future.
2. Career dialogues serve a variety of personal needs.
3. Bosses gain by helping subordinates with their careers.
4. Bosses can bring realism about the future to subordinates.
5. Promises or predictions about advancement are not required.
6. Comparisons with others competing for a position are not needed.
7. Frequency and timing of career dialogues can affect the outcomes.

These guidelines are useful in developing and using career dialogue skills. Every career dialogue involves some of these guidelines.

1. A career dialogue is an investment in the future. Individuals at all levels in an organization are concerned about their future job situation. When there's no chance to talk with the boss about the future, subordinates may assume their future in the organization is dim. They may seek greener pastures, and the organization may lose valuable personnel. Periodic career dialogues help an individual have a better perspective, with a longer time frame, on the present and the future. Useful information can relieve anxiety. Meaningful development efforts can relieve subordinates' impatience.

Each position in an organization requires certain abilities. Each employee has certain abilities and potential to learn and grow. The organization needs the current abilities of the individual now, hence the employer-employee relationship. The organization will have need in the future for a wide variety of talents. Therefore, new assignments, transfers, or advancements lie ahead for most individuals. Managers have the responsibility to invest in the development, use, motivation, and retention of talent in the organization. The current and future success of the organization can be enhanced by the outcomes of effective career dialogues.

2. Career dialogues serve a variety of personal needs. The needs of individuals vary. Some are intent on advancement; some fear what others will think if they don't appear to want advancement. Some want a change of jobs so they'll be moved to another location; some fear they might be uprooted. Some worry about being successful in a new job; some worry about job security in their present situation. Career dialogues can be used to meet all kinds of personal needs while serving the best interests of the organization.

To be successful, an individual must be in a job he or she is capable of performing. Then positive reinforcement is possible. Indications of success are powerful motivators for future performance. A career dialogue should help assure that an individual is in a job where success is possible and where personal needs are given proper consideration. Also, preparation for the future should be tied in as closely as possible with success in the current job assignment.

3. Bosses gain by helping subordinates with their careers. A reputation for developing subordinates and helping them move ahead has to be earned. The price of such a reputation is the time and effort invested plus the likelihood that your subordinates will be moving on to other positions in the organization.

The benefits of such a reputation are: The top talent in an organization seeks the opportunity to work for such managers. A justifiable fear of talented individuals is that they might be hoarded or hidden by bosses who don't want to lose their valuable services, or "knifed" by bosses who feel threatened by their talents. Second, top talent quickly becomes valuable in any setting. Highly talented people pick up a new assignment and become fully productive in minimal time. They contribute to the boss's success each day. Third, as the talented individuals move ahead in the organization, the manager has a growing circle of associates with whom there is a mutual respect and trust, as well as friendship.

4. *Bosses can bring realism about the future to subordinates.* Desirable outcomes of a career dialogue include the subordinate's being realistic about the requirements for success in a given assignment, future opportunities, and the existing competition.

Requirements for success might also be termed job specifications. Managers use these specifications in identifying the development needs of an individual preparing for a new position, in making appointments to fill openings, and in identifying the development needs of a new subordinate before job performance information is available. By knowing the job specifications, subordinates can compare their current qualifications with the requirements of the job. And the boss's evaluation can then be shared with the subordinates. From this dual evaluation, subordinates can learn of their competitive strengths and development needs.

The possibility of future opportunities may be revealed by a look at the way openings have occurred in the past. New positions may be created as a result of growth or of restructuring to improve operations or meet new demands of the business. People are selected to meet organizational needs, not the other way around. Knowing the facts about opportunities that do exist or may exist in the future helps bring realism to a career discussion with a subordinate.

There should be competition for every job opening. Without competition, the selection standards might be lowered and a host of problems could follow. Bosses may not know exactly how tough the competition is, but they are likely to know far more than subordinates about what it takes to be selected for a given position. Sharing their views on the standards used in the selection process adds to the realism a subordinate needs in planning for the future.

5. Promises or predictions about advancement are not required. Many bosses have avoided career dialogues because they felt they had to tell the subordinates whether they would be promoted or not. Final decisions on promotions are made one or more levels above the subordinate's boss. The most a boss can do is make recommendations. It just isn't necessary to make promises about advancement during a career dialogue. To tell subordinates they will never be promoted is equally unnecessary. Organizational changes have a way of making long odds come through in many cases. Help individuals to be realistic about the probabilities. Slamming the door may cut subordinates' motivation to perform well on a current assignment or to prepare for new or more challenging assignments in the future.

6. Comparisons with others competing for a given position are not required. Focusing on the requirements for success in a given position makes it unnecessary to make comparisons with other candidates for the position. Comparing an individual's current qualifications with the requirements is useful for all candidates. This approach permits the precise identification of a candidate's development needs.

Candidates know there is competition for job openings; they know that meeting the position requirements, in the eyes of their boss, is no guarantee they will be selected, but that failure to meet the critical position specifications will almost surely disqualify them from being selected. So, if the subordinate wants to be considered, and does not now fully qualify on each critical requirement, development efforts should be planned and implemented.

7. Frequency and timing of career dialogues can affect the outcomes. The proper frequency of career dialogues depends on the needs of the individual and the needs of the organization. Subordinates with high aspirations are likely to have more urgent need for career dialogues than those who are content with being where they are. Young subordinates and those with fewer years of service and less familiarity with the organization may need more frequent dialogues. The dialogues should take place when the subordinate is most likely to be receptive to the help. It's difficult for a subordinate to keep out emotions and maintain objectivity just after missing out on a promotion, or just before a decision on filling a position is to be made.

The Process of Conducting Effective Career Dialogues

An effective career dialogue helps the subordinates to be realistic about the future and motivates them to prepare for future responsibilities. The process has much in common with the process suggested for other managerial dialogues, but in some respects it's quite different. As mentioned before, recognizing the similarity and differences aids in learning the skill.

The guidelines and the process for conducting a career dialogue can help you analyze what you do that is effective and what you do that is not effective in conducting these dialogues. The process includes the following:

1. Prepare for the career dialogue.
2. Maintain a helpful, motivational climate.
3. Explore aspirations and opportunities.
4. Explain the requirements for success in a given position.
5. Compare qualifications with requirements.
6. Agree on an action plan.

1. Prepare for the career dialogue. In order to prepare for a career dialogue, you need to have some advance knowledge of the thinking and career concerns of your subordinate. Then you can gather pertinent information, do your preliminary analysis, and plan how you can be most helpful. The dialogue will likely include most, if not all, of the following topics:

• Your subordinate's interests, aspirations, and career concerns.
• The roles of subordinate, superior, and higher management in furthering your subordinate's career.
• The requirements for success in a given position (position specifications).
• Your subordinate's qualifications compared with the requirements for success in a given position.
• The competitive situation with regard to a given position.
• Action plans to prepare your subordinate for future responsibilities.

If you know the interests, aspirations, and career concerns of your subordinates, the dialogue preparation can focus on the remaining topics. If you don't know them, encourage your subordinates to place this information in their personnel file and to keep it current. (See Chapter 18 for specific suggestions on this issue.) With subordinates who choose not to have this information in the file, a brief discussion is required to allow you to proceed with your preparation for the career dialogue.

Based on your existing knowledge, and/or the written or verbal inputs, you can decide where help is most needed by your subordinates. Focusing on specific needs will increase your effectiveness in handling the dialogue and reduce your preparation time and effort. You may need to get information and help from your superior or others in the organization in preparing to discuss position openings, future opportunities, and position specifications with your subordinates. Personnel specialists may be of help in all of these career matters. Also, you may wish to consult specific individuals about position openings on their staff. And you may need to consult higher management about future opportunities in the business and specifications for top-level positions.

Either when you set up the time and place for the career dialogue or at the beginning of the career dialogue, explain your desire to fulfill your responsibilities as a manager in developing and utilizing your subordinate's talents, and in building the organization to meet the needs of the future. Explain, if you feel it's necessary or that it would be helpful, such things as the following: (1) the way promotion decisions are made in the organization; that is, who is involved, the steps in the process, who makes the final decisions; (2) the need to be successful in a current assignment as a prerequisite to being considered for advancement; (3) the need to excel compared to the competition in order to be selected to fill a given opening; and (4) the importance of higher management's recognition of abilities and accomplishments.

2. Maintain a helpful, motivational climate. The suggestions for maintaining a helpful, motivational climate in a career dialogue are the same as for a performance dialogue. Briefly, they are: *Let your subordinate do it.* Set up the situation so your subordinate can take the initiative. As soon as possible, and at every opportunity, let your subordinate run with the ball. *Reinforce your subordinate's contributions.* Give evidence of agreement, approval, acceptance at every opportunity. *Be a coach and counselor to your subordinate.* When it would be helpful to provide information, share your experience, or give suggestions, do it.

But do it at the proper time; be sure your assistance does not come prematurely.

3. Explore aspirations and opportunities. Discuss your subordinate's aspirations and career concerns first, including your subordinate's current feelings about the written information he or she may have submitted to you. Take the time to be sure you understand your subordinate's concerns about the future.

Then share your knowledge about current and future opportunities that would be of interest and importance to your subordinate. Provide data, cite examples, and refer to organizational objectives, strategic plans, or budgets whenever possible to show the staffing requirements of the future.

4. Explain the requirements for success in a given position. As you explain position specifications, or the requirements for success in a given position, encourage your subordinate to ask probing questions to gain a deeper understanding of them. Use of the worksheet shown in Figure 17 is suggested when a particular position (such as that used in the example) is being considered as a possible next move. More general specifications are adequate when discussing the requirements of a given position two or more levels above your subordinate's current position. Use of the worksheet shown in Figure 18 is suggested for this situation.

Provide your subordinate with a copy of the worksheet you will be using. Both of you should have the position requirements in specific or general form for use in the next step.

5. Compare qualifications with requirements. The suggested sequence for this step is as follows:

- Ask your subordinate to evaluate the extent to which he or she currently meets each critical requirement. Use the rating key shown on the worksheet. Mark the evaluation by your subordinate for each critical requirement on the worksheets.
- Share your evaluation of how well your subordinate currently meets each requirement. Add your coded evaluations to the worksheets.
- Note the similarities and differences in your evaluations. Differences need to be talked over in depth. Explain that your evaluations can change whenever you see evidence in your subordinate's behavior and job performance to change your thinking.
- Identify the areas where development efforts are needed.

Figure 17. Worksheet for the specific requirements for a position.

POSITION REQUIREMENTS — SPECIFIC

Position:___Department Manager_____   Date: _____

Most Important Results to Be Achieved

1. Accelerate growth through new accounts.
2. Eliminate low-profit product lines.
3. Upgrade department and field personnel.
4. Build an aggressive distributor organization.

Evaluation of
Subordinate's
Current
Qualifications

	By Subordinate	By Superior
Most Critical Requirements for Success 1. Experience in field operations management (at least five years).		
2. Sound judgment on financial matters related to growth of the business.		
3. Skillful in communicating and motivating (influencing, persuading, training).		
4. Effective in building an organization (selecting, developing, using, motivating, and retaining talent).		
5. Effective in using all the processes of management in administering a large and diverse organization.		
Overall		

Rating key: ✓✓ Fully meets requirements, no reservations.
          ✓ Generally meets requirements, minor reservations.
          – Does not meet requirements currently.
          ? Don't know qualifications, unable to rate.

Figure 18. Worksheet for the general requirements for a position.

POSITION REQUIREMENTS — GENERAL

Position: _____ Date: _____

Evaluation of
Subordinate's
Current
Qualifications

	By Subordinate	By Superior

Experience
- Relevant work experience
- Supervisory experience
- Education and special training

What it takes to manage the entire job
- Time, effort, intellectual ability, emotional maturity, achievement motivation
- Technical competence
- Working with and through others

Standards of excellence
- Communications (oral and written)
- Development and use of subordinates
- Systematic management practices

Physical health, stamina, appearance

Special requirements

Overall

Rating key: √√ Fully meets requirements, no reservations.
        √ Generally meets requirements, minor reservations.
        − Does not meet requirements currently.
        ? Don't know qualifications, unable to rate,

6. Agree on an action plan. An action plan increases the likelihood that steps will be taken to further the career of the subordinate. Written action plans document the commitment to action and provide a means of self-discipline. The boss should do the writing of whatever action plans are formulated. This allows the boss to control the dialogue more easily.

As previously suggested, get your subordinate to take the initiative in suggesting action steps. The action plan may cover one or more of the following areas where development efforts are needed:

- Improvement of current job performance to the level required for continued progress toward his or her career aspirations.
- Correction of inappropriate behavior that might disqualify your subordinate from consideration for positions in which he or she has an interest.
- Increasing the extent to which current qualifications meet the critical requirements for success in position(s) for which he or she has career interests.

Self-Critique of a Career Dialogue: Checklist

1. *Preparation*
   Specific guidelines used well? Ignored? Misused?
   Specific process suggestions used well? Ignored? Misused?
2. *Dialogue Climate*
   Subordinate initiative encouraged? Discouraged?
   Subordinate contributions reinforced? Ignored?
   Coaching/counseling help provided? At proper time?
3. *Aspirations/Opportunities*
   Interests, aspirations, concerns clarified? Ignored?
   Current and/or future opportunities discussed? Ignored?
4. *Position Requirements*
   Requirements explained? Discussed?
5. *Qualifications*
   Evaluated by subordinate first? Then by superior?
   Evaluations discussed?
6. *Action Plans*
   Plans developed jointly? Not at all?
   Plans specific? General?
   Plans in writing? Verbal only?

Applications of the Model for Career Dialogues

The model presented for conducting a career dialogue is used in four situations: (1) when the subordinate asks for a career dialogue; (2) when the boss senses a specific need for a career dialogue because the subordinate's concerns about the future should be handled now, or because a position the subordinate will be interested in will be opening and the subordinate should be helped to become a qualified candidate, or because a position will be opening that calls for the present and/or potential talents of the subordinate, who should therefore be guided and encouraged to become a qualified candidate; (3) when the request or need for a career dialogue is an outgrowth of a job performance or behavior dialogue; and (4) when the boss elects to conduct career dialogues periodically with some or all subordinates.

Conclusion

The guidelines and process suggestions in this chapter are offered to encourage you to increase your present level of effectiveness in conducting career dialogues with your subordinates. The process suggestions can be adapted to the needs of the situation. If necessary, you can begin with a general discussion of the aspirations and concerns of the subordinate, and the broad spectrum of opportunities afforded by the organization, and then move toward being more specific. As soon as possible, focus on the requirements of a specific position and the individual's qualifications compared with those requirements. The process for career dialogues encourages meaningful and realistic development efforts.

IV

THE MANAGEMENT SYSTEM AND ORGANIZATIONWIDE NEEDS

In the preceding two sections, we focused on how to manage individual jobs, and how to have effective superior-subordinate dialogues on matters important to the business. In this section, we'll focus on organizational issues, matters involving individuals, superior-subordinate relationships, groups, and the entire organization.

To some degree, we have already handled the organizational issues when we set up each job to contribute to the success of the business and to develop and use the talents and fulfill the drives of the individual doing the job. But it really isn't that simple. The world of business is dynamic, not static. Jobs are forever being changed in small or large ways. Positions are filled with those considered to be the right selections. Still, people fail, or leave, or are unfulfilled, or have morale problems that affect job performance. Some of these problems can and should be handled by the boss and the subordinate. But some of these problems are truly organizational issues.

Planning organizational behavior is a matter of visualizing how the organization will behave or function as particular changes are made. For an effective organization, each position must be set up not only as an independent productive effort to contribute to the business, but also as part of the overall system. A systematic approach to correlating job content of individuals and setting up structural relationships is required.

Resolving power issues is an ongoing process in any organization. The risks of handling power confrontations must be weighed against the adverse effects of unresolved power problems. Systematic approaches to managing power are needed as part of the correlation of efforts in an organization.

The process of selecting an individual to fill a given position should be a joint endeavor, taking into account the individual's interests and aspirations, and qualifications and potential to grow in the assignment. Job content and structural relationships might need to be altered to use the talents of an individual.

A variety of controls are required to operate a business organization. If a successful and effective organization is the desired end, then the control system should provide a climate for achievement motivation. Control data and reports, budgets, and compensation should complement the other management processes. The interrelationships should be synergistic.

A systematic approach to career development takes into account what needs to be handled by or for each employee on a one-to-one basis with the boss, by bosses with respect to their key subordinates at the two next lower levels, and by personnel specialists on an organizationwide basis. Keeping the people pipeline full to assure continuity in running the business is part of the challenge. A more important challenge is building the organization by developing and using the talents of individuals.

Finally, the search for a better way of managing uses feedback from many sources and is based on the truism that improvement requires change. Change for the sake of change, of course, may not lead to improvement. Change in the search for improvement has to be managed. And improvement has to be accepted as a way of life if the organization is to identify the future it desires and then make it happen.

16

How to Select Structure and Personnel and Correlate Efforts for Optimum Results

In planning organizational behavior, we must visualize how the organization will perform as changes are made in one or more of three closely related areas: (1) the correlation of individual work efforts, (2) the establishment of optimal structural relationships, and (3) the selection of personnel who will succeed on the job. Upgrading the practices connected with these issues can increase the effectiveness of individual and organizationwide efforts to accomplish what's important to the business.

The Correlation of Individual Work Efforts

An individual has a set of responsibilities and objectives to use as a management tool. The objectives guide the individual's work efforts. The process of deciding how individual efforts can be set up to contribute to organizational success has to begin somewhere. It usually begins with the joint efforts of the individual and the boss.

Getting correlation started. In setting up a system for managing what's important to a business, each participant develops, with the boss's approval, a job content document. The responsibilities and objectives of the subordinate are deliberately defined to achieve correlation with the boss's responsibilities.

The initial correlation with the boss then has to be extended to others on the boss's immediate team. Job content documents often need to be modified to correlate with the efforts of others on the team, even after each member of the team has gone through the initial correlation effort with the same boss. This simply underscores the complexity of managing a business and the need for correlation of individual efforts.

Further correlation may be required with individuals or groups throughout the organization. It may be needed to resolve conflicts in the objectives themselves, and several levels of management may be involved before full correlation is achieved. Correlation may be needed to achieve teamwork for accomplishing shared objectives. It is then required in action plans, that is, what you do and what I do to achieve the common objective.

Correlation as an ongoing process. Correlation is not a one-time event. It is an ongoing process. From the initial correlation of objectives an awareness develops of what is going on in the organization; further correlation needs are likely to be identified as changes occur in individual jobs.

In addition, structural changes call for reexamination of the correlation of individual work efforts. Personnel changes call for starting over, in a sense, in clarifying job content and the correlation of efforts so the newcomer can quickly become productive in the new position.

Correlation and Power Issues

With structural relationships and personnel determined, the issues of who has the power to decide and act and which freedoms and restraints must be observed in carrying out job responsibilities can be resolved. This is also part of the ongoing process of correlation of individual work efforts. An individual who can make things happen, who has an impact on decisions and actions, is said to have organizational power. But power can be used to hinder as well as to help the organization achieve its objectives. So power has to be managed to accomplish what's important to the success of the business.

There are three forms of managerial power. The first is position authority. The exercise of legitimate authority that comes with a position can minimize behavior opposed to organizational objectives, but it does not maximize enthusiastic support. The idea of the voluntary "consent of the governed" becomes meaningful in this regard. The second form of power is the direct control of extrinsic rewards and punishments. The third form of power comes from identification with the purpose of the organization and with a leader.

Managing power means managing how power is exercised in an organization. This includes how power is delegated and how prevailing practices are reviewed and modified. Effective managers understand power issues and exercise their own power in deliberate ways so that power exercised by their subordinates contributes to the achievement of organizational objectives.

In managing power, freedoms and restraints to be observed by the individuals and groups must be defined in connection with the power to make specific decisions, to take specific actions, to influence decisions, to veto decisions, to audit, to share in joint decisions, to protest decisions, to review decisions and react to them before they are carried out.

There are risks involved in resolving power issues. Managers are encouraged to face up to the adverse effects of unresolved power problems and to take action to resolve the problems. The use of certain methods can lead to solutions in which both sides "win."

Resolving power issues always involves more than one person, and a confrontation is usually required. A method for working through to a resolution is suggested for four common types of power issues: superior-subordinate delegation, peer-group role clarification, multigroup work flow, and line-staff role clarification.

Superior-subordinate delegation. This situation involves the exercise of vertical power, and the method facilitates the making of changes. These are the steps to be followed:

STEP 1. A list of important decisions and/or actions related to the highest-priority objectives of the subordinate's job is prepared. The items can be selected by either the boss or the subordinate.

STEP 2. For each item on the list, boss and subordinate separately indicate which of the following responses best describes the freedoms/restraints under which the subordinate operates:

1. Subordinate does nothing without being told what to do.
2. Subordinate recommends, boss or someone else decides/takes action.

3. Subordinate discusses the situation with boss or someone else, then decides/takes action.
4. Subordinate decides/takes action, then informs boss.
5. Subordinate decides/takes action without discussion with anyone.

STEP 3. Boss's and subordinate's responses are compared. Differences are discussed and resolved.

STEP 4. Changes in degree of freedom to decide/act are suggested by either party, discussed, and resolved.

STEP 5. Decisions/actions handled by the boss that might be delegated to the subordinate are suggested by either party, discussed, and resolved.

Peer-group role clarification. This process is for resolving conflicts between two peer groups. (The process works when more than two groups are involved, but it takes longer.) A neutral party is usually required to assist in carrying out the process. These are the steps:

STEP 1. Both groups prepare a list of decisions important to both groups.

STEP 2. For each item on the list, each group defines its own role and the role of the other group.

STEP 3. Similarities and differences in the understanding of group roles are identified and discussed in a confrontation session. Resolutions of critical differences of opinion are based on the good of the whole organization. The results of the confrontation session form the basis of reference documents such as statements of policy and procedures.

Multigroup work flow. This process is for resolving conflicts that involve several groups in the work flow. A neutral party is usually required to assist in carrying out the process. The steps are as follows:

STEP 1. Major decisions or actions to be taken in the work flow are listed. All groups contribute to the list.

STEP 2. For each item on the list, each group defines what its contribution should be. Inputs are collected and charted.

STEP 3. The groups meet together to discuss the charted data, gain an understanding of the responsibilities of the others involved in the work flow, and work out improvements. Results of the session can be set up as a reference manual.

Line-staff role clarification. This process is for resolving conflicts between line and staff groups. A neutral party is usually required to assist in carrying out the process. These are the steps:

STEP 1. A list of staff contributions to the line organization is prepared. The list should include contributions currently being made, as seen by the staff, and contributions the staff could make, as seen by either line or staff.

STEP 2. For each item on the list, each group indicates the frequency of the staff contribution (very often, often, occasionally, rarely, never) and, looking to the future, whether more or less effort should be put into making the contribution (should do more, no change, should do less, should not do at all).

STEP 3. The data are discussed in a confrontation session. Each group learns the views and priorities of the other. Effort is made to resolve differences so that the critical objectives of both groups are considered and therefore both groups "win."

In summary, the correlation of individual work efforts is an ongoing process of deciding who needs to do what to make the business succeed. Now let's consider another factor affecting organizational behavior—structure.

The Establishment of Optimal Structural Relationships

The best organizational structure will not guarantee the achievement of desired business results. But the wrong structure can guarantee nonperformance because it may produce wasted motion, work gaps or overlap, inhibited behavior, higher costs, slower responses, friction, and frustration. Having the best possible structure, then, is prerequisite to business success.

Changes in positions and structure are often made shortly after a new top executive is appointed. The desired outcome of these changes is improved performance of the organization. Sometimes, however, the changes are used by an executive to "buy time," that is, to show superiors evidence of management activity when business results are not forthcoming and it's no longer possible to blame the previous management. Making changes in positions and structure to meet new objectives, to adapt to new conditions, and to overcome new obstacles is an ongoing managerial responsibility.

Structural relationships can help or hinder the achievement of organizational objectives. In setting up the positions and structure for a new organization or group, in analyzing a current structure, or in considering changes to achieve improvements, the task is to visualize how the organization will perform. A model for making an analysis of existing positions in a given structure and for considering structural changes includes the following:

STEP 1. Identify the most important organizational objectives to be achieved and the major obstacles to their achievement.

STEP 2. Identify the key activities required to achieve the objectives and overcome the obstacles.

STEP 3. Identify the positions needed to carry out the key activities.

STEP 4. Identify the best way of organizing the needed positions in a structure.

Let's look at each of these steps in more detail to understand how using the model can facilitate the accomplishment of what's important to the business.

Step 1: Organizational Objectives and Obstacles

The business objectives used in planning organizational structure may not be identical to the objectives on a top manager's job content document. Major obstacles to organizational success do not appear as such on a job content document. Yet both objectives and obstacles are important in planning organizational structure. And both grow out of the major responsibility of the top executive of the organization—to make the organization succeed.

The most important organizational objectives. Business objectives define what the business is, what the business will be, what the business should be in the future. In establishing major business objectives, the top executive spells out strong convictions about the future. The need is to visualize these objectives on a long-term basis—say, five years ahead.

The major obstacles to organizational success. An obstacle is any condition, either current or anticipated, internal or external, that adversely affects the achievement of business objectives. Obstacles to the achievement of objectives affect business results whether we like it or not. Therefore, major obstacles to achieving business objectives must be identified and dealt with just as systematically as the objectives themselves. They may or may not require structural changes, but they must be handled.

Identifying obstacles is possible only after the objectives have been established. Major objectives are often drafted by the top executive and then refined as an outcome of discussions with the staff. Major obstacles, however, may be identified by the executive, the executive's staff, or a special task force, depending on the need for in-depth analysis of internal and external conditions, either current or anticipated, which could affect results.

Step 2: Key Activities to Achieve Objectives and Overcome Obstacles

Work has to be done to achieve results. In this step, we are looking for key activities only, not the detailed activities found on action plans to achieve a specific objective of an individual. The key activities identified in this step should be stated as precisely as is practical. Detail is not required as long as clarity is achieved. This step is only a means to an end—to identify needed positions in the organization.

Step 3. Positions Needed to Carry Out Key Activities

Key activities have to be carried out to achieve desired results; positions are set up and filled in order for these activities to be carried out.

Four basic uses of positions should be considered in analyzing a current organization and its performance. These basic uses help in visualizing how the organization will perform with a changed structure. They represent benefits that are available from positions in a structure. An increase in one benefit to the organization is likely to come at the expense of some other benefit.

The benefits of a position must be justified on the basis of cost effectiveness. There must be some special reason, some unique contribution, to justify adding or retaining a position. The purpose of positions—to achieve objectives and overcome obstacles—comes first; the purposes should then be achieved as economically as possible. Some combination of the following four benefits can be expected from a given structural position: (1) concentration, (2) teamwork, (3) attention, and (4) personnel development.

Achieving concentration of effort on specific results. When an individual or a group has responsibility to concentrate on an important objective or obstacle, things happen, and the job is more likely to get done. Concentration on a particular assignment can lead to competence and high levels of performance. However, assigning an individual or a group to focus its efforts and resources on achieving specific business objectives can also lead to egocentricity, that is, little concern for teamwork and the success of the overall effort.

The benefit is realized by identifying objectives or obstacles where concentration is most needed. Then, if the need for emphasis on specific results is not adequately met with existing positions, new positions are inserted into the structure. These specialized positions see that the work gets done.

A position set up to achieve the benefit of concentration on specific results also ensures that the work gets done "right." For example, a quality-control position might be established that reports to the same top manager responsible for manufacturing and marketing. This position provides insurance that product quality will be maintained. Another example is an auditor, whose function is to ensure that certain standards are maintained or certain procedures followed.

The benefits of concentration of effort may have to be considered as a trade-off against teamwork. As with each benefit, costs associated with the position must be justified by the importance of the outcomes of the position to the success of the business.

Achieving teamwork. Correlation of job content and action plans goes hand in hand with structural positions set up to achieve teamwork. Teamwork needs to be increased when decision making takes too much time and adversely affects business results and morale. Too many meetings to coordinate the work may signal a teamwork problem. Whenever accountability is unclear, problems with teamwork are likely to occur.

Positions such as program manager, project manager, and product manager are set up to achieve teamwork. Sometimes assistant or assistant-to positions are set up for this purpose. The benefit is being realized when the time required for the top manager to achieve full correlation of effort is at a minimum, and the team effort produces the desired results without time delays.

Achieving appropriate attention to a specific area of responsibility. When an important responsibility is apt to be neglected by management, a position might be set up to ensure that it receives appropriate attention. For example, responsibility for safety or human resources development might result in the position of safety director or human resources development director being added to the structure. The holder of a position created to get the benefit of management attention in a particular area stimulates, guides, and encourages others in the organization to accept specific responsibilities and manage them to achieve the desired business results.

Achieving personnel development. Competent personnel are necessary for the health and long-term success of an organization. The development, motivation, and retention of top talent in an organization becomes increasingly important as business becomes more complex and competition becomes more keen. Positions can be set up for the express purpose of training and developing personnel for higher-level positions. The assistant manager position might be used for this purpose. In addition to the developmental benefit, the position may also motivate and retain impatient managers eager to move on to greater challenges. At a high level, the group vice president position is often used with this in mind.

To avoid an obvious pitfall, positions set up for personnel development should be created for a series of individuals, not one specific person. This type of position is costly, so the need for such a position must be considered carefully.

Step 4: Organizing Needed Positions in a Structure

Various structural approaches to organizing needed positions should be examined to see which will contribute most to achieving the objectives and overcoming the obstacles that have been identified. And structural hazards should be avoided as much as possible.

Structural approaches. Seven structural approaches to organizing key activities are in common use: the functional approach, the product or service approach, the matrix approach, the process approach, the customer approach, the geographic approach, and the knowledge approach.

The positive and negative characteristics of each approach can be found in much of the literature on organization planning, so they will not be repeated here. Knowing what these characteristics are helps in selecting the optimum structure for a specific situation.

Structural hazards. The model for analyzing an existing structure or considering structural changes suggests that a structure be selected that provides optimum benefits and avoids structural hazards. The following ten structural hazards are not in themselves entirely bad. However, each presents potential problems that are readily recognized. The organization planner should consider these potential difficulties and either correct the structure or make plans to deal with the difficulties.

Hazard 1. Too many levels. For example, each manager from the top to the bottom of an organization with only one or two immediate subordinates.

Hazard 2. Duplication of effort. For example, a plant manager with a Staff Specialist, Maintenance, and also a Manager, Engineering and Maintenance, as immediate subordinates.

Hazard 3. Conflicting objectives. For example, a Director with a Manager, Field Sales, and a Manager, Market Research, as immediate subordinates.

Hazard 4. More than one boss. For example, an individual assigned as an administrative assistant to two bosses.

Hazard 5. Improper/unclear use of assistants. For example, a general manager with three department managers and an assistant general manager as immediate subordinates.

Hazard 6. Boss spread too thin. For example, a plant manager with 6 satellite plant managers and a plant staff of 12 as immediate subordinates.

Hazard 7. One over one. For example, a department manager with an assistant department manager as the only immediate subordinate.

Hazard 8. Workloads out of balance. For example, Manager A is responsible for Purchasing and Traffic; Manager B is responsible for Industrial Relations; Manager C is responsible for Production, Engineering, Maintenance, Technical Support, Accounting, Field Sales.

Hazard 9. Functions misplaced. For example, a Market Research Director reports to Sales Director E, one of five Sales Directors who report to a Director of Marketing.

Hazard 10. Improper organizational emphasis. For example, a production manager reports to the engineering manager, who is on the immediate staff of a plant manager.

The Selection of Personnel Who Will Succeed on the Job

Selecting the right person to fill a position opening is a critical decision for both the individual and the organization. Ideally, selection should consist in choosing from among several qualified candidates the one most likely to be successful in the position. Qualifications include both ability and willingness to do the work. Knowledge, skill, experience, motivation, mental ability, personal characteristics, physical ability, and willingness to relocate may be considerations in the final selection.

In actual practice, selection often becomes a compromise between the ideal and handling real-life staffing problems. In some cases, the tail wags the dog; an individual is selected and job content and structure are changed to fit the individual. The impact of such decisions on the effectiveness of the organization needs to be understood by those planning organizational behavior. Fortunately, a trend in many organizations is to involve individuals in planning their careers. Selection for a particular position becomes a joint undertaking in which long-term career aspirations receive consideration. Training in conducting effective career dialogues is a requirement in many cases, to provide know-how or to overcome counterproductive practices. The final decision on who is to fill an opening is a joint venture involving those who offer the position and the candidate who accepts.

A selection/acceptance dialogue with a viable candidate precedes a final decision. It's a special kind of managerial dialogue with a potential subordinate. There are guidelines to follow and a suggested process to use in selecting an individual who will be successful in managing the entire job and accomplishing important results. And in using the guidelines and the process, the individual selected will be encouraged to accept the offer and will join the new environment with useful information and appropriate attitudes.

Guidelines for Selection/Acceptance Dialogues

Filling an open position is very much a two-way street. Those responsible make the selection from among available candidates. The person selected must accept the offer.

The final decision on filling an opening should be made after giving full consideration to each viable candidate, which includes securing and analyzing available data, and then having a face-to-face discussion to put into focus the total picture of the candidate. The dialogue is likely to be the most critical part of the final selection decision. Likewise, the final decision by the applicant is likely to be reserved until the dialogue has taken place and the applicant's questions and concerns have been fully aired.

The guidelines for conducting helpful and motivational selection/acceptance dialogues are:

1. Past performance helps predict future performance.
2. Evaluate new data in light of what is known.
3. Use tentative hypotheses.
4. Compare aspirations with potential.
5. Look for achievement motivation.
6. The right decision is right for all.

Every selection/acceptance dialogue involves these guidelines. A brief outline of what is meant by each guideline follows.

1. Past performance helps predict future performance. It's not a perfect measure, but past performance is often the most reliable basis for predicting future performance. The selection/acceptance dialogue, out of necessity, deals with both the past and the future. The past provides data that give evidence of achievement motivation, actual achievement under a specific set of circumstances, and the processes used to arrive at the results achieved. The past is analyzed in terms of a future situation and the critical requirements for success in that situation.

Data from the recent past are more likely to be useful than data from many years ago. Accomplishments in a current position, or perhaps in one or two prior positions, provide insight into the accumulated experience, knowledge, skill, ability, and motivation that the candidate would bring to a new assignment.

2. Evaluate new data in light of what is known. No single fact should be used alone. Like a jigsaw puzzle, all the pieces need to be put together to see the full picture. New pieces can add to the clarity of the picture, or they can change the picture abruptly. With each added piece, the picture takes on a new dimension. Integrate each piece of data as it comes along. Don't wait until after the dialogue to put the pieces together. Putting it all together is not a simple task; as with the jigsaw puzzle, it's easier to do it one piece at a time.

3. Use tentative hypotheses. This guideline has to do with efficiency in gathering and processing data. Decide what answer you expect to a given question. Anticipate what your judgment will be on a given matter. Then use those hypotheses to improve your listening. If the response is what you expected, it will be easy to spot and you can move on to other items. If the response is different from what you expected, it will be easy to spot and you can probe further for more facts and explanations, processing the data as they're received.

One note of caution: A tentative hypothesis is just that. You must be just as willing to change your hypothesis in the light of new data as to make it in the first place on the basis of very little data.

4. Compare aspirations with potential. Aspirations have to do with what the candidate wants for a future situation. Potential has to do with the realities of what the candidate will be able to do in the future. For candidates who appear to be overaspiring, you'll need to stress the need to be successful in each position held, the experience requirements that must be fulfilled, the competition for jobs, and the realities of the numbers of position openings in which they will have interest and outstanding qualifications. For candidates who appear to be underaspiring, you'll need to stress the current and future needs of the organization for talent, the continual search for individuals who distinguish themselves in their current assignments and who are actively preparing themselves for greater responsibilities, and the rewards available for those who excel.

Another variable to keep in mind is that a candidate may be an overachiever or an underachiever. Overachievers get things done in spite of the people who think they can't. Underachievers may have developed habits of laziness, often stemming from being bright and bored. These are cases where ability and willingness factors need to be explored. Both underachievers and overachievers need help in being realistic; both need position assignments that take into account the motivational forces that will result in their success on the job.

5. Look for achievement motivation. Asking the candidate to tell you about the most significant accomplishments in recent work assignments is one way to obtain evidence of motivation to work. Listen for what kinds of accomplishments are considered memorable by the applicant, and the circumstances involved. Did the individual seek and assume personal responsibilities? Set challenging targets? Take calculated risks? Make full use of feedback? Expect recognition for jobs well done?

6. *The right decision is right for all.* A selection/acceptance decision affects many lives. It's not enough for the decision to benefit only one party. The right decision is right for all: The candidate accepts the position believing there is the chance to learn, grow, succeed, and move closer to the fulfillment of career aspirations. The manager makes the selection believing the candidate is the best choice, considering the needs of the organization and the individual's qualifications, aspirations, and potential. The continuity of the organization itself depends on the selection of individuals who can succeed in given assignments, and who will learn, grow, and prepare for future responsibilities.

The Process of Conducting Selection/Acceptance Dialogues

An effective selection/acceptance dialogue helps the manager and the candidate to make the right decision on a position opening. This dialogue skill is needed by managers who are required to make the selection from the available candidates, to encourage the candidate selected to accept the position, and to see that the other candidates maintain a high regard for the organization and a full appreciation of the selection/acceptance process.

The guidelines and the process for conducting a selection/acceptance dialogue can help you analyze what you do that is effective and what you do that is not effective in conducting the dialogue. The process includes the following:

1. Prepare for the selection/acceptance dialogue.
2. Maintain a helpful, motivational climate.
3. Explore aspirations and opportunities.
4. Explore background areas relevant to position requirements.
5. Compare qualifications with requirements.
6. Agree on an action plan.

Since the final decision on filling an open position may involve several candidates, the assumption is that the selection/acceptance dialogue will not produce an immediate decision; rather, it is part of the process that leads to selection of a candidate.

1. Prepare for the selection/acceptance dialogue. Preparing for the dialogue includes the following:

- Know the requirements for success in the position. It's suggested that the requirements be listed on a worksheet for use during the dialogue.
- Review all available data concerning the candidate. Look for areas you'll want to probe for further information during the dialogue.
- Check relevant references. Ask current or former superiors about the candidate's most significant accomplishments; try to find the reasons behind any failure to live up to expectations; ask about areas where close supervision was required and where great freedom was extended.
- Develop tentative hypotheses. What do you expect the candidate's interests and aspirations to be? What concerns would the candidate have if offered the position? For which of the critical position requirements do you expect to find the candidate fully qualified? Partially qualified? Not qualified? How quickly would you expect the candidate to become fully productive in the position? How would you expect to rate the candidate's performance and potential a year from now?
- Be ready to discuss future opportunities. Include this in the dialogue if the candidate has talent and potential you hope to obtain or retain in the organization regardless of who is selected to fill the immediate position opening.

2. Maintain a helpful, motivational climate. The suggestions for maintaining a helpful, motivational climate in a selection/acceptance dialogue are:

- Let the candidate do it. Set up the situation so the candidate can respond freely to your inquiries and can ask whatever questions are of interest or concern. As soon as possible, and at every opportunity, let the candidate run with the ball.
- Reinforce the candidate's contribution. Show that you are interested in the candidate as a person, that you are hearing what is said, that you understand what is said, that you are listening for content and meaning rather than merely for the words.

• Be a coach and counselor to the candidate. When it would be helpful to provide information, share your experience, or give suggestions, do it. But do it at the proper time; be sure your assistance does not come prematurely.

3. *Explore aspirations and opportunities.* Talk about the candidate's interests, aspirations, and career concerns first. Let your tentative hypotheses guide you in listening to what is said and learning what is meant as the candidate talks. One way to get dialogue started is to refer to some item in the data you have about the candidate, and ask a question. In response to the candidate's comments, you can share your knowledge about current and future opportunities that would be of interest and importance to the candidate. Whatever the facts are, help the candidate understand them. In doing this, you are helping the candidate make the decision to accept or not accept the position if it is offered.

In this step, the dialogue gets moving, and the stage is set for discussing the background of the candidate as it relates to the position requirements. The time this step takes should be carefully controlled. Invest just enough time to get a good feel for the candidate's career aspirations and to share your views on the opportunities that lie ahead for those who can meet the requirements.

4. *Explore background areas relevant to position requirements. You know the critical requirements* for success in the position; the candidate is not likely to have this information. An exception would be a candidate who has had a career dialogue in which this position was discussed in depth for developmental reasons. In this dialogue, you are seeking information to aid in the selection decision. Therefore, the process is different, and the critical requirements are not explained to the candidate in the same way as in a career dialogue.

Since every position is created to accomplish results of some kind, it's appropriate to explore what has been accomplished by the candidate in the past to get a picture of how the individual might perform in the future. Consider the following areas for questions:

• What was accomplished? The question might be posed this way: "Tell me about some of your recent accomplishments, and why you feel they were important." This calls for more than cold data on accomplishments; it pushes for the value of the accomplishment to the success of the business.

- What contributed to your success? The reasons given might tell you something about the candidate's managerial abilities, personal characteristics, experience, special training or knowledge. Probe further as needed to get responses that are relevant to the critical requirements for success in the open position.
- What results were not up to your expectations? This refers to plans not carried out, hopes not realized, disappointments of some importance.
- What contributed to your disappointments? Here you're looking for willingness to accept responsiblity for results and how disappointments are handled.

In this step, and the previous one, you are collecting and processing information. You are checking out your tentative hypotheses and either confirming your convictions, or forming new convictions, about the candidate's potential.

5. Compare qualifications with requirements. When you have adequate information, you'll be able to evaluate the qualifications of the candidate on each of the critical position requirements. If you are uncomfortable in making an evaluation on a requirement for success in the position, perhaps you need more information. If so, continue the dialogue until you get the information. This step ensures that you have the information to make the necessary judgments regarding the candidate.

This step also prepares the way for ending the dialogue with an action plan. A comparison of the candidate's qualifications with the position requirements should tell you whether there is a possibility that the candidate will be offered the position.

The use of a checklist of the critical position requirements is suggested. The requirements need not be explained to the candidate, and your evaluations need not be divulged. Your coded evaluations against each requirement are insurance that the dialogue is productive. This record of your evaluations can also be used in the years ahead to develop your ability to select candidates who will be successful.

6. Agree on an action plan. In all fairness to the candidate, the dialogue should not end until an action plan has been agreed upon. First, find out whether the individual still wishes to be considered for the position. If so, the next steps should be understood. It's likely the action plan will include some of the following: When, how, and by whom will the candidate be informed of the decision regarding the open position? If the position is offered to the candidate, when will the acceptance decision be expected? If the position is offered and accepted, when will the candidate be expected to report for work?

In summary, the suggestions for carrying out the process and the guidelines for conducting a selection/acceptance dialogue are to assist you and the candidate in making the right decision regarding a position opening. They are offered as a model to encourage you to increase your present level of effectiveness in filling open positions.

The process suggestions can be adapted to the needs of the situation; that is, the suggestions may be used in dialogues with candidates from inside or outside the organization and with candidates with extensive work experience or mostly academic backgrounds.

Conclusion

Organizational behavior can be changed by making changes in structure, personnel, and the effectiveness of the correlation of individual work efforts. Virtually all managers are involved in the correlation of work efforts. And all managers may be required to select new subordinates from the available candidates and to consider structural changes for their organizations.

The relationship of these parts can be seen in the following hypothetical sequence of events in setting up a new organization. First, the most important organizational objectives and the major obstacles to their achievement are identified. Then, positions needed to carry out the necessary work activities to achieve the objectives and overcome the obstacles are identified. Next, the positions are organized into a structure that provides most of the possible benefits from structure. Next, the critical requirements for success in each position are identified, and personnel are selected on the basis of their qualifications and potential for success. Then, the job content for each position is drafted and subsequently goes through the process of correlation with the job content of others in the organization so that power to decide and act is properly managed. As conditions call for change, changes in one area or another may justify other changes to maintain organizational excellence and to achieve optimum business results.

17

How to Use Controls to Set Up Achievement Motivation

Controls are a means to an end. The end is control. Control by management means keeping the business moving toward its objectives at the desired rate. It involves directing, coordinating, and supervising work while the work is in progress and appraising the quality of the work after it has been completed.

A system for managing based on the use of responsibilities and objectives is sometimes referred to as a system for planning and control. Planning deals with the future, with desired outcomes and the steps to be taken to achieve those outcomes. Control also deals with the future, with direction and expectations, with what ought to be.

Controls, on the other hand, provide measurement, information, facts; they deal with the past; they are concerned with analysis of what has taken place. Thanks to modern computer technology, we can process and analyze great quantities of data very rapidly. Improved controls of this kind can assist managers in exercising control. But controlling involves more than the use of data from easily measured events.

Controls must help us focus on results if they are to make a significant contribution to managing a business. Internal results are usually associated with costs that are relatively easy to define. External results, those connected with the customer, the economy, or society, are often more difficult to measure. Further, controls are needed for both easy-to-measure and difficult-to-measure results. From a practical standpoint, some important results cannot be measured precisely, yet are very tangible. An example in the people area would be attracting and retaining top talent, with its profound effect on the long-term success of the business. Setting up ideal controls is a continuing management challenge.

Ideal controls satisfy the following specifications:

1. *Practicality.* Controls should provide the minimum information needed for control. The information should provide the basis for effective management action, and at a cost that can be justified.

2. *Significance.* Controls should be established for events that can have a critical impact on performance and results. Controls should be related to major objectives, high priorities, key activities that define the business. Control by "exception" should apply to less essential objectives.

3. *Usefulness.* Controls should give a picture of the reality of the situation, and not mislead through meaningless precision of measurement; the control data should be available when they're needed for control purposes; the controls should be understandable to the user.

The following discussion about control contains information that is important to the operation of an effective management system and that is relevant to achievement motivation. The control system can have a profound influence on achievement-oriented behavior. The relationship of the control system to achievement motivation is discussed; guidelines for analyzing and improving control data and reports are suggested. Budgets are discussed in relation to the objectives of the organization. The purpose of budgeting, the proper use of budgets, and the timing in setting up budgets are reviewed. Compensation is included because it's a powerful control tool that can complement or wreck a business management system. An innovative approach to compensation is presented.

The Control System and Achievement Motivation

The way we behave depends on our motives or needs and the characteristics of our environment. Our motivation to satisfy a need in a given situation depends on the strength of the need, our expectation that the need can be satisfied, and the amount of satisfaction we expect to receive.

Every personality is made up of a network of needs. Some of the more important needs that have been studied are: (1) the need for success in life as measured against some standard of excellence; (2) the need for power to make things happen, for personal influence, and for control over the means of influencing others; (3) the need for friendship and close interpersonal relationships; (4) the need to avoid failure or criticism in connection with an activity that is to be evaluated. Needs are developed early in life and remain relatively unchanged in later years. However, motivation to satisfy needs comes from the combination of the person and the environment. Therefore, a person's behavior may change radically throughout life.

In a business situation, we are concerned with the motivation to accomplish certain results. In studies conducted by psychologist David C. McClelland it was found that persons with a high need to achieve tend to: seek personal responsibility; take calculated risks; set challenging, but realistic targets for themselves; develop appropriate plans to help them achieve what they set out to do; make use of the available feedback on the results of their actions; look for opportunities where their desires to achieve will be recognized and where they will be rewarded for their accomplishments. This suggests that high achievers tend to be attracted to business environments that encourage and reinforce these behaviors.

Management control processes can be set up so that achievement-oriented behavior is rewarded and reinforced. Once aroused, achievement-oriented behavior becomes self-rewarding and self-sustaining. The guidelines presented here suggest what to look for in a management system to evaluate its impact on achievement motivation and thus business results. The guidelines can be identified with parts of the system for managing what's important presented earlier. They also relate the parts of the system, yet to be presented, to a method of encouraging achievement motivation.

1. *Establish clear objectives.* By definition, achievement motivation refers to competition with a standard of excellence.

2. *Establish objectives with a moderate degree of risk for the individuals involved.* The subjective probability should be about 50-50.

3. *Make provisions for adjusting objectives when the chances of success/failure change significantly from the 50-50 level.* There should be provision for systematic review and adjustment of objectives built into the management control system. By insisting that objectives remain challenging (that is, with a 50-50 chance of achieving them), the en-

tire organization can be injected with excitement and an orientation toward achievement of important business results.

4. *Reinforce the setting of moderately risky objectives.* As part of the evaluation of individuals, provide positive reinforcement (rewards rather than punishment) for setting moderately risky objectives. A pitfall to be avoided is placing heavy stress on 100-percent achievement of every objective. The system should require that every objective be managed well, that is, that every objective receive attention appropriate to its importance to the business. Emphasis should be placed on achieving results that contribute the most to the success of the business.

5. *Provide appropriate feedback on progress toward objectives.* High achievers characteristically want concrete feedback of the results of their efforts. The feedback should be prompt, unbiased, and relevant.

6. *Emphasize individual responsibility.* In setting objectives and reviewing progress, the acceptance of responsibility is encouraged by a results orientation. The system should call for the subordinate to take the initiative as much as possible in establishing objectives and reporting results. The boss then functions in the role of coach and counselor.

7. *Reward important accomplishments.* When achievement motivation is high, achievement itself becomes the most important reward. Formal organizational rewards are important also because they symbolize success and satisfy other personal needs. Accomplishments need to be reinforced with all available forms of reward according to the importance of the accomplishments and all the factors that were involved. Failure to differentiate performance levels in the formal reward system means the system will have relatively little effect on accomplishments. To arouse achievement motivation, the system should reward individuals who excel, whether or not the group of which they are part has accomplished its objectives.

8. *Provide a supportive climate.* To stimulate achievement motivation, encouragement and support should be task-related. Coaching and counseling sessions, both formal and informal, provide opportunity to give help and encouragement related to specific objectives. A supportive environment is self-generating. The anxiety and resulting negative effects that fear of failure has on continued high performance are reduced in a supportive environment.

In summary, achievement motivation is desirable in a business organization. The development and use of talent and the accomplishment of business results are enhanced when individuals have the characteristics of high achievers. Achievement-oriented behavior can be encouraged by creating the right kind of environment in the organization. The organizational environment is determined by the design and the implementation of the control system, combined with the attitudes and values each manager brings to the job of control. Because of its organizationwide impact on behavior and results, the design of the control system is the responsibility of top management. The responsibility for implementation of the suggested control processes must be with line management—each boss.

Control Data and Reports

Reports providing control data are essential for most businesses. Managers tend to use the reports provided, grateful when the data are accurate and timely. Seldom do managers push for improvements in control reports. Rarely do managers request their names be dropped from distribution lists.

As more sophisticated equipment for preparing reports becomes available, more control data are produced, and distributed sooner, to more and more people on the list. The growth of control reports in an organization has been likened to the growth of a cancer in the body. Prevention is most desirable; surgery may be necesary, followed by preventive maintenance.

The following guidelines are suggested for analyzing current control reports and considering possible improvements:

1. Control data should be provided at the lowest level where the individual is permitted to take action based on the data.

2. Control data provided to higher levels should be condensed and simplified to include only the information needed to understand the situation and take action appropriate for that higher level.

3. Control data should enable an individual to track progress toward the achievement of objectives.

4. Control data should be provided frequently enough to permit concurrent control, and infrequently enough to make the data meaningful.

Data can be presented in control reports in a variety of ways:
Data only. These might be termed raw data. Raw data are the

basis for all other forms of presentation, but raw data alone do not lead to action. Raw data must be compared with some standard of measurement before variances can be identified that lead to remedial action. Raw data are common in control reports, but they're likely to be the least desirable for control purposes when other forms for presenting data are available.

Data compared with a standard. Examples of this reporting method are: figures for this year to date compared with the same period last year, showing increases or decreases, and current results compared with budget, showing over or under figures. With this report form, the first step in using raw data has been completed for the user. The analysis process then continues; that is, variances that require attention must be identified. The user must decide which increase/decrease or over/under figures are significant enough to warrant action.

Data compared with a standard and with items identified as requiring action. The identification of items that require remedial action is done for the user in this reporting method. The acceptable tolerances for variances are established in advance. For example, items that are more than 5 percent over budget might be identified in the report.

Exception only. This report shows only the items requiring attention. No data, data/standard, or data/standard/action information is provided.

How the data are presented in control reports affects efficiency in using the data. But who gets the data, what data they get, and when they get the data affects achievement motivation.

The Control System and Budgets

Budgets are plans in numerical terms. Budgets are used as controls, to assist managers in achieving control. Budgetary control consists of preparation of a plan that reflects the objectives of the business, comparison of actual results with the planned results, explanation of deviations from the plan, and appropriate action.

Plans are only good intentions until they are translated into work. In setting up a budget, management commits resources to be used in doing the work. People are assigned to the work, accountability is defined, materials and equipment are provided, deadlines are set, measurements are established, and feedback from what happens leads to further plans. In this sense, it might be said that some form of formal or informal budgets are involved in all work to achieve all objectives.

Budgets and Objectives

Consider the linkages between objectives and budgets. Long-term objectives define what the business is and what it should be in the future. Short-term objectives define the end results needed in the current period to move at an appropriate pace toward the long-term objectives. Action plans define what it will take to achieve the short-term objectives: the work, the activities, the resources, the people, the timing of events. Budgets define who spends time where, and what expenses, revenues, or units of physical input or output will be involved.

Budgets, then, are based on objectives, and objectives look to the future. In setting objectives, the immediate future has to be balanced against the long term; objectives have to be balanced against each other, and the trade-offs have to be considered; objectives always require a decision on where to take the risks. In setting and balancing objectives, the budget is a useful tool to express the decisions behind the objectives.

Budgeting is often thought of as a financial process. It would be more appropriate to consider it a means of expressing the priorities that management has set. Priorities reflect the results of the balancing of objectives. Even when a budget is approved, it shouldn't be seen as a rigid plan of action. Important unforeseen changes in internal or external conditions may call for budget revisions during the budget period.

Zero-Base Budgeting, Performance Auditing, and the Sunset Concept

In recent years, the concept of zero-base budgeting has received publicity. It offers advantages over the typical budgeting approach, but it has its disadvantages. It's not practical in every organizational setting.

The essence of zero-base budgeting is to justify each activity's projected level of expenditures. No expenditure is to be taken for granted. Instead of upgrading the figures from the previous budget, the idea is to start from base zero and take a fresh look at activities and priorities. It's a tool for reviewing, analyzing, and evaluating budget requests. The process has three steps: (1) Each discrete activity is described in a "decision package." (2) The decision packages are evaluated and ranked, using a cost-benefits approach. (3) The resources are allocated accordingly.

Zero-base budgeting requires a lot of time, money, and paperwork. The time and effort required for budget preparation have been considered a very serious problem by those using the approach. Another major problem is the temptation to beat the system by hiding inefficiencies, "scratching each other's backs," and labeling featherbedding items as essential.

The principal advantage to the zero-base budgeting approach is that every discretionary cost is defined and categorized. Incremental changes or additions to the previous budgets are not accepted without question; they are instead evaluated on a cost-benefits basis.

Two alternatives to zero-base budgeting deserve mention. In *performance auditing,* the effectiveness, efficiency, and economy of specific activities are reviewed. This alternative does not call for rankings and priorities, and it can be done on one or many activities, and on a time schedule convenient to all. Performance auditing can be done by internal teams or key external help. Since each manager must be involved in analyzing the efficiency and effectiveness of each program or activity, appropriate measurements must be set up if they are not already in use. An advantage for top management is the freedom to review the performance audits made at lower levels on a selective basis, and on its own schedule. For all its advantages, however, it is not a systematic approach to managing the entire job. It is what its name implies, a performance audit of a selected activity.

According to the *sunset concept,* each activity is abolished automatically, per plan, on a given "sunset" date. In order to be continued, the activity must pass the same type of scrutiny involved in a performance audit to justify its existence. The idea is that the review will be in sufficient depth so that outdated and low-priority activities, and the costs associated with them, will be weeded out. The sunset concept has proved useful in requiring management to give its attention to particular activities. The sunset concept is, for all practical purposes, a performance audit with a specific deadline.

The basic purpose of zero-base budgeting, performance audits, and the sunset concept are realized in an effective system for managing what's important. Every effort has been made to build into the management control system the advantages available from these other approaches, while taking care to avoid the pitfalls.

The Timing Sequence in Establishing Budgets

A sequence to be followed in setting objectives and establishing budgets has not yet been suggested here. Budgets are numerical reflections of objectives, and objectives reflect decisions about the future and the priorities of the business. If budgets are seen as the same thing as objectives, although expressed in different terms, it doesn't matter much which comes first. The danger is that when budgets are set first, the tendency is to adjust the previous budget figures, and then set objectives and plan activities and the use of resources to fit the budget. Trade-offs and priorities may not receive consideration they deserve.

When the system for managing what's important is functioning, the trade-offs among objectives are considered and priorities are set. Then, the available resources are allocated to activities that will produce the greatest payback. Highest-priority activities get the people and the money to maximize the possibility of success. Low-priority activites may have to be dropped or cut back because all the available resources are already committed. Budgets are then set to reflect those decisions and commitments.

The Control System and Compensation

Whenever management is making a significant effort to increase its managerial effectiveness, it's appropriate to examine the compensation system to make sure that it's compatible with other processes and that the organization is getting the maximum motivational impact from each compensation dollar.

In order for a compensation program to be motivational, the employees involved must feel there has been an equitable distribution of the available funds to those who actually make the contributions to company performance. Compensation programs should be used to reward those who actually do make significant contributions to the performance of the company each year and to create a climate that will encourage all those eligible for financial awards to make significant contributions to the performance of the company each year.

The Compensation System as a Control

A company requires the efforts of its employees to achieve its business objectives. In return, working for a company satisfies many important needs of the employees. The more the important needs of the employees are satisfied, the more highly motivated they will be to continue performing the activities that lead to those satisfactions.

Financial rewards fill several needs. They provide life's basic necessities and some of the luxuries for the employees and their families. They are also a *symbol* of success, status, growth, competence, personal worth, power, responsibility, achievement.

Financial rewards are very important to most employees in a business organization. If you want evidence of this fact of life, implement a 50-percent reduction in pay and observe the reactions of those affected by your edict. This demonstrates the importance of the monetary value of financial rewards as a maintenance factor related to past performance, but it does not demonstrate the limitations of monetary value as a motivator of future performance. The personal or symbolic value attached to financial rewards, on the other hand, is a very significant motivator of performance.

In order for maximum motivational impact from each compensation dollar to be achieved: (1) The compensation system should consistently provide for internal and external equity in the distribution of financial rewards. (2) Each superior and subordinate should understand the compensation system and how compensation decisions are reached. (3) Each superior should accept the full responsibility for administering the system, including full use of its freedoms and adherence to its restraints. (4) Each superior should understand the motivational aspects of compensation and be able to assist subordinates in seeing both the personal and the monetary value of rewards for performance.

Control of the financial reward system, then, is an important control over human needs satisfaction and the motivation to work. The decision regarding adjustments in the compensation of an individual should be based on the contributions of the individual to the business. The decision should not be made as a reaction to a single event or result—no matter what it might be. The value of the contributions and the management characteristics that brought about the results should be given due consideration.

Compensation and Management Characteristics

A compensation system can either support or wreck a business management system. Managing the business comes first; the compensation system must complement the management system. Compensation decisions are based on comparisons of one individual's contributions against another's. Each situation, each set of responsibilities and objectives, is unique. Thus compensation decisions are subjective judgments, which makes having a systematic approach to making them equitable all the more important. By following the procedures in the system for managing what's important, a boss gains in-depth insight into the management characteristics and the achievements of each subordinate. This insight prepares a boss to make compensation decisions that are fair to each subordinate, and further, these decisions are more likely to be accepted by the subordinates themselves as equitable.

Three management characteristics should be considered in evaluating the contributions of an individual to the success of the business. These characteristics are seen in how the individual manages the job day after day. The detail behind these management characteristics provides a basis for development efforts. This matter is discussed in Chapter 18 on career development. The detail summarized under these three headings is useful in making compensation decisions:

Job content. To what extent were the responsibilities, controls, and objectives of the individual useful, practical, motivational, correlated with those of others, and important to the short-term and long-term success of the business? Only after the fact can all the factors involved in accomplishments, or lack of accomplishments, be given full consideration. Compensation decisions involve evaluating the results achieved, looking at all the factors involved with the benefit of hindsight.

Having exemplary management characteristics with regard to job content is important not only for the superior but also for the subordinates under his or her supervision. A boss who provides the proper job content model can strongly influence the climate for achievement motivation in the organization.

Managing the entire job. How appropriately were effort and resources allocated to each area of responsibility; was the emphasis on accomplishments of greatest importance to the business? On the basis of day-to-day contacts and stewardship reviews, the boss gains insight into whether systematic management practices have been and are being used, and what the managerial capabilities of the subordinate are. Using the evidence gathered, the boss can exert the kind of control that encourages achievement motivation.

Standards of excellence. Is the individual exemplary in systematic management practices, in the development and use of the talent of subordinates, and in oral and written communications? Again, this is a subjective judgment concerning one individual in comparison with others in the organization. Exemplary means a model worthy of imitation. It implies a relative degree of perfection. The person is better than others but is still striving for further improvement.

Compensation and the Value of Accomplishments

The value of an individual's contributions to the success of the business is the major consideration in classifying subordinates into categories for financial rewards. The link between results achieved and compensation should not be a mechanical one. Setting up a compensation system such that achieving X percent over objective means Y percent salary increase leads to all the abuses connected with traditional methods of using objectives. However, to produce internal equity, and encourage achievement motivation, results achieved and compensation do have to be closely related. As noted before, compensation decisions are subjective judgments that should take into account how well the job was managed and the significance of what was achieved. Every area of responsibility and each objective needs to be considered in making the compensation decisions, along with all the other factors involved in the total contribution of the subordinate to the success of the business.

The Compensation Decision

In the traditional compensation program, all too often the superior, for reasons known only to the superior, decides what a subordinate's compensation will be. Then the necessary paperwork is completed to justify the decision—an appropriate performance rating is selected, and comments that fit the performance rating on strengths, weaknesses, potential, development needs, and plans are made. To put it bluntly, this approach goes against all we know about reinforcement, motivation, and fairness; it teaches all the wrong things.

Contrast that approach to one that provides for making compensation decisions on the basis of (1) documented evidence in a tracking system of how well each part of the job was managed by the subordinate throughout the year, (2) documented evidence in the form of the subordinate's own evaluation of accomplishments compared to objectives, the value of the accomplishments to the organization, and what it took to achieve them, (3) documented evidence from the boss as a control on the honesty of the subordinate's accomplishments report, (4) documented evidence of the boss's judgments in comparing one subordinate's performance with another's, and (5) the next level higher's review of the documented evidence as control on the boss's judgments. The compensation decision comes after, not before, thorough and honest consideration of the facts and of all known factors influencing performance.

The chart provided for classifying subordinates into compensation categories (see Figure 19) combines the evaluations of management characteristics and results achieved so that both are considered in the basic compensation decision.

Control of the Awards

In order to maintain internal and external equity in the compensation system, managers should have guidelines each year indicating an appropriate range for financial awards in each compensation category. The guidelines for a given year might be:

Category	Award Guidelines
Top award	20% and up
Above-average award	10–20%
Average award	5–10%
No award	0

Control of the award from a financial point of view comes through the use of compensation budgets. Consider these policy issues:

1. The overall compensation budget should be based on the financial achievement of the company and the amount required to achieve/maintain external and internal equity.

2. Budget allocations to groups should be based on current ex-

Figure 19. Guidelines for classifying subordinates for compensation purposes.

CLASSIFYING SUBORDINATES FOR COMPENSATION PURPOSES

Ratings should be relative to the performance of others in the organization.

CATEGORIES

Top Award 1 in 10*	Above-Average Award 3 in 10*	Average Award 5 in 10*	No Award 1 in 10*

ACCOMPLISHMENTS

Top Award	Above-Average Award	Average Award	No Award
1. Results exceptional on all major objectives; value of contribution more than could be expected.	Results exceptional on many major objectives	Results exceptional on several major objectives.	Results not satisfactory on major objectives.
2. No exceptions to satisfactory results on all aspects of the job.	No exceptions to satisfactory results on all aspects of the job.	No exceptions to satisfactory results on all aspects of the job.	Many exceptions to satisfactory results, considering all aspects of the job.

MANAGEMENT CHARACTERISTICS (Identify point on each continuum to represent summary.)

1. **Job Content:** Responsibilities, controls, and objectives useful, practical, motivational, correlated with others', important to short-term and long-term success of the business.

◄───►

Exemplary   Improvement Required

2. **Managing the Entire Job:** Appropriate allocation of effort and resources to each area of responsibility, with emphasis on accomplishments of greatest importance to the business.

◄───►

Exemplary   Improvement Required

3. **Standards of Excellence:** In systematic management practices, in the development and use of talent of subordinates, in oral and written communications.

◄───►

Exemplary   Improvement Required

*Likely number of subordinates in category.

ternal and internal equity in compensation of the group as a whole and on group contribution to company financial achievement.

3. Flexibility should be allowed in granting individual awards; that is, budget allocations should never become an excuse for internal inequities. Each award should be justified when compared to other awards in the entire organization, not just in the immediate peer group.

4. Responsibility for differentiation to achieve equity among a manager's immediate subordinates should rest with the manager.

5. Responsibility for adjustments to achieve equity across managers should rest at the next higher level.

Benefits of the Innovative Approach to Compensation

An innovative application of the basic approach to compensation outlined here is a performance-award program that has both base salary and bonus elements. But it also has several striking departures from traditional compensation programs that could be classified as salary and bonus plans. The important benefits of this approach in relation to achievement motivation are:

• The approach can be used equally well for staff and line positions; at all management levels; in organizations of all sizes.

• There are no penalties for top performers. Traditional approaches have maximum amounts for each salary range. Those whose performance moves them toward the top of their range before they are promoted to a position with a higher range are penalized—the salary increase they have earned is often reduced "in order to have the proper salary curve." A similar, but harsher, penalty is imposed on those who have reached their salary-range ceiling, have no possibility of upward mobility, and yet are making exceptional contributions year after year. The range ceiling often leads to reclassification of jobs so that the individuals can be properly rewarded. This handles the problem temporarily, but doesn't solve it.

• It can replace a straight salary program, or a salary-plus-bonus program. No extra funds have to be allocated.

• It provides a record of the judgments and adjustments involved in the total award granted, not just the dollar amount of the award. The use of the dollar amount of awards without other information is one of the problems associated with traditional compensation programs; that is, the history of salary increases, and the evaluations of the individual's promotability, have too great an influence on current compensation decisions.

• It ensures maximum motivational impact from each compensation dollar. Participants can understand how compensation decisions are made. The process of arriving at compensation decisions is auditable. No damaging labels are attached to the awards granted. Awards have to be earned each and every year. There are no limits to the award an individual can earn in competition with others in the organization.

• The compensation decision cannot be made first by the boss, who would then have to complete all the paperwork in such a way as to justify the decision. The reverse is required. Objectives, tracking, dialogues, and reviews lead up to accomplishment highlights, the most important reference document for compensation decisions. The basic compensation decision, made by comparing the performance of one individual with the performance of others, has to be justified by what is already documented.

How the Model Compensation Program Works

1. For each position, a "minimum" and "market value" salary is established. These are based on external and internal surveys and are upgraded as required. Market value represents a competitive salary for fully productive professionals; it may be equal to the midpoint of a traditional salary range for a position.

2. Budget allocations are made to each manager covering the total subordinate group, and guidelines are provided for awards in each category (top, above average, average).

3. Recommendations are made by line managers for awards to their immediate subordinates. The next higher level of management either approves the recommendations or changes the budget allocation (either increases or decreases the allocation), and requires the manager to adjust the awards for the subordinates accordingly. The control at the next higher level takes care of managers who tend to be either too generous ("Santa Claus") or too frugal ("Scrooge") in making compensation recommendations. It serves as a teaching/learning device to prevent extremes that lead to inequities. The manager retains ultimate responsibility for differentiation of awards among subordinates.

4. The granting of awards for those whose base salary is below market value is handled as follows: (1) The award is used first to increase base salary; base salary may not exceed market value; an increase in base salary in a given year may not exceed one half of the difference between the minimum and market value salaries for the position. (2) If there is award money remaining after considering the base salary increase, it's given as a performance award for the year, usually in a lump sum.

5. The granting of awards for those whose base salary is at market value is handled in this way: The entire amount is granted as a performance award for the year, usually in a lump sum. (In setting up the program, there may be those whose base salary exceeds the market value of the position. They are treated as if their salary were at market value; over a period of time, assuming inflationary trends continue, market value will catch up with their base salary. Meanwhile, they are not penalized by the compensation program. Each individual must earn whatever award is granted each year, and there is no ceiling—each individual gets what is earned.)

The steps a boss takes in making compensation recommendations are as follows:

STEP 1. Set up the compensation planning worksheets (see Figures 20 and 21), one for each subordinate and one for the group, with current status information regarding salaries, the assigned compensation budgets, and the award guidelines for the year.

STEP 2. Classify each subordinate into one of the four categories for compensation purposes: Top Award, Above-Average Award, Average Award, No Award. (Example: A. Allen to receive above-average award.)

STEP 3. Assign a tentative award, percentage of base salary and dollar amount, to each individual, using the current guideline. (Example: Tentative award to A. Allen set at 18% or $306 per month.)

STEP 4. Add the tentative awards for each subordinate and compare with the assigned budget for the group. Decide whether there should be an adjustment for the budget. If you are over, under, or right on the budget, can you justify your recommendations? (Example: Tentative awards were over budget by a total of $49 per month, or 8%. The decision was made to adjust the tentative awards downward 8% to more nearly achieve equity with others in the organization.)

STEP 5. Make the adjustments for budget, if any, to the tentative awards for each subordinate. Round the figures to the nearest $5.00. Do not recommend awards smaller than a practical minimum. (Example: The tentative award to A. Allen was reduced 8% and rounded to a total award of $280. The total award, annualized, amounted to 16.5%.)

STEP 6. Break down the total award into the portion for an increase in base salary if current salary is not at market value for the position, and into the portion for a lump-sum performance bonus—whatever remains of the total award after the salary increase is considered. (Example: A. Allen's salary increased by $170 per month; the performance bonus amounted to the equivalent of $110 per month, to be granted as a lump sum of $1,320.)

STEP 7. If the next higher level of management judges the recommendations to be too liberal or too conservative compared to others in the organization, a further budget adjustment will be required. The process for adjusting for the budget should be repeated. Such final changes, when required by management, are added to the worksheet for the individual.

STEP 8. The completed individual compensation planning worksheet should be retained in each subordinate's personnel file.

In conclusion, the controls used in setting up a climate for achievement motivation call for self-control by boss and subordinates. Self-control in managing requires self-discipline. It makes large demands. The subordinate has the challenge of taking the initiative, as much as possible, in managing the entire job. The boss has the challenge of not interfering with the subordinate as long as the agreed-upon actions and communications are taking place, and of doing what is necessary to maintain a helpful, motivational climate in all interactions with the subordinate. The long-term success of the business may depend on whether the controls used encourage achievement motivation.

Figure 20. Format of the compensation planning worksheet (individual).

COMPENSATION PLANNING (INDIVIDUAL)

Name: _α. αllen_   Title: _Manager, Product A_

Grade: _18_   Range Minimum: $ _1600_   Market Value: $_2000_

Current Salary: $ _1700_   Compensation Rate: _0.85_

Category for Award Consideration   Guideline for this Year

____ Top Award   From _20%_ up

_X_ Above Average Award   From _10%_ to _20%_

____ Average Award   From _5%_ to _10%_

____ No Award   No Award

Tentative Award Based on Category and Guideline

                                    | _18%_ | | $ _306_ |

Budget Adjustment (if any)
used for all subordinates   Total Award
in making recommendations   Recommended | $_280_ |

(+)   (−) _− 8%_

Recommendations

Salary Increase (per month)	New Salary	New Compen- sation Rate	Performance Bonus Equivalent per month	Lump-Sum amount	Total Award (annualized)	Date Effective
$ _170_	$_1,870_	_0.94_	$_110_	$_1,320_	_16.5%_	

Signature:_____   Date:_____

Approved Awards (Complete only for changes in above.)

$	$		$	$	%	

Figure 21. Format of the compensation planning worksheet (group).

	Current Status			Tentative Award	Adjustment for Budget	Salary Increase	Recommendations		Performance Bonus		Award (annualized) %
Name	Salary	Market Value	Compensation Rate				New Salary	New Compensation Rate	(equivalent per month)	Lump Sum	
1. A. Allen	1700	2000	0.85	306	280	170	1870	0.94	110	1320	16.5
2. B. Brown	1330	1510	0.88	—	—	—	1330	0.88	—	—	—
3. C. Carter	1230	1130	1.09	148	135	—	1230	1.09	135	1620	11.0
4. D. Doe	820	850	0.96	205	190	30	850	1.00	160	1920	23.2
5.											
6.											
7.											
Totals	$5080	$5490	0.93	$659	$605	$200	$5280	0.96	$405	$4860	11.9%

Assigned Budget ___12%___

Over/Under Budget ___$610___

Adjustment for Budget (if any) ___$49___

$\dfrac{\$ \text{Over/Under Budget}}{\$ \text{Assigned Budget}} = \dfrac{\$49}{\$610} = \boxed{(+) (-)} \ -8\%$

18

How to Handle
Career Development
Organizationwide

Nothing is more important to managing a business than the people who make it happen. People manage the business. Where do the people come from who fill position openings? Two sources, obviously. They're brought in from outside, or they're selected from among current employees.

Every employee was at some time a nonemployee who applied for a job, was selected from among the available candidates, and accepted the offer of employment. People brought in from the outside ultimately form the pool that is the internal source of candidates for openings. Therefore, the hiring decision has an immediate and also a long-term effect on the success of the business.

Once inside the organization, the matter of career development becomes important for both the employee and management. An interesting exercise is to estimate the dollar costs and/or the dollar contribution to profits from effective or ineffective selection and development efforts. Effective career development means systematically doing the right things to manage the most basic resource of the business—people.

A systematic approach to career development takes into account what needs to be handled by and/or for each employee on a one-to-one basis with the boss, what needs to be done by bosses for their subordinates one and two levels below them, and what needs to be handled on an organizationwide basis.

Career Development by/for Each Employee

Each employee participating in the system for managing what's important has opportunities to make career development a joint venture involving the boss and others in the organization. Each of the following is linked to the career development of the individual:

1. The initial hiring decision. Initial selection, and extension of a job offer, are based on the indications from all available inputs of the likely success of the individual on the job—the first step in the individual's career with the organization. But the job offer has to be accepted before the individual is hired. That is, the individual has to choose to join the organization. Again, this is done in the belief that the decision is the best available choice in terms of the individual's career interests and aspirations. Hiring is a joint decision.

2. Setting up and updating job content. Newcomers usually have to rely on the boss for help in identifying responsibilities, controls, and objectives connected with the position. However, even newcomers can make suggestions about their personal development. As experience on the job and with the organization increases, both the individuals and the boss are in a better position to identify developmental needs. Ideally, self-improvement objectives grow out of the interests and aspirations of the subordinates, and the coaching and counseling of the boss.

3. Managerial dialogues. Every managerial dialogue has an impact on the career of the subordinate. In every managerial dialogue, learning takes place—academic and/or emotional—that changes the subordinate in some way. Behavior and ultimately job performance are affected. The boss learns from managerial dialogues too. What the boss learns influences coaching and counseling activities, work assignments, and promotion recommendations.

4. Career interests and aspirations shared organizationwide. All individuals should be invited, not coerced, to place in their personnel file a record of their career interests and aspirations. Figure 22 shows the suggested format for this record. Updating of the information should be allowed at any time, and a reminder to consider updating the information should be given the individual each year. With this kind of information, the boss and personnel staff specialists can try to make available appropriate work assignments, education experiences, and

Figure 22. Format of the career interests and aspirations worksheet.

INTERESTS AND ASPIRATIONS

Name:_____   Date:_____

Your career development is a joint responsibility involving you and the company. This worksheet is intended to help you, your superior, and others concerned with your career development communicate your interests and aspirations. With these in mind, developmental activities become more meaningful. Therefore, you are encouraged to be candid in your responses, and you are permitted to update your responses whenever you wish.

1. *Present Position.* In what areas of your work would you like more coaching, counseling, training, education, or broadened experience?

2. *Next Position.* What specific position, or type of position, would you prefer as the next move in your career?

3. *Future Positions.* What kind of work do you hope to be doing five to ten years from now?

4. *Future Organizational Responsibility.* What size organization would you like to be in charge of five to ten years from now? (Number of employees, volume of business)

5. *Special Considerations.* What special considerations need to be taken into account in planning your career over the next five to ten years (personal or family needs, amount of travel required, location, willingness to relocate)?

---

rotational moves to broaden the individual in preparation for increased responsibilities in present and future assignments.

5. *Selection for, and acceptance of, another position within the organization.* This is much the same as the hiring decision, except it can occur any number of times during a person's career. Career development efforts are not aimed at the next job only, or even the one after that. An entire career is involved, and developmental efforts are required at all ages and stages.

Each time a move is made to a new position, or to a higher level of responsibility, a career crisis occurs. To be successful in a new assignment, an individual must adapt to the new circumstances. This means letting go of certain routines and picking up new ones. New job content means there are things to learn, new relationships to develop. A change in self-concept is required—and it does occur—if there is to be success in a new assignment.

6. *Analysis of performance for purposes of individual development.* Few management processes are as destructive as the traditional performance appraisal. A better way of managing calls for changing the performance appraisal from a destructive to a developmental process. The traditional performance appraisal has been appropriately dubbed "the annual doomsday appraisal." In spite of warnings about its value, such as those in "Split Roles in Performance Appraisal," the classic article by Herbert H. Meyer, Emanuel Kay, and John K. P. French first published in the *Harvard Business Review* in 1965, many companies continue to use traditional appraisals that accomplish the opposite of what they are supposed to accomplish.

Most traditional performance appraisal programs provide a performance summary as a way to simplify communications. Numbers (1, 2, 3, 4, 5), letters (A, B, C, D, E), words (outstanding, excellent, good, fair, unsatisfactory), and phrases (consistently exceeds requirements, meets requirements, fails to meet requirements) are typical of the various approaches to labeling performance. Detailed definitions are usually provided for each label.

There are many problems with performance labels. Let's mention a few. (1) Labels are imprecise. Standards of measurement vary with the rater; an individual who is rated a 2 may be nearly a 1 or nearly a 3 performer; most organizations don't have a system for providing evidence to support the rating so that it is considered fair by the individual being rated. (2) Labels are unreliable. In addition to the problem of the standards of the rater, ratings are often changed by successive levels of authority; initial ratings are often changed to accommodate some form of forced distribution of ratings. (3) Labels are damaging. The current superior-subordinate relationship is more likely to be damaged than it is to be improved when performance labels are used; others who see the labels—personnel specialists, managers considering the individual as a potential subordinate, higher levels of management involved in career decisions—may be influenced to make decisions not in the best interests of the individual or the organization.

Another aspect of the traditional performance appraisal that lingers in one form or another is trait-based ratings such as for loyalty, dependability, and self-confidence. It's often difficult to relate these to specific job activities, raising a potential problem with Equal Employment Opportunity requirements.

Behavior-based rating scales are being developed in a number of companies today. Behavior-based ratings provide feedback to the individual that could be useful in planning developmental activities. However, the problem of labels remains—excellent behaviors are described and then the descriptions continue down to unacceptable behaviors—and the motivational aspect of the appraisal is as destructive as ever. In addition, there are problems in setting up the scales to fit individual jobs. Another problem is the staggering amount of time and effort required to set up the system. So far it hasn't been shown to be practical.

Effectiveness-based ratings, such as those connected with the achievement of objectives, are attempts to measure results, not behaviors or activities. As discussed earlier, there are problems with traditional approaches that stress *meeting* objectives rather than *using* objectives to manage the entire job and make important contributions to the success of the business.

Still, performance must be appraised for development, compensation, and promotion decisions. A better way is needed for dealing with these ongoing problems of performance appraisal. First, there is the subjectivity of human judgments. Second, even with conscientious raters, the information they have may be inadequate or erroneous. Third, the basis on which performance will be judged may not be adequately defined by the boss or understood by the subordinate. Fourth, the purpose of the appraisal may not be clear, or there may be an attempt to use a single appraisal approach for development, compensation, and promotion decisions. Fifth, the dynamic nature of jobs, and the uniqueness of each job situation, may not be taken into account in appraising the performance of the individual.

A better way of managing is to recognize the traditional performance appraisal as obsolete and to use an approach that accomplishes the important purposes of performance appraisal without the destructive side effects so common in prevailing systems. The benefits of effectiveness-based appraisal are realized by following the procedures described in Section II for managing the entire job, with special emphasis on the value of accomplishments as contributions to the success of the business.

The benefits of behavior-based appraisal have to do with its value as a developmental device. In order for it to be effective, destructive labels have to be eliminated, and the process has to be seen as nonthreatening by both boss and subordinate. Also, development efforts have to be related intimately with success on the job—effectiveness in making contributions of importance. Therefore, the behaviors to be considered are those connected with managing the entire job and accomplishing what's important.

In the place of ratings of the various behaviors, boss and subordinate jointly decide on the priority for improvement in connection with each behavior. This removes defensiveness on the part of the subordinate, since low or high priority for improvement has nothing to do with an arbitrary standard. Yet it allows the boss to function as coach and counselor in identifying where improvement efforts will pay off the most for the individual and the organization.

The use of this approach to identify developmental priorities has all the benefits of a behavior-based appraisal, yet avoids the problems of labels, relevancy, and practicality. An example of the format suggested is shown in Figure 23. The analysis is conducted jointly, and both boss and subordinate keep current copies for their own use; outdated analysis forms are destroyed. The analysis should be made at least annually; more often if either boss or subordinate feels it would be worthwhile.

Career Development Handled by the Boss

A systematic approach to career development of subordinates, from the boss's point of view, takes into account individual performance, interests and aspirations, promotability predictions, position

Figure 23. Format of the developmental priorities worksheet.

DEVELOPMENTAL PRIORITIES

Name: _J. Doe_   Position: _V.P. Security_

Prepared jointly with (superior) _B. Brown_   Date: _2/7/82_

Factors Contributing to Performance

Priority for Improvement

(Check priority. Circle items selected for improvement.)   Low   High

1. Job Content
   - All major responsibilities being managed.
   - Useful and practical controls.
   - Objectives important to the success of the business.
   - ⊙ Probability of success 50-50 in setting objectives.
   - Correlation of short-term and long-term objectives for self and with others.

   ☐ ✓ ☐ ☐

2. Tracking
   - All available data used in making evaluations.
   - System used as springboard to improvement efforts.
   - Priority for action based on importance of objectives.

   ✓ ☐ ☐ ☐

3. No Surprises
   - Early identification of problems.
   - ⊙ Early identification of improvement opportunities.
   - ⊙ Early identification of business potential.

   ☐ ☐ ☐ ✓

4. Homework Before Help
   - Appropriate amount of homework.
   - Problem-solving skill.
   - ⊙ Planning to seize opportunities.
   - Appropriate use of superior's time as coach.
   - Use of coaching and counseling help.

   ☐ ✓ ☐ ☐

5. Action Plans
   - Effective use of own time.
   - ⊙ Right amount of "insurance" for each objective.
   - Plans useful, practical, innovative.

   ☐ ✓ ☐ ☐

6. Stewardship Reviews
   - Knowledge of status of each objective.
   - Ability to adapt to changing priorities and standards.
   - Willingness to adapt to changes required.

   ✓ ☐ ☐ ☐

7. Accomplishment Highlights
   - Accuracy of information.
   - Understanding of value of accomplishments.
   - Evidence that results were achieved through management effort.

   ✓ ☐ ☐ ☐

8. Development & Use of Subordinates
   - Flexibility in leadership.
   - ⊙ Delegation skills.
   - ⊙ Coaching and counseling effectiveness.

   ☐ ☐ ✓ ☐

9. Teamwork & Relationships
   - Clarity combined with brevity in all communications.
   - Correlation of action plans on shared objectives.
   - Contributions to efforts of others.
   - Achievement of cooperation of others.
   - Company image enhanced in contacts with outsiders.

   ✓ ☐ ☐ ☐

10. Technical Competence
    - Technical job knowledge both broad and current.
    - Interrelationships with other jobs understood.
    - ⊙ Innovation in planning and achieving results.

    ☐ ✓ ☐ ☐

COMMENTS
   By position holder:
   By others:

projections, people projections, and individual development plans. The approach suggested is intended for use by top managers and their staffs, thereby giving the top managers information on the first and second levels below them. The needs of the organization (usually related to the number of levels of employees) determine how far down in the organization the use of the process is justified.

Comments on each segment of career development to be handled by the boss follow. The parts are assembled in a career development manual for the convenience of the manager and others, such as personnel specialists and higher levels of management.

1. *Interests and aspirations.* The option of the subordinate to have this information in the personnel file has been mentioned. The form suggested was shown in Figure 22. Interests and aspirations cannot guarantee success on the job, but interests do relate to persistence and the likelihood of job satisfaction. Knowing the interests and aspirations of an individual helps in understanding the individual and in planning developmental activities and organizational moves.

2. *Developmental priorities.* The joint responsibility of boss and subordinate for making this analysis has been discussed. The form suggested was shown in Figure 23. Both retain copies for use in planning developmental activities for the subordinate. This analysis provides input in summarizing the management characteristics of the individual as part of an overall summary of performance and as part of the guideline for classifying subordinates for compensation purposes.

3. *Performance summary.* A summary can be a useful tool for an executive. Figure 24 presents a practical one-page summary of performance. Note that the summary must be based on information in other, more detailed documents. For example, the "management characteristics" summary will reflect the joint decisions made in the developmental priorities analysis, which in turn is based on dialogues and reviews using job content and the tracking system throughout the year. "Most important results achieved" will be a digest of what appears in the accomplishment highlights. "Important results not up to expectations," if any, will have been identified in the tracking system and action planning. The "compensation category" takes total performance into account.

The involvement of the subordinate in the basic reference documents, and the review by the boss's boss, help make the summary a useful, reliable tool for career development in the organization. The

Figure 24. Format of the performance summary worksheet.

PERFORMANCE SUMMARY

Name:_____   Position:_____

Period from:_____ to:_____   Length of time in position:_____

Prepared by:_____   Years as supervisor of employee:_____

MANAGEMENT CHARACTERISTICS (Place check on each continuum to represent summary.)

1. **Job Content:** Responsibilities, controls, and objectives useful, practical, motivational, correlated with others', important to short-term and long-term success of the business.

◄――――――――――――――――――――――――――――――――►

Exemplary   Improvement Required

2. **Managing the Entire Job:** Appropriate allocation of effort and resources to each area of responsibility, with emphasis on accomplishments of greatest importance to the business.

◄――――――――――――――――――――――――――――――――►

Exemplary   Improvement Required

3. **Standards of Excellence:** In systematic management practices, in the development and use of talent of subordinates, in oral and written communications.

◄――――――――――――――――――――――――――――――――►

Exemplary   Improvement Required

ACCOMPLISHMENTS

1. *Most Important Results Achieved.* (Be specific. Add comments on value of results.)

2. *Important Results Not up to Expectations (if any).* (Be specific. Add your opinion of why.)

COMPENSATION CATEGORY
_____ Top Award ____Above-Average Award ____ Average Award ____No Award

summary gives the big picture for planning developmental activities and predicting promotability. It should be updated annually. Outdated forms should be destroyed.

4. *Promotability predictions.* This part of the career development program is completed for each key position reporting to the boss. A format is suggested in Figure 25.

"Most important results to be achieved" can be gleaned from the subordinate's job content document supplemented by the boss's knowledge about future results desired. "Most critical requirements for success" are selected by analyzing the action steps required to achieve the desired results. Certain experience, knowledge, skills, drives, and abilities are deemed critical to doing the work and achieving success on the job. Individual names and ratings can be added or changed at any time. A major change in important results to be achieved on a given job calls for an update promptly. A thorough review and update are recommended annually for all positions.

In searching for individuals who will be well qualified in the future to handle a given position, managers have reason to communicate with each other and with personnel specialists. Career dialogues may be set up to ensure that individuals receive appropriate coaching and counseling in developmental activities and that they are encouraged to consider the position as a possible career opportunity in the future.

Prediction of the individuals who will be well qualified to handle the position within five years requires a manager to have some estimate of the current abilities and potential of the individuals. The performance summary is helpful in this regard, especially in cases where the manager is not intimately acquainted with the individual's performance record. For immediate subordinates, the procedures for using objectives, along with the insights from managerial dialogues, help a manager make the predictions. Rating current qualifications against each of the critical requirements pinpoints current strengths and developmental needs.

A given manager may not be aware of all the individuals in the organization who have the potential to handle the job. The larger the organization, the more it is spread geographically, and the fewer the communications among employees, the more acute this problem becomes. In such cases, the need for coordination, usually involving the personnel function, becomes very important.

Figure 25. Format of the promotability predictions worksheet.

PROMOTABILITY PREDICTIONS

Position: ___Planning Manager_____

Prepared by:_____ Date:_____

Most Important Results to Be Achieved

1. Upgrade effectiveness of field management planning systems.

2. Improve accuracy of forecasting to within 5% of actual.

3. Reduce time lag in management information systems.

Most Critical Requirements for Success

1. Experience in management connected with field operations (at least five years).
2. Skill in management planning processes (analytical, methodical).
3. Sound judgment in evaluating business opportunities and solutions to financial problems.
4. Innovation in methods and approaches to business problems and opportunities.
5. Capable of working closely with top management in planning the direction of the business.

Prediction of Individuals Who Will Be
Well Qualified Within Five Years   Current Qualifications vs. Requirements

Name	1	2	3	4	5	Overall	Ranking
F. Fayol	✓✓	✓	–	–	✓	–	4
G. Gregory	✓	✓✓	✓	✓✓	✓	✓	1
H. Hunter	✓	✓	✓	✓	✓	✓	2
I. Ingram	✓	✓	–	?	✓	–	3

Rating Key: ✓✓ Fully meets requirements, no reservations.
✓ Generally meets requirements, minor reservations.
— Does not meet requirements currently.
? Don't know qualifications, unable to rate.

Figure 26. Format of the position projections worksheet.

POSITION PROJECTIONS	
Prepared by:_____	Date:_____
Current Organization Position Titles (Your position) (Subordinates' positions)	Possible changes within five years due to expansion, reorganization.
Division President	No change
Vice President, Finance	No change
Vice President, Product Planning & Distribution	To become new position of Vice President, Operations, and supervise current operations managers
Manager of Operations (2)	To be moved under Vice President, Operations
Vice President, Marketing	To supervise regional sales managers; new organization to have five regions
Vice President, Engineering	No change
Vice President, Administration	To be eliminated, activities assigned to others
Director, Industrial Relations	No change
Regional Sales Manager (2)	To be moved under Vice President, Marketing
_____	New position, Vice President, Technology, to be created

5. *Position projections.* This part of the program concerns bosses and their immediate subordinates. For each position in the current organization, possible changes within five years, due to expansion or reorganization, are listed. (Figure 26 shows a form filled out by the division president for the division president and the immediate subordinates.) Often there will be no changes planned. When changes are projected, attention is called to the item so that advance preparations can be made and last-minute crisis situations avoided. Changes can be made on the form at any time. A thorough review and update are recommended annually.

6. *People projections.* This part of the program has to do with personnel moves connected with positions in the boss's organization. See Figure 27. For each position, timing projections are made. If a change is projected, the individual's next assignment and replacement candidates are listed. This step reveals the sense of urgency connected with developmental activities, and alerts the organization when no viable replacement candidates have been identified. Changes can be made on the form at any time. A thorough review and update are recommended annually.

7. *Individual development plans.* This part of the program grows out of all the interactions of the boss and the subordinate. The suggested form is shown in Figure 28. This step encourages managers to think through three areas of developmental activity. Many managers avoid their responsibility for developing subordinates by having as a developmental plan nothing more than "should attend course X," or "needs more time on present assignments." Managers are challenged to identify the purpose of special work assignments or educational experiences, to plan the time schedule, and to specify areas where their coaching and counseling skills will be used in developing the subordinate's talent. Changes can be made on the form at any time. An update may be called for as a result of changes in the subordinate's interests and aspirations, as an outgrowth of a managerial dialogue or review, or as a result of a joint analysis of developmental priorities. A thorough review and update are recommended at least annually.

When a manager has set up a career development program and has begun to use it regularly as a management tool, anxiety and guilt over personnel decisions disappear. The program adds evidence that the selection, development, motivation, use, and retention of key personnel are being well managed. People make the business succeed,

Figure 27. Format of the people projections worksheet.

PEOPLE PROJECTIONS						
Prepared by:_____ Date_____						
Position	Timing (years)					Comments
Incumbent Years in position	1	2	3	4	5	Incumbent's possible next assignment Replacement Candidate(s)
Director of Personnel			X			
Mr. Allen 9 years						Retirement Conner
Manager, Employment			X			
Ms. Brown 1 year						Manager, Training & Development Abbot, Adams, Anderson, Avery
Manager, Training & Development			X			
Ms. Conner 2 years						Director of Personnel Brown, Bell, Beard
Manager, Pay & Benefits	X					
Mr. Davis 5 years						Early retirement due to health Cassidy
Manager, Labor Relations				X		
Mr. Edwards 1 year						Corporate Industrial Relations Daley, Daniel
Manager, Safety				X		
Mr. Franklin new						Edgar, Eden

Figure 28. **Format of the worksheet for individual development plans.**

INDIVIDUAL DEVELOPMENT PLANS

Name:_____   Position:_____

Prepared by:_____   Date:_____

1. Work Assignments. (specify special assignments to be given; identify their developmental purpose; state time schedule.)

    Assign as chairman of task force on project X, with personal responsibility for reporting progress and final outcomes. Purposes: Experience in achieving cooperation of others and in developing oral and written communication skills. Completion of project targeted for 8/1.

2. Coaching and Counseling. (Specify areas for improvement where coaching and counseling skills of immediate supervisor will be utilized.)

    Critique homework for appropriate amount in relation to importance of the problem or opportunity.

    Coach on appropriate use of my time in reviewing homework and giving help. Discourage coming to me on insignificant items.

3. Educational Experiences. (Specify courses, seminars, independent study, personal visits, industry events, etc.; identify their developmental purpose; state time schedule.)

    Business communication correspondence course. Completed this year.

---

and important business results include the career development of those people.

Career Development Organizationwide

Career development is aimed, first, at helping individuals succeed in their current assignments. However, people at all levels move out of their jobs or leave the organization for a variety of reasons and have to be replaced. Therefore, career development is also aimed at keeping the "pipeline" full of qualified replacements. It is an organizationwide effort. It involves intake, selection, and the variety of activities that contribute to the development and use of talent.

Effective personnel specialists can assist individual employees and their bosses in their respective roles in career development, and make other contributions that require organizationwide activities. The following activities are relevant in an organization of any size.

1. *Intake should meet both short- and long-term needs for people.* People are usually brought into the organization in response to a specific need to fill an opening. Most often these are entry-level or low-level positions. Because newcomers often become the source of candidates for higher-level positions, planning the intake, in terms of numbers and potential abilities, with future needs in mind is part of managing what's important.

For example, in one large organization, approximately 600 exempt employees are recruited each year. Each recruit joined the organization with expectations of rising to mid-management levels in the organization. Each year approximately 80 employees actually made it to mid-management positions. What happened to those who didn't make it? What happened when the newcomers realized what was happening? How much top talent left before it could be developed and used? How many in effect "retired" before age 30? How many stayed, with a disillusionment that affected others?

An organization needs many kinds of talent. It can accommodate people with different aspirations, interests, and drives. It needs people of different ages, with various kinds of experience and abilities. A personnel specialist can coordinate intake with immediate needs and at the same time be sure the pipeline will supply the needs of the future.

2. *Selection should be based on consideration of all viable candidates.*
Hoarding talent is a temptation to every manager. But it's not in the
best interests of the organization, or the individual. In the long run, it
also hurts the manager who tries it. Who would choose to work for
such a person?

Business policy should demand that consideration be given to all
viable candidates in the organization before a selection decision is
reached. This usually calls for specific efforts on the part of personnel
specialists. The following items are minimal requirements of the staff
contribution:

• The personnel specialist should make sure the position specifications reflect the critical requirements for success in the job in the
near future. The immediate superior should be in the best position to
prepare position specifications for a subordinate position. The staff
person needs to have an in-depth understanding of the specifications
in order to search out and screen potential candidates.

• The personnel specialist should screen employees (1) who have
an interest in the position, (2) who have been recommended as viable
candidates, or (3) who have qualifications that make them potential
candidates. Some large organizations use computer technology to
keep track of historical information related to employee job experience, skills, and education. When the right information is in the computer system, every employee who should receive consideration can at
least be screened by a staff specialist. In most organizations, however,
the information available from the computer system is not adequate
to produce all the viable candidates.

Personnel specialists are responsible for finding out the interests,
aspirations, and qualifications of employees. Employees' interests,
managers' predictions, performance summaries, and other information in the individual's personnel file, such as accomplishment highlights, are available for staff use. Screening is an initial step aimed at
producing enough viable candidates—those whose current qualifications are a reasonable match with position requirements to make the
final selection a tough choice—and reducing the number of candidates, if necessary, to a practical number worthy of final consideration. Screening is done among candidates from inside the organization whenever it's possible, and from outside, whenever it's necessary
for maintaining high standards in the selection of personnel. The pro-

cess of screening applies to position openings, developmental moves, and the identification of individuals with high potential for executive positions.

• The personnel specialist should provide information to those who must make the final selection. More and better data on candidates lead to better selections and growing confidence that the screening process is producing high-caliber candidates. Perspective is gained in the final selection process when the staff specialist provides information on those eliminated in the initial screening. Knowing the identity of these candidates and the principal reasons for their elimination allows a possible second consideration, and by comparison shows the caliber of those recommended for final consideration.

3. *In-depth personnel reviews should be held annually.* Each manager who has subordinates has their career development as a major area of responsibility. This can be expressed as responsibility for the selection, training and development, motivation, use, and retention of talent in the organization. Specific objectives are set up, tracked, and reviewed with the boss, and action plans are developed and implemented as the need arises, the same as for any other responsibility. In support of these personnel objectives, and to fit in with organizationwide needs, each manager should use the systematic approach to career development suggested here.

But there is one more important part to a career development program—the annual in-depth personnel review. This review reinforces the importance of career development, permits the exchange of important information, and ensures that important action steps dealing with people are planned and implemented.

The annual in-depth personnel review can be held at a time convenient for the individuals involved. Some executives prefer it to be held in connection with the annual stewardship review. Some executives prefer to schedule it early in the new annual cycle. The choice depends on having adequate time to conduct the review and having the right people there.

Who should be there? The manager, the manager's boss, and the appropriate personnel representative. At the top of an organization, for example, the chief executive would conduct the review with one subordinate at a time, with the top personnel executive present.

What takes place at the review? An agenda planned well in advance is followed. The manager, therefore, has the opportunity to be fully prepared. The agenda requires the manager to exhibit in-depth knowledge and systematic approaches in the people area just as in the operating areas of the business. Preparation for the review is largely a matter of familiarity with the data in the manager's career development manual. Basic items for a personnel review agenda follow. Other items should be added to meet the current needs of the organization.

Personnel Review Agenda

1. Discussion of each immediate subordinate.
   A. How is A (B, C, . . .) doing? (Use performance summary.)
   B. What does A want to do? (Use interests and aspirations.)
   C. What is A's potential? (Use performance summary, interests and aspirations, promotability predictions. Should this individual receive special attention to develop his or her high potential?)
   D. What developmental activities are planned for A? (Use developmental priorities, individual development plans.)
   E. How satisfied are you with A's efforts in the career development of subordinates at the next lower level? To what extent is there agreement on evaluations, predictions, projections, and development plans? What are your plans in this regard?

2. Discussion of individuals at the next lower level.
   A. Who are the top performers (if any), and what are the plans to develop, use, and retain their talents in the organization? (Use performance summary, promotability predictions, people projections, individual development plans.)
   B. Who are the marginal performers (if any), and what are the plans to upgrade their performance? (Use developmental priorities, performance summary, individual development plans.) If these plans are not successful, what alternatives are under consideration for each individual?

3. Discussion of changes and needs over the next five years.
   A. What changes in the business situation will affect personnel needs?
   B. What changes in positions or organizational structure are possible? (Use position projections.)

    C. What replacement needs do you anticipate due to departures for personal reasons, health, retirement? (Use interests and aspirations, people projections.)

    D. What replacement needs or additional personnel do you anticipate due to organizational changes, transfers, promotions? (Use position projections, people projections.)

4. Discussion of depth and quality of replacement candidates.

    A. For what needs will hiring from outside the organization be required or preferred? (Use promotability predictions, people projections.)

    B. If current replacement projections become a reality, will the resulting organization be stronger or weaker? If stronger, what are your plans for the interim with your existing organization? If weaker, what special plans do you have to overcome the problems?

5. Discussion of other personnel topics. (optional)

    A. Analysis of controllable turnover.

    B. Analysis of age distribution of key personnel.

    C. Analysis of management skills and needs for training and development.

    D. Analysis of need for developmental moves (cross-function, cross-business.)

In summary, a systematic approach to career development is just as essential as systematic approaches to managing other aspects of a business. The system of managing what's important makes the career development of employees an integral part of managing the business. Each employee and each boss, along with personnel specialists, have roles in career development activities that are designed to meet both individual and organizational needs.

A new approach to identifying developmental priorities is part of a better way of handling performance appraisal, one that makes traditional approaches obsolete. Practical methods have been suggested for planning various aspects of career development and communicating relevant information. The likelihood of the long-term success of a business is enhanced by systematic use of these career development tools to aid in realizing the potential of each employee.

19

How to Make Organizational Improvement a Way of Life

Finding a better way of managing and accomplishing what's important to a business is more than a nice thing to do once in a while; over the long haul, it's a business imperative. One individual, alone, can make important improvements. When each member upgrades some aspect of performance, so much the better. Best of all is for the search for a better way, and for finding and implementing that better way, to be an *organizationwide* effort.

The seach for improved ways of doing things should go on with each of the basic management functions. A manager's responsibility for planning calls not only for planning end results and the action steps to achieve those end results, but by our definition of innovation in a business organization, for introducing new and better ways of planning as well. This responsibility for innovation applies equally to each of the other management functions of organizing, directing, and controlling. As was said earlier, we need to adopt as a philosophy the saying, "The best way hasn't been found yet."

An accepted standard is nothing more than a current performance plateau. Someone sets a standard to be achieved, and we innovate in order to reach it. If we are successful in reaching the plateau, our performance is usually rewarded, or at the very least we are not punished. We have a chance to "catch our breath." But circumstances change, and what was acceptable yesterday may not be good enough today. Higher-level plateaus are established by achievement-oriented individuals who set their sights on exceeding current standards and take the right risks as a result of innovative thinking. Emphasis on the value of accomplishments, rather than on merely meeting objectives, encourages innovation and adds an atmosphere of excitement to raising performance plateaus. The cycle of control and improvement encompasses all managerial activity, and innovation is essential in maintaining performance at acceptable levels and in moving to higher levels.

The aim of innovation is improvement. Innovation means better solutions to problems, better ways of handling work procedures, better approaches in dealing with opportunities, better ways of dealing with people. Managers are paid to become more effective themselves and to manage increasingly effective organizations. A characteristic of the innovative manager is a healthy dissatisfaction with the status quo and a focused concern for improvement.

Getting Change for the Better

There are four elements involved in getting individuals and organizations to innovate, to improve in management perfomance: (1) the systematic study of principles and guidelines, (2) the use of available knowledge, (3) analysis of our own performance, and (4) the willingness to make innovation on the job a regular practice.

Acceptance of the philosophy that the best way hasn't been found yet means that improvement efforts have to be ongoing. No book, including this one, has all the answers a manager needs. Nor will all the answers be discovered tomorrow, or even next year. But that is no excuse for not working to increase managerial effectiveness.

When the dominant orientation of an individual or an organization is to the future, change and improvement are accepted, even welcomed. Those with this orientation also believe that they can have an impact in shaping the future. It's a matter of attitude. Those who believe they are helpless to alter fate will be helpless. Those who believe they can have an impact on the future will have an impact. Fortunately, attitudes are learned and they can change in the right circumstances.

As an organization grows in size and complexity, individuals depend less and less on firsthand experience and more and more on data that have been through the information processing system. It's a characteristic of information systems that raw data not readily expressed in words or numbers, or able to be condensed into categories by procedures currently available, are omitted or filtered out. The system thus filters out information critical to understanding the real situation—the emotions, mood, and feelings that are part of all situations involving people.

This does not imply that the information processing system is of no value. How could modern business cope without it? But it does suggest that individuals need to make full use of information that has not been heavily processed and filtered. It suggests that a certain amount of firsthand experience combined with inputs from superiors, peers, subordinates, and perhaps many other individuals is needed in forming a picture of reality.

Organizations change in many ways as they evolve. Small organizations tend to be characterized by simplicity, flexibility, and openness in communications. Large organizations often have the advantages that go with size—financial resources to meet needs, economies based on volume, internal capabilities. As organizations grow larger, however, there is a tendency to glorify forms and formalities, to grow cumbersome, to become more complex and less adaptable.

It's difficult to grow more simple, almost impossible to become disencumbered without radical surgery. Organizational improvement is dedicated to achieving the advantages of both small and large organizations and to avoiding the problems associated with each. In this chapter we'll look at the kinds of information on which an individual can base a personal performance evaluation and performance improvement.

Sources of Information on Which to Base Improvement Efforts

Sources of feedback discussed in earlier chapters that are useful in improving managerial performance include the clients we serve in carrying out our job responsibilities, peers, superiors, subordinates, and ourselves. One source not previously discussed—the organizational improvement process—is added to the list. Each source will be reviewed as a springboard to individual improvement and thus organizational improvement.

Clients

The clients, the customers, the users of the products or services of a business, are one source of information that can lead to improvement efforts. Since most individuals receive work from others and supply work to others in the work flow of the business, organizational improvement is aided by feedback on what facilitates and what blocks the achievement of results. Some individuals, of course, have as clients outsiders to the organization. Outsiders who buy the product or service are likely to provide the most meaningful feedback for encouraging innovation.

The answers to a few incisive questions provide useful feedback from clients. Does your work output meet the needs of the user? Does your work output create problems for the user because of quality or timing? What complaints do you receive, directly or indirectly, from the user? What opportunities could be seized by the user if changes and improvements were accomplished in your area of responsibility?

Finding the answers to questions such as these takes more than the reading of processed and filtered information. The use of all available sources of feedback will likely be required to answer these questions. The processes suggested in Chapter 16 for correlating individual work efforts, especially for resolving power issues, are avenues to improvement efforts.

Peers

Feedback from peers is provided by their reactions in one-to-one discussions, at operating meetings, and at team progress reviews. Their comments and observations may help you face up to the need for innovation, and their suggestions may be useful.

When an objective is shared with one or more peers, the struggle to decide who will do what often provides initial planning that leads to innovation. Special assignments, such as to a project task force, encourage the exploration of ideas. There is appropriate peer pressure to participate and contribute useful ideas at a meeting, and then innovate back on the job as required to make your contribution to the success of the team.

Superiors

Agreement on job content provides the initial direction from the boss that leads to innovation. All coaching and counseling are related to the agreed-upon responsibilities and objectives. When the boss initiates a performance dialogue, it's for the purpose of achieving some change that will mean improvement. Action plans document the steps to achieve the desired improvement.

Reactions from the boss to homework either reinforce what has been done, or lead to innovation as a result of the boss's questions, comments, suggestions, or requests. Reactions from the boss during stewardship reviews have the same effect. Work assignments and promotions provide a certain amount of feedback on how others see your past experiences, current qualifications, and potential. They can be a springboard to innovation by providing a new situation, a fresh challenge.

Subordinates

The success of your subordinates is your success. You see a reflection of how you're doing by looking at their achievements and growth. You can see a bit of yourself in their homework, their preparation and handling of stewardship reviews, their response to your coaching and counseling.

During managerial dialogues, and at individual and group review sessions, you can gather evidence of how the organizational structure is functioning, how well the controls are serving, how accurate your judgment was in selecting an individual for a particular position or assignment.

You gain useful feedback through your subordinates' disclosure of problems and viewpoints, their analysis of the causes of problems, and their reasons for their successes and disappointments. This reveals not only their value as employees, but also your to-date accomplishments as coach and counselor—and the need for continuing to innovate to achieve production targets and to further develop and use your subordinates' talents.

Information Systems and Self-Management Processes

The data in the various management information systems allow you to compare actual results with the projected or desired results. Budgets, quotas, forecasts, and objectives are set up as reference points. Comparisons with actual results provide the information needed for improvement planning.

The tracking system is a device to help you identify where attention is needed and to take action. Most often the need is for more time, effort, and resources to be applied to ensure that the desired result will be achieved. However, because of business priorities, the need may be for an innovation to reduce what it takes to achieve one acceptable result. You use the tracking system to identify specific needs for innovation to balance the overall effort.

Action plans are developed when innovation is called for. As action plans are implemented step by step, there is an ongoing search for just what is needed—not too much in the way of effort and resources and not too little—to reach the objective. Action plans usually evolve somewhat while they are being implemented. Action plans and innovation are, or should be, somewhat synonymous. The plans themselves are attempts to find the best way to achieve the desired result.

The Organizational Improvement Process

How do you get managers (and the organization) to change for the better? Specifically, how do you get more effective managerial communications? How do you identify and get corrective action on factors that affect the ability and/or willingness of subordinates to do what's expected of them? How do you get individuals and teams to improve their teamwork? And is it possible to accomplish these things cost effectively?

There is a way: the organizational improvement process. In my experience, it's the most cost-effective way to make organizational improvement a way of life. And in addition to getting change for the better, the process helps managers (and organizations) know what they're doing that's helping them succeed. It's the pat on the back that says, "Great! Keep it up!"

What's involved in the process? How does it work? Here are the elements: data collection, processing, feedback, analysis, and action planning. What's new, different, and better about this process compared to the many similar sounding approaches available?

1. The process gets candid, reliable data that are relevant to achieving important business results. The data are not self-evaluations. And they are not available from peers or the boss. Subordinates supply the data that help a manager decide what conditions or practices in the organization are helpful in achieving business results and where changes might be desirable. The data are collected with specially designed survey instruments.

2. Integrity in the collection, processing, and use of the data is safeguarded. Experience has shown that when the data are processed internally the process is perceived as a device for assessing and rating the effectiveness of managers by personnel specialists and higher levels of management. This virtually assures that the process will not produce reliable data or the results it was designed to achieve. Therefore, as an external consultant, I oversee the collection of the data, do the processing, protect the confidentiality of the reports, and train the managers in the proper use of the data.

3. The data are reported in a unique, copyrighted format that combines the measures (effort and satisfaction; importance and satisfaction), permits positives and negatives in the data to be identified quickly, and provides detail for comparisons and analysis. Group and individual reports are prepared with strict adherence to the following two rules: (1) responses are not identified with individual subordinates in the data, and (2) the manager is the only one in the organization to receive his or her confidential report. This ensures candid responses from subordinates to survey questions and allows the manager to analyze and act on the data without defensiveness.

4. Managers learn to work with the data in a group session using group results. Individual managers can then compare their confidential data with group data. This provides perspective, reinforcement of positive conditions and practices, and motivation for improvement efforts.

5. Improvement efforts begin with a manager's simple action plan to correct a high-priority concern identified in the data. Action plans and success experiences are shared openly. Then the improvement process is repeated for another item of concern. And again, and again, for up to two years.

6. Progress is measured by gathering and analyzing new data. Fresh insights reinforce past improvement efforts and give direction and motivation to continued organizational improvement.

Did you notice:

- The absence of "typical" training in the process?
- That no one "tells" the manager what to do; that the manager decides?
- That confidential data are never shared, but action plans and success experiences are?

- That the process is totally positive; that there is opportunity for coaching, support, and praise, but no place for criticism?
- That behavioral theory on motivation and change is built into the process?

The organizational improvement process is designed for internal use. It can be used alone, or in connection with other training and development efforts; for one manager and the manager's staff, or for special groups of managers; for one group at a time, or for a whole department, division, or company.

The factor and item content in the survey instruments shows what effective managers do and the conditions that are critical in most management situations. This knowledge is extremely important in training aimed at developing managerial skills. But training is not the most important benefit. The process sets up, directs, motivates, and reinforces improvement efforts and managerial effectiveness. The organizational improvement process is divided into three parts: managerial communications, organizational climate, and organizational teamwork. We'll review the measures used and the factor and item content of each part.

Managerial Communications

SUBJECT: Effective superior-subordinate communication practices.
MEASURES: Effort devoted to the practice or activity.
  Satisfaction of subordinate with the practice or activity.
  CONTENT: 10 factors, 40 items.
  1. Two-way communications.
  2. Knowing the needs of the business.
  3. Knowing what is expected of you.
  4. Delegation and follow-up.
  5. Knowing how you're doing.
  6. Getting help when you need it.
  7. Learning and growing.
  8. Career discussions.
  9. Group discussions.
  10. Reinforcement of results.

The practices of effective bosses in the area of managerial communications serve as guidelines for conducting performance dialogues. These practices were discussed in Chapter 13, and therefore will not be repeated here.

Survey results are summarized for each item, each factor, and the total survey by means of a communication grid. The grid provides an instant, visual summary of the data. Detailed survey data are also provided to assist in analysis and action planning. The report format makes possible the rapid and accurate identification of the items, factors, or themes that have the greatest positive and the greatest negative impact on business results and morale. Reinforcement is thus provided on the positives; the negatives become improvement targets.

Organizational Climate

SUBJECT: Conditions that affect the ability and/or willingness of subordinates to achieve expected results.

MEASURES: Importance of the condition to the subordinate.

Satisfaction of the subordinate with the existing condition.

Overall job satisfaction of each subordinate.

Comments and suggestions on selected items.

CONTENT: 9 factors, 36 items.

1. Information flow.
2. Job content.
3. Job context.
4. Supervision.
5. Work relationships.
6. Reinforcement system.
7. Organization.
8. Resources and support.
9. Personal development.

A variety of conditions in a work situation can affect a subordinate's ability or willingness to do what is expected. Together, these conditions represent the climate in which the subordinate works. Each item represents a condition important to managerial effectiveness, and also a potential improvement challenge to the organization.

1. *Information flow.* Information flow implies more than the existence of information. It's information that gets through, that's received, that's understood. This includes knowing the objectives of the overall organization, knowing what's going on in the organization, knowing what's expected in a particular assignment, and having ad-

vance knowledge of changes that will affect the individual. Even though the information may originate elsewhere, the boss is the key link in making sure the subordinate gets and understands the information.

2. *Job content.* In setting up job content, an attempt is made to meet both organizational and human needs. The job should make the fullest possible use of the abilities of the subordinate. In performing the work, the subordinate should be able to understand its significance. And the job should allow as much freedom as possible for the subordinate in accomplishing what's expected. When these areas need attention, improvement efforts begin with redesign of the job and continue as the procedures for managing the job are carried out.

3. *Job context.* Ability and willingness to work are affected by environmental factors. The environment on the job should be conducive to work. When the job context cannot be improved, increased effort should go into improving job content and the other climate factors.

4. *Supervision.* The quality of supervision affects the climate in which a subordinate works. This could be a sensitive subject for the boss. But the ground rules that the subordinates' responses are anonymous and that the survey data are provided on a confidential basis to the boss alone make defensive reactions unnecessary and open the way to improvement efforts.

5. *Work relationships.* Climate is improved as work relationships become more effective among peers, with the boss, and with other groups. Having clearly defined lines of responsibility and authority and being part of a group that can influence important business decisions also contribute to a desirable climate.

These conditions are not all entirely within the control of the boss, but the boss can see that the work relationships are clearly defined. The boss can set the example in handling day-to-day interactions. And the boss can do much to influence important business decisions.

6. *Reinforcement system.* Receiving praise and recognition based on work accomplishments gives an individual a feeling of success that reinforces the effort behind the success. The boss is in the best position to provide this reinforcement to a subordinate. The boss is also responsible for differentiating among the performances of subordinates and for relating each subordinate's compensation to work accom-

plishments. Another reinforcement device available to the boss is giving work assignments based on subordinates' current performance and personal development needs.

Outside the boss's direct control is the matter of promotions for immediate subordinates. But the boss has great influence in evaluating and reporting on subordinates' current performance and qualifications for another specific assignment.

7. *Organization.* In an organization with a healthy climate, the objectives of top management provide a clear sense of direction to employees. And throughout the organization, there is a sense of urgency, a voluntary force driving individuals and teams to contribute to the achievement of those objectives. This direction and vitality are ingredients in a viable organization, one in which employees can take pride. A thriving, growing organization means advancement opportunities are continually being created. This adds another important dimension to the climate.

8. *Resources and support.* To do the job, a subordinate needs certain resources—people, money, information. Cooperation from other groups and individuals not directly involved in a particular project is also needed at times. Having decisions made by higher levels of management, at the time they are needed, represents both a resource and support. And the encouragement from superiors to introduce improvements in methods and procedures adds to a healthy climate. Bosses are involved in providing each of these items so subordinates can succeed on their jobs.

9. *Personal development.* By functioning as a coach and counselor, the boss can, without losing control, let subordinates think, decide, and act on their own in doing their work. The boss can make work assignments that aid subordinates' personal development. The boss can provide reactions, give suggestions, and pass along information about career opportunities as a guide to subordinates' personal development. So, though all development is self-development, the boss can establish a climate that encourages growth.

The results of the organizational climate survey are summarized for each item, each factor, and the total survey by means of action-priority profiles. The profiles provide an instant, visual summary of the data, showing the priority for improvement efforts. Detailed survey data are also provided to assist in analysis and action planning. The report format permits the rapid and accurate identification of the items, factors, or themes that have the greatest positive and the greatest negative impact on business results and morale. Reinforcement is thus provided on the positives; the negatives become improvement targets.

A job satisfaction score is calculated for each subordinate. The score is a measure of morale, and is useful information in analyzing survey results and planning action steps to achieve improvement. Again, subordinates are not identified in the data.

Comments and suggestions are solicited in addition to responses to specific survey items. The comments are restricted to a limited number of items in the survey. The purpose of this is to focus on the items that are most important to the subordinate. The report lists these anonymous comments for each item, thus providing a convenient summary of strong reactions and convictions to supplement the basic survey data for analysis and action planning.

Organizational Teamwork

SUBJECT: Behavior patterns of leader and group members on teamwork issues.

MEASURES: Importance of the pattern to the subordinate.
Satisfaction of subordinates with the existing pattern.
Overall teamwork satisfaction of each subordinate.
Comments and suggestions on selected items.
CONTENT: 6 factors, 24 items.
1. Response to a challenge.
2. Role of leader in group sessions.
3. Role of members in group sessions.
4. Resolving differences and conflicts.
5. The process of making decisions.
6. Attitude toward teamwork.

Business results can be affected by the behavior patterns of the leader and group members when teamwork is involved. The following items are important to most organizations.

1. *Response to a challenge.* Organizational effectiveness is enhanced when group members react to tough challenges with a positive attitude of "we can do it," when there is a problem or a crisis and everyone works together as a team, when group members try to resolve problems without blaming each other, and when group members try

to resolve problems without passing them on to higher management. The very idea of challenge invites innovation.

2. *Role of leader in group sessions.* The behavior of the leader in group sessions can help or hinder the achievement of business results. In handling group sessions, effective leaders encourage subordinates to express their own positions openly and honestly. And when there are differences of opinion among group members, and conflicts to be resolved, group discussions lead to the innovation required.

3. *Role of members in group sessions.* Group members need to feel free to challenge each other and to disagree in group sessions. They also need to feel free to challenge the leader's opinions and ideas. Group members should act on the basis of their independent thinking, rather than on what they suppose the leader wants. And group members should be more concerned about working together and getting the job done than about who has the responsibility for the job. These attitudes and behaviors spawn innovation.

4. *Resolving differences and conflicts.* Effective leaders resolve differences and conflicts without bias and so that all parties "win." They dig for the real reasons for differences of opinion on important matters. And they make sure group members don't waste energy on interpersonal differences and conflicts. Regulations and procedures are not likely to offer ready solutions to differences and conflicts. Solutions must be found through innovation—the finding of new and better ways to work together.

5. *The process of making decisions.* The steps in decision making have been described in detail by many authors and will not be repeated here. However, in connection with organizational teamwork, there are four patterns to consider. (1) The leader responsible for the decision should make the decision without delay. This does not suggest haste, but proper consideration of the cost of unnecessary delay on business results and morale. (2) Since there are no riskless decisions, the leader and group members should take risks in making decisions based on the potential benefits from the decision. (3) The leader who makes decisions should do so without being unduly influenced by policies, procedures, or tradition. And (4) the wise leader sees to it that expertise is the basis on which group members influence decisions made at higher levels.

6. *Attitude toward teamwork.* Attitudes influence behavior, and we can observe the behaviors that result from attitudes. A noticeable

amount of teamplay among group members reveals their positive attitude toward teamwork. So does evidence of enthusiasm for doing the work. Group members' each feeling personally responsible for the results expected of the overall organization and each being willing to make personal sacrifices to achieve results important to the success of the business are evidence of their positive attitude toward teamwork. An individual's point of view is not easily changed. But an organization dedicated to innovation fosters attitudes that encourage flexibility, teamwork, and accomplishment.

Organizational teamwork survey results are presented in the same way as data from the organizational climate survey. Action-priority profiles, detailed data, teamwork satisfaction scores, and comments and suggestions are included in the report for both confidential individual results and group results.

Analysis and Action Planning

The process for analyzing the survey data and planning action steps to achieve improvements has four major steps: raw data highlights, data analysis, response analysis, action plans. The steps apply to all three surveys in the organizational improvement process.

Step 1. Raw data highlights. The items in the report data with the most positive or favorable responses are listed. Approximately a fourth of the survey items might be listed. A similar list is prepared of the most negative or unfavorable responses.

Step 2. Data analysis. Your personal knowledge and judgment are required in this step. From the list of positives generated in Step 1, select those items, factors, or themes that you feel have the greatest positive impact on business results and morale in your organization. Five of these positives would be a practical number to provide perspective in relation to the negatives in the data.

From the list of negatives generated in Step 1, consider which have the greatest negative impact on business results and morale in your organization. Again, five negatives is a practical number to begin with—enough to provide perspective in your further analysis and action planning.

Step 3. Response analysis. One item is selected from your list of top negatives for further analysis and action planning. There are four parts to this step: First, list the possible reasons for the survey responses. Brainstorming is suggested; that is, without evaluating the items on the list, list as many reasons or causes for the negative responses as you can think of. Try for at least ten possible reasons. Second, evaluate the items on your list, and select one or more as the most likely reasons for the survey responses. Third, referring to the most likely reason(s), brainstorm a list of possible action steps to take to improve the situation. Fourth, from your list of possible action steps, formulate a tentative plan of action.

Step 4. Action plans. Discuss your tentative plan of action with your subordinates—those who supplied the data on which the plan is based. In doing so, you give evidence of your desire to improve and of your willingness to accept and use the data they have provided. Your subordinates may be able to offer suggestions that will be helpful in finalizing your plans. And they will have increased ownership in the outcomes of the improvement efforts.

Your tentative plan of action should be reviewed and approved by your boss before it is finalized. Knowing your plans, your boss can provide encouragement and support, and reinforcement as the results of your improvement efforts become apparent.

The improvement process is ongoing. When one plan of action to achieve a particular improvement has been implemented, select another item from your list of top negatives, and repeat Steps 3 and 4. When your list of top negatives is exhausted, go back to Step 2 and put a second group of negatives on your list, and so on. The data can be used in this way for up to two years. This allows time to make significant improvements. Then a resurvey is suggested to measure progress and make sure your ongoing improvement efforts are aimed at what's currently most important to your organization.

Sharing success experiences in using the process has proved to be the best way of making organizational improvement a way of life. The process is totally positive even though it deals with both positive and negative data, because there is abundant opportunity for coaching and counseling, and support and praise, but no place for criticism. Behavioral theory on motivation and change is built into the process.

Epilogue

Operating Instructions Summary

The most important function of a management system is to accomplish what's important—to realize human potential and achieve optimum business results. If you have concluded your quest for a better way of managing what's important and have determined that you already have the perfect management system and that it's being fully utilized, you'll have no use for the theory or the operating instructions detailed throughout this book.

If you choose to continue the quest with the rest of us, however, you'll appreciate the words of Eugene O'Neill: "A man's work is in danger of deteriorating when he thinks he has found the one best formula for doing it. If he thinks that, he is likely to feel that all he needs is merely to go on repeating himself. . . . So long as a person is searching for better ways of doing his work he is fairly safe."

The claim that the system for managing what's important represents a better way than traditional approaches to dealing with organizational effectiveness invites the improvement-oriented individual to try it out. The invitation to use the system includes, in large print, the reminder that the potential benefits accrue from using the entire system, not from using only parts of it. The temptation to select replacement parts, at random, to patch up a traditional management system that doesn't work must be steadfastly resisted.

However, the system you are using may already have many parts of advanced design and high quality. There is no reason to discard these parts if one condition is met: They must supplement and complement the other parts, fitting together to make one functional unit suited to the particular needs of your situation.

How do you test the appropriateness of a given part? Here are three checks:

- Does it fit with the concepts outlined for effective use of human resources? Does it contribute to realizing human potential?
- Does it fit with the procedures for managing the entire job and accomplishing what's important?
- Does it hold up in use? Is it more than *another* way? Is it actually a *better* way?

If virtually the entire management system is needed to replace an obsolete model, remember the advice of British Prime Minister David Lloyd George: "Don't be afraid to take a big step if one is indicated. You can't cross a chasm in two small jumps."

And in case some parts presented herein don't quite meet your exacting standards, here is a comforting thought and a challenge: Built into the workings of the system for managing what's important are the mechanisms necessary to encourage and support the continuing search for a better way of managing. Therefore, you are encouraged to contribute your ideas and share your experience to help the rest of us see a better way. There's reason to cheer whenever a better way of managing is found.

In the meantime, the operating instructions are: Use the system to develop talent, to produce important achievements, to provide appropriate reinforcement, and through these means, to realize human potential and achieve optimum business results.

The system works. Use it as if you had conceived the design, created each of the parts, and written the operating instructions yourself.

Index